CaliforniaBabylon

ALSO BY **KRISTAN LAWSON** AND **ANNELI RUFUS**

Weird Europe

America Off the Wall: The West Coast

Europe Off the Wall

Goddess Sites: Europe

BY KRISTAN LAWSON

The Rules of Speed Chess

BY ANNELI RUFUS

Magnificent Corpses

The World Holiday Book

CaliforniaBabylon

A GUIDE TO SITES OF **SCANDAL**,
MAYHEM, AND **CELLULOID**
IN THE GOLDEN STATE

KristanLawson
AND **AnneliRufus**

St. Martin's Griffin New York

www.stmartins.com

Book design by Judith Stagnitto Abbate/Abbate Design

Library of Congress Cataloging-in-Publication Data
Lawson, Kristan.
    California Babylon : a guide to sites of scandal, mayhem, and celluloid
in the Golden State / Kristan Lawson and Anneli Rufus.
        p. cm.
    Includes bibliographical references (p.   ) and index.
    ISBN 0-312-26385-6
    1. California—Guidebooks. 2. California—History, Local. 3. Scandals—
California—History. 4. Celebrities—California—History. I. Rufus, Anneli
S. II. Title.

F859.3 .L35 2000
917.9404'53—dc21

                                                            00-024868

First Edition: October 2000

10 9 8 7 6 5 4 3 2 1

CONTENTS

TheCentralCoast

ACKNOWLEDGMENTS

The authors would like to thank Nadine Bass, Marcia Rufus, Jennifer Cherniss, and David Simon for showing us around; Marji, Jan, and Marc Morrow for their generosity; Jerry Pohlen for suggestions and research on dozens of locations; Marc Wanamaker, Richard Senate, Chris Morrow, Sayre Van Young of the Berkeley Public Library, Robert Kehlmann of the Berkeley Architectural Heritage Association, Koleen Hamblin of Koli Company, and Carolyn Elayne Alexander of the Venice Historical Society for sharing their expertise; the Academy Center for Motion Picture Study, the San Francisco Public Library, the Berkeley Historical Society, the Los Angeles Central Public Library, and the San Pedro Historical Society Archives for the use of their resources and facilities; various film commissions and chambers of commerce throughout the state; the authors of all the books mentioned in our bibliography (and many that aren't); and the hundreds of helpful people we encountered on our travels.

A lot of stuff happens in California. Not the Yalta Conference, perhaps. But this is where trends are set, cults go crazy, stars are born. Where flesh and fantasy merge on film and mass killers lurk while riots rage. So much goes down here that sometimes the earth below cannot contain itself and shudders, sending houses crashing down and cars careening.

How many times have you heard a really stirring bit of news—a restaurant massacre; a cult's hideout revealed; a favorite singer married, jailed, or dead—and found yourself wondering, *Where?* We crave details: the color of the walls, the view out the window. We want to see for ourselves. It makes us a part of things. It makes things more real.

The same goes for history. Certain moments have changed the world—discoveries, concerts, disasters. And each happened *somewhere.* Each unfolded in a particular location, on a specific roadside or beach, even at a specific address.

California Babylon is about seeing those places where "it" happened—and, in some cases, where it is still happening. Exactly where *was* Patty Hearst kidnapped? Where *did* the Manson Family hatch its plans? Where did they film *Vertigo, The Graduate, Chinatown,* and *Pulp Fiction?* Where did Hugh Grant hire Divine Brown? Where do fans still leave flowers on Karen Carpenter's grave? Where do the stars savor blintzes? Such things, for better or worse, are essential parts of the California heritage, the California soul.

Appearances mean a lot in California. Call it shallow if you like, but you need to know what something looks like before you can completely understand it. You can *hear* till the cows come home about Altamont Speedway or the Viper Room or the Heaven's Gate house. But hearing about it just isn't enough. Like a pilgrim seeking the Holy Land, you want to see *in person* where it all happened: the manger, the tomb, the motel, the bullet holes, the stain on the sidewalk.

Let's do it.

The chapters in this book are arranged south to north, starting in San Diego and ending up at the Oregon border. *California Babylon* is foremost a hands-on guidebook to be used while traveling; so, wherever possible, entries within each chapter are arranged geographically "in a row," as a walking or driving tour. Some of the locations mentioned in the book are private homes: do not trespass or disturb the occupants. If you are looking for a particular site but don't know its exact location, the index at the back of the book contains a detailed listing of every person, place, and topic mentioned in the text.

All information in this book was extensively researched and double-checked, and to the best of our knowledge is true at the time of this writing. The authors personally visited nearly every site mentioned in *California Babylon,* interviewed current residents, owners, employees, and witnesses (when they were willing to talk), and verified facts with local historians and reliable sources. We've done our best to correct common errors and misperceptions, so you may come across some details here that differ from those presented in other books. But be aware that things change quickly (especially in California), so by the time you read this a few buildings may have been torn down or restaurants gone out of business. We welcome your updates, comments, questions, or suggestions.

Kristan Lawson and Anneli Rufus
P.O. Box 295
Berkeley, CA 94701

San Diego

SAN YSIDRO

McDonald's Massacre Site
Final score: James Huberty 21–Police 1.

Now the Southwestern College Education Center at San Ysidro, 460 W. San Ysidro Boule-
vard, about a mile north of the Mexican border. The monument to the victims is near the
front door of the center. (619) 690-6083. Yum-Yum Donut Shop is at 482 W. San Ysidro
Boulevard, just a few yards away. (619) 428-9221.

Repressed madman James Huberty awoke on July 18, 1984, and announced calmly to his wife that he was going out to "hunt humans." He loaded up on bullets and walked over to a nearby McDonald's. Then he started shooting. In short order he had massacred twenty-one total strangers. Police quickly surrounded the place and positioned snipers in the nearby Yum-Yum Donut Shop and in a post office. After a standoff a sharpshooter felled Huberty with a single shot, thus obviating the spectacle of a trial. Huberty's record-setting spree remains one of the all-time worst mass shootings in U.S. history, its sheer scale untouched by the spate of shootings that followed in the 1990s. Fearful of bad vibes, McDonald's never reopened the restaurant; instead they tore it down and gave the land away. A new branch of a local community college was built in its place, and the school was thoughtful enough to erect a circular monument with twenty-one columns, each in memory of one of the victims. But the Yum-Yum Donut Shop is still standing. (Note: There is a different McDonald's a few blocks away that is unrelated to the Huberty incident.)

Hotel Del Coronado
Where they filmed Some Like It Hot.

> 1500 Orange Avenue, directly on the beach in Coronado. (619) 435-6611 or (800) HOTEL-DEL.

From Lucy and Desi to LBJ, a phalanx of celebrities has lapped up the sun at the West Coast's largest beach resort since it opened in 1888. L. Frank Baum wrote some of his Oz tales here. And legend has it that this is where in 1920 Edward, Prince of Wales, may have first seen the woman named Wallis Simpson, whom he later married and for whom he abdicated the throne. The guest list stuns: Charlie Chaplin; Charles Lindbergh; a spate of presidents including FDR, Nixon, and Reagan. Ray Bradbury has been a regular Christmastime guest for more than thirty years. In 1958 Billy Wilder chose the hotel as a location for *Some Like It Hot* with Jack Lemmon, Tony Curtis, and Marilyn Monroe; the actress's

PHOTO COURTESY OF HOTEL DEL CORONADO, 1999

Hotel del Coronado

pathological lateness drove her director crazy. Other productions, including Peter O'Toole's film *The Stunt Man* and *Baywatch,* have been filmed here, and stars spotted staying here include Madonna, Jack Nicholson, Demi Moore, and Dustin Hoffman. Palm-fringed and palatial, "the Del" offers guided walks for those who can't afford to stay.

Croce's
Chow down with Leroy Brown.

> 850 Fifth Avenue, at F Street, in the Gaslamp District of downtown San Diego. Jazz Bar and Jazz Restaurant open daily 5:00 P.M.–midnight; Blues Bar open daily 11:00 A.M.–1:45 A.M.; Blues Restaurant open daily 7:30 A.M.–3:00 P.M. and 5:00 P.M.–midnight. (619) 233-4355.

In the early 1970s Jim Croce tried to rescue the Top 40 from the musical doldrums with raucous hits like "Bad, Bad Leroy Brown." But like Buddy Holly before him, Croce died young in a tragic plane crash, ending his career just moments before he

THE ANDREW CUNANAN TOUR

He always wanted to be famous. As a teenager he vowed he would be. Later to kill five men and then himself at age twenty-seven, Andrew Cunanan spent nearly all his life amid the sun-splashed landscapes of San Diego. As his parents' favored child, living in a ranch-style home at **5777 Watercrest Drive** in **Bonita** (a suburban area of San Diego, southeast of downtown near National City and Chula Vista), he attended **Sunnyside Elementary School,** where teachers found him clever. He had a passion for fashion even then. After **Bonita Vista Junior High** he went on to tony **Bishop's School** in **La Jolla.** There he acted flamboyantly and told his wealthy classmates lies that made his family seem fabulously rich. Upon graduation he was voted "least likely to be forgotten."

When his stockbroker dad ditched the family and went home to the Philippines, Andrew dropped out of the **University of California at San Diego**, where he had been majoring in history. After a stint in the Bay Area (where he proudly told friends he had met Gianni Versace) he moved back south. Living with his mother in a **Rancho Bernardo** apartment, he clerked for three years at the nearby **Thrifty Drugstore**. He hid these plebe details from friends at gay bars in San Diego's **Hillcrest district** (north of downtown), where he was known as Andrew De Silva, a bon vivant who flaunted cash and connections. Some who socialized with him at the lively night spot **Flicks (1017 University Avenue, at Tenth Avenue)** and chic **California Cuisine (1027 University Avenue)** say he dealt drugs, did drugs, and was a procurer and part-time hustler who specialized in May–September (not quite December) sex. His fancy clothes and ability to talk about art charmed some, but Cunanan's fibs (about working for Israel's Mossad, for instance) left others cold. Champagne flowed at his going-away party April 24, 1997, at California Cuisine. The heavily-in-debt Andrew lived a couple blocks away in **a 1960s-style apartment complex at 1234 Robinson Avenue**.

Unrequited love for a Minneapolis architect may have been what launched Andrew eastward on what would become a three-month killing spree. A gigantic manhunt ended when Andrew shot himself in a Miami houseboat on July 23. Today Hillcrest wants very much to forget him.

reached superstardom. In a valiant attempt to save time in a bottle, Jim's wife and one-time musical partner Ingrid founded Croce's Restaurants and Nightclubs in his memory (it's actually four separate venues rolled into one: two bars and two restaurants, one of each devoted to jazz and blues). The walls of all four display Jim Croce memorabilia, including photos, his jacket, his guitar, and (of course) some used guitar picks.

EL CAJON

Unarius Academy of Science World Headquarters
Awaiting aliens.

> 145 S. Magnolia Avenue, at Main Street. Open Mon.–Sat., 10:00 A.M.–5:00 P.M. (619) 444-7062.

After Ernest Norman met his future wife Ruth at a psychics' convention in 1954, the pair founded the Unarius Academy of Science. Members believe that by the year 2001 thirty-two spaceships will have come to Earth from the planet Myton. At that point the aliens will invite Earth to join the Interplanetary Confederation of Planets. Claiming hundreds of thousands of adherents worldwide, Unarius has published well over a hundred books—many of them authored with "help" from beings on other planes, and many recounting past lives. Ruth Norman claimed to have lived previous lives as the Buddha, Mona Lisa, King Arthur, Socrates, Ben Franklin, Henry VIII, Charlemagne, Confucius, and dozens of other people. Ernest claimed to have lived before as Osiris, Jesus, and Satan. Today the roomy headquarters are adorned with members' paintings and other artwork depicting what they call "the nature of consciousness substantiated by an interdimensional science of life"—on the planet Vixall, for example. Though the Normans are no longer on this planet, you may see headlines about Unarius in 2001, when Ruth predicted Space Brothers would land on Earth (with luck, at Unarius's own landing site in nearby Jamul). If Ruth is wrong, the group will have to reexamine itself. If she's right—hey, we might *all* be Unarians by 2002.

Elsewhere in San Diego County

RANCHO SANTA FE

Heaven's Gate Cult Suicide Site
> Former address: 18241 Colina Norte.
> New address: 18241 Paseo Victoria.
> The unincorporated town of Rancho Santa Fe is in northern San Diego County, just inland

from Encinitas. From Highway 5 in downtown Encinitas, take Encinitas Boulevard 3 miles east, turn north on Rancho Santa Fe Road for 1 mile, then turn east on El Camino del Norte. After about 1½ miles, look for a small street called Paseo Victoria on the north side of the road.

Thirty-nine decomposing bodies were found here on March 26, 1997, all wearing identical outfits: black shirts and pants and Nike sneakers, all covered with purple shrouds. Baffled at first, police soon discovered a videotape explaining what had happened. All thirty-nine were members of an apocalyptic cult called Heaven's Gate who had intentionally "shed their earthly containers to achieve a higher level of being"—in other words, they'd committed suicide. The arrival of an eagerly anticipated but ultimately disappointing comet named Hale-Bopp triggered the cult's end-of-the-world mood. They believed a UFO was waiting in the comet's tail to take them all away to a better place. But the only way to board the UFO was to get rid of those pesky earthbound bodies. So they did. The group's leaders, "Do" (Marshall Applewhite) and "Ti" (Bonnie Lu Nettles), had in recent years transformed their confused, moribund twenty-year-old spiritual commune into a space-age UFO cult, using the Internet to recruit new, computer-savvy members. By the mid-1990s they were making a nice income designing slick Web pages, using as a front a consulting company they named Higher Source. Millions of earthlings were glued to their TVs watching coverage of the largest-ever mass suicide on U.S. soil. Satellite uplink trucks clogged the streets of Rancho Santa Fe, and TV news anchors were elbow-to-elbow on the sidewalks. Residents couldn't take it anymore; not long after the suicides, in an effort to discourage gawkers, local officials changed the street's name to Paseo Victoria. The house was sold in June 1999 to a new owner who announced plans to tear it down and build a new one in its place.

CARLSBAD

Marie Callender's
Where the Heaven's Gate members ate their last meal.

5980 Avenida Encinas, off Palomar Airport Road, next to Highway 5. Open Mon.–Fri., 7:00 A.M.–9:30 P.M.; Sat.–Sun., 8:00 A.M.–9:30 P.M. (760) 438-3929.

They dressed alike, they talked alike—sometimes they even ate alike. On a mild spring evening in 1997 thirty-nine members of the Heaven's Gate cult politely ordered and ate identical meals at this branch of the pie chain. All had turkey pot pie. ("Pot pie to die for," restaurant staff later joked.) Then they went home and killed themselves, believing a spaceship hidden in the Hale-Bopp comet was going to take them somewhere nice.

ESCONDIDO

Lawrence Welk Museum

8860 Lawrence Welk Drive, off Champagne Boulevard in the Welk Resort, 6 miles north of Escondido, off Highway 15; enter the museum through the lobby of the Welk Resort Theatre. Open Mondays and Fridays, 9:00 A.M.–4:30 P.M.; Wednesdays and Sundays, 9:00 A.M.–1:00 P.M.; Tuesdays, Thursdays, and Saturdays, 9:00 A.M.–1:00 P.M. and 4:30 –7:00 P.M. (760) 749-3000.

Today few under fifty still remember Lawrence Welk's lilting brand of "champagne music" and his voice chanting, "Wonderful! Wonderful!" as the band played gentle melodies. Welk bought property in pokey Escondido circa 1965, ten years after launching his famous TV show. Today it's a resort better avoided by those who dislike golf carts and musical theater. The museum has relics from the show including photos, instruments, a bandstand, and the world's largest champagne glass, six feet high and five feet across. Also here is Welk's accordion—viewers went wild when he played it.

BORREGO SPRINGS

Peg Leg Monument
Where a fortune in gold was found and lost.

At the intersection of Henderson Canyon Road and County Road S-22. From downtown Borrego Springs, go east 2 miles on Palm Canyon Drive, past the airport, and follow the road as it turns north until you reach the Y-shaped intersection with Henderson Canyon Road. The monument looks like a pile of rocks on the north side of the intersection.

Around 1850 a one-legged rascal named Peg Leg Smith claimed to have found gold nuggets scattered profusely on the ground somewhere in this section of desert. The problem was, he said, he had made his discovery many years earlier while carrying a load of pelts to California. After a decade or two of intervening adventures he returned and tried to find the field that was littered with hunks of free gold—to no avail. Several expeditions in the 1850s came home empty-handed. So Peg Leg retired to a life of drinking and schmoozing, embroidering his tale ever more extravagantly with each passing season. The story of Peg Leg's gold spread throughout the West. As the years passed, hundreds of men wasted the better part of their lives searching for the elusive treasure, but all they ever came back with was more tall tales. This monument marks the approximate site of Peg Leg's supposed discovery. A sign at the site encourages seekers to add rocks to the pile that constitutes the focal point of the monument. On the first Saturday in April (or a week earlier if Easter falls on the first Sunday in April), fibbers convene here from all points for the Peg Leg Liars' Contest, to spin the least believable mining-related tales they can concoct.

Palm Springs Area

CABAZON

Cabazon Dinosaurs

Browse the bronto's bowels.

Dinosaur Delights: 50800 Seminole Drive, at Main Street, north of Highway 10, Cabazon; open daily 9:00 A.M.–7:00 P.M. (closing time varies). (909) 849-8309. Wheel Inn: 50900 Seminole Drive; open daily 24 hours. (909) 849-7012.

Claude Bell had big, big dreams when he purchased around seventy-five acres of desert and opened his Wheel Inn coffee shop in 1958. In 1964 he started building a big hollow steel-and-concrete brontosaurus right nearby, air-conditioned and actually larger than life. When that was done he started building a fifty-five-foot-tall *Tyrannosaurus rex* to keep it company. But Bell died before this second beast was completed. Perhaps you saw the enormous pair in *Pee-Wee's Big Adventure, National Lampoon's Vacation,* or in many a music video. While you cannot enter the *T. rex,* a gift shop thrives in the belly of its long-tailed companion—

The Cabazon dinosaurs

which is, to be hairsplittingly precise, an apatosaurus. Peek at the desert through portholes in the animal's flank and peruse saurian-themed T-shirts, magnets, cards, novelties, rocks, fossils, jewelry, and educational toys.

PALM SPRINGS

Palm Springs's Walk of Stars
Like Hollywood's, but hotter.

Along Palm Canyon Drive, downtown Palm Springs.

M any a Hollywood sun worshipper has been lured out here to the desert. Palm Springs gloats over this, and manifests its gloating with star shapes set into the sidewalk. Sound familiar? On the town's main shopping drag this Walk of Stars immortalizes Bob Hope, Frank Sinatra, Sophia Loren, Ginger Rogers, and many others.

Korakia Pensione
Where Churchill indulged.

257 S. Patencio Road, just south of Palm Springs Desert Museum, at the far western edge of Palm Springs. (760) 864-6411.

O ccupying two villas tucked against a mountainside, this romantic retreat is so popular that at last report Brad Pitt had called repeatedly in search of lodgings but found the place fully booked every time. The whitewashed 1924 Moroccan-style villa was home to Scots artist Gordon Coutts, who was nostalgic for days spent in Tangier. One early visitor was Winston Churchill, who took advantage of its serene surroundings to practice his hobby, painting. The art studio he enjoyed is now outfitted as a guest suite. Formerly owned by early screen star J. Carol Nash, the adjacent Mediterranean-style villa boasts a mosaicked pool. Elisabeth Shue has been spotted here, as have Laura Dern, Randy Quaid, Christina Applegate, and many other notables. Keep trying, Brad.

CATHEDRAL CITY

Desert Memorial Park
Where the beat goes on and on and on.

69920 E. Ramon Road, at Da Vall Drive, just north of Mission Hills North Golf Course, at the far eastern edge of Cathedral City. Open daily 7:00 A.M.–6:00 P.M. (760) 328-3316.

H e's got you, babe. The marker on Sonny Bono's grave (B-35, number 294) is chiseled with a replica of his autograph as well as the words "And the beat goes on." The pop star–turned–Palm Springs congressman was killed while skiing in

1998—his funeral put Palm Springs on news broadcasts worldwide. Frank Sinatra (B-8, number 151) rests near his parents. Considering the Rat Packer's reputation, some might debate the chiseled tribute on his grave marker: "Beloved husband & father." Also buried here are producer-choreographer Busby Berkeley, composer Frederick Loewe, actor William Powell, and the Gabor sisters' mom.

RANCHO MIRAGE

Betty Ford Center
Where stars dry out.

> 39000 Bob Hope Drive, on the Eisenhower Medical Center campus. (760) 773-4100 or (800) 854-9211.

The former first lady opened this treatment center in 1982 after bravely admitting she was an alcoholic with an addiction to painkillers. Today the fourteen-acre, eighty-bed facility—an average monthly stay costs about $13,000—makes headlines when big names check in. The tens of thousands of alumni reportedly include Tammy Faye Bakker, Stevie Nicks, Liz Taylor, Jerry Lee Lewis, and many others. A Valium-addicted and alcoholic Liza Minnelli once checked herself in, vowing to escape her mother's fate; and the filming of *Frasier* took a break in 1996 after a DUI Kelsey Grammer smashed his car and wound up at Betty Ford.

STAR STREETS OF RANCHO MIRAGE

The chichi little town of Rancho Mirage has named streets after some of the best-loved stars who have emigrated here over the decades. Cruise down **Dinah Shore Drive, Bob Hope Drive,** and **Frank Sinatra Drive.** Or stumble patriotically along **Gerald Ford Drive,** named for the ex-president whose wife Betty established her famous clinic in Rancho Mirage.

LA QUINTA

La Quinta Resort
Where Capra courted his muse.

49–499 Eisenhower Drive, east of Palm Desert. (760) 564-4111 or (800) 598-3828.

E ver since this super-exclusive desert retreat was erected in 1926, Hollywood types have been making a continuous beeline for it. With its cute Spanish-style casitas snug against dry mountains, La Quinta inspired Frank Capra to write *It Happened One Night*. And this is where he came to work on the script for *Lost Horizon*. Tiled roofs, heavily beamed ceilings, picture windows, and fields of desert flowers flanking golf and tennis facilities are the deal here. A set of swimming pools are named after former guests—Gable, Dietrich, Lombard, and Garbo—and the original casitas bear shiny metal wall plaques telling which stars stayed in each, and when. Look for the names of Capra and Gable, et al., as well as those of Desi Arnaz and Ricardo Montalban, and more.

Mojave Desert Region

LANDERS

The Integratron
Mysterious dome built by a UFO pioneer.

2477 Belfield Boulevard, Landers. From either Yucca Valley or Barstow, take Old Woman Springs Road (Highway 247) until you reach Reche Road in Landers; turn east on Reche Road and go 2 miles; turn north (left) on Belfield Boulevard and go 2 miles; the Integratron is near the end of the paved road close to Linn Road, across the street from Gubler Orchids. Visitors are asked to give a $7 donation for the tour, which is given on Sundays, noon–4:00 P.M.; or call ahead to schedule a private tour: (760) 364-3126 or (760) 366-8138. Giant Rock is 3 miles northeast of the Integratron, near Giant Rock Airport.

W hat may look to the untrained eye like a run-of-the-mill fifty-foot-in-diameter white dome in the middle of the desert was actually built with the help of a "seventeen-inch-long equation" given to mankind by beings from another world. So said George Van Tassel, the man who built and named the intriguing, spherical Integratron. Van Tassel was one of the very first people who claimed to be a "contactee"—that is, while others in the early '50s were merely seeing UFOs from a distance, Van Tassel said he had actually spoken to the saucers' inhabitants and been invited aboard. This was long before the era of anal probes and Men in Black: Van Tassel's aliens were friendly and wise. The Integratron and a giant rock nearby (named, oddly, Giant Rock) for decades played host to Van Tassel's UFO conventions, which became the Woodstocks of the fringe community. After Van Tassel's death in 1978 the Integratron was in legal limbo for years, but now it's back in friendly hands, and the new owners offer tours of the spiritually charged building, including discussions on the history of the UFO movement. After the tour, visitors are invited to stay for an orgone-rich drumming circle inside the dome.

Landers Earthquake Epicenters

The first epicenter was near the intersection of Old Woman Springs Road (Highway 247) and Pipes Canyon Road, midway between Landers and Yucca Valley; the second was about 1½ miles north of Reche Road, about one-quarter mile east of Old Woman Springs Road (Highway 247), along an unnamed dirt road on the outskirts of Landers.

Though not well known outside California, the Landers quake was the United States' third largest in the twentieth century. The 7.4 temblor struck at 4:58 A.M. on June 28, 1992, and actually had two epicenters just a few miles apart: the first one snapped at Pipes Canyon Road, and the next one broke less than a second later, just north, near Reche Road. Though it killed only one unfortunate, it caused over $100 million in damage, and half ruined the towns of Landers and Yucca Valley. Residents describe the thirty seconds of shaking as cataclysmic, earth-shattering: it was felt as far away as Idaho. Although the original magnitude estimate of 8.1 was later downgraded to 7.6, and then 7.4, many locals believed the downgrading was false, that it was propaganda to prevent panic elsewhere in the state and that their quake really *was* an 8.1; even at a "mere" 7.4, it was three times more powerful than the much more famous Loma Prieta quake that struck northern California a few years earlier.

JOSHUA TREE

Gram Parsons Memorial Room and Cremation Site

Joshua Tree Inn, 61259 Twenty-nine Palms Highway (Highway 62), at Outpost Road, in the city of Joshua Tree. (760) 366-1188. Cap Rock is in Joshua Tree National Park: From the city of Joshua Tree, take Quail Springs Road southeast until you get to a Y-intersection with one road going east to Jumbo Rocks and another going south to Keys View. Take the road south (on your right) and after a short way turn left into the parking lot for Cap Rock. Park Ranger: (760) 367-5500.

Gram Parsons never had a hit song. He never appeared on *American Bandstand* or *Don Kirshner's Rock Concert.* His music had little mass appeal. Yet for some reason he retains a large cult following today, nearly thirty years after his death. Why? Was it his friendship with the Rolling Stones; his relationship with Emmylou Harris; his short stint as a member of the Byrds? Was it the embarrassing name of his most successful band, the Flying Burrito Brothers? Or is it his reputation as the creator of a rather dismal musical genre now known as country rock? Perhaps it was the events surrounding his tragic death at age twenty-six that made him a legend.

Parsons checked into room 8 of the Joshua Tree Inn on September 19, 1973, reportedly drank way too much tequila and took way too much morphine, and died of heart failure. (Oddly, Jim Croce died the very next day and stole all the headlines.) Relatives took his body to Los Angeles Airport for a flight to New Orleans. But Parsons's road manager Phil Kaufman and buddy Michael Martin had a different idea: they went to the airport at the last moment, conned a cargo handler into giving them the corpse, and absconded with it back to the desert. Following Parsons's wishes, they attempted to cremate him at the base of a boulder called Cap Rock. The remains were eventually reclaimed and transported to New Orleans, but Cap Rock has become the Lourdes of the country-rock world, a top destination for "Gram fans." The Joshua Tree Inn has decorated the popular room 8 with pictures of Parsons and other items donated by the faithful. Every few years, organizers stage a GramFest at venues around Joshua Tree.

CALICO

Calico Early Man Archaeological Site
Where amazing discoveries are ignored.

Fifteen miles northeast of Barstow: take Highway 15 east about 12 miles, exit at the Minneola turnoff, and follow the signs 2½ miles north to the site. Open for self-guided tours Wed.–Sun., 9:00 A.M.–4:00 P.M.; guided tours Wed., 1:30 and 3:30 P.M., Thurs.–Sun., 9:30 and 11:30 A.M. and 1:30 and 3:30 P.M. No phone at the site, but the Bureau of Land Management maintains it: (760) 252-6000.

The bizarre goings-on at this archaeological dig are a case study in the scientific community's tendency toward closed-minded skepticism. Actually, what's bizarre is what's *not* going on. Prevailing theory holds that the first ancestors of Native Americans did not arrive in the New World until about 12,000 or 14,000 B.C.— 20,000 B.C. at the very earliest, crossing over from Asia on a land bridge connecting Siberia and Alaska. The oldest human remains ever found in North America date from this era, so the theory has become entrenched as fact. Then, along comes Calico.

First seriously excavated in the '60s, Calico has yielded no human remains but, instead, hundreds of stone tools—choppers, slicers, picks, and the like—manufactured in a style and out of a material similar to other stone-age tools discovered in Africa and elsewhere. The problem? Highly accurate uranium-thorium dating of the material in which the tools were encased positively fixes their age at two hundred thousand years. Now, we know *animals* don't make advanced tools. Hoaxers, no matter how sophisticated, could not fake two hundred thousand–year-old calcium carbonate, nor construct a huge archaeological site and then bury it. So the tools must have been made by early humans or a related species such as *Homo erectus* or Neanderthals. Louis Leakey of Olduvai Gorge fame, one of the world's most respected paleontologists, thought the site so important that he spent the last eight years of his life directing the excavations and studying their results.

So this is an important place, right? Revolutionized our theories of humans in America, right? Not on your life. Calico is now ridiculed, scoffed at, and—worst of all—ignored by the entire archaeological establishment. Most New World paleontologists have based their entire careers on the "no earlier than twenty thousand years" theory, and Calico upsets the apple cart; so its discoveries are dismissed and swept under the rug. Young archaeologists who mention Calico in a paper or examine its evidence risk losing their credibility and stature in the scientific community. But at least you can see the archaeological pits and tools for yourself. A self-guided trail gives you a good sense of the site and what was discovered there, and the guided tours (at the hours given above) are even more informative. Keep that mind open.

LANCASTER

Edwards Air Force Base
Where the sound barrier was broken and spy planes are tested.

The base has three entrance gates: on 120th Street East, from the eastern side of Lancaster; on Rosamond Boulevard, just east of the town of Rosamond; and at the other end of Rosamond Boulevard, south of the town of North Edwards. You will not be admitted to the base if you have not made an advance reservation for one of the tours. The Air Force tour is on Fridays only, at 10:00 A.M.; call (661) 277-3517 to reserve a spot. The NASA tour is given Mon.–Fri. at 10:15 A.M. and 1:15 P.M.; call (661) 258-3446 or -3460. The guards at the entrance gates will give directions to the exact meeting site once you show up. Both tours are free.

For years it was thought that man could never travel faster than the speed of sound. But that didn't stop pilot Chuck Yeager from climbing into an experimental rocket plane right here at Edwards in 1947 and blasting into history, creating the first man-made sonic boom. Edwards has since become the center for aeronautic innovation: almost all new military craft are tested here extensively, long before they become public knowledge. Until very recently Edwards was also the landing site for the space shuttle, but now they only use it when the weather is bad in Florida, so your chances of seeing the *Enterprise* touch down are pretty slim. A small historical museum was being relocated at the time of this writing to a new location on Rosamond Boulevard at Lancaster Boulevard, but both NASA and the Air Force offer their own in-depth tours here. If you have to choose just one, the Air Force tour takes you deeper into the base: visitors get to ride a bus along the Rogers Lake "flight line," where experimental planes take off and land. NASA gives a walking tour of the Dryden Flight Research Center that shows hangars, historic airplanes, and a video about the base.

Whatever you do, *don't* start chatting about formerly top-secret airplanes you may have read about in *Newsweek* or the *New York Times*. It was widely reported in the early '90s that the Aurora, an astounding new spy plane that flies at Mach 8—that's 5,280 mph—was being tested here at Edwards. But the tour leaders will not speak of it or even acknowledge its existence, though they will talk freely about many other futuristic spacecraft and fighter jets that seem just as militarily sensitive, such as the Mach 7 X-43A, the Centurion (which skims along the top of the earth's atmosphere), and next-generation space shuttles.

Cypress

Forest Lawn Cypress
The final resting place of Karen Carpenter and Eddie Cochran.

4471 Lincoln Avenue. From central Los Angeles, take the San Diego Freeway (Highway 405) south through Long Beach; exit onto Highway 605 heading north, then exit at the Carson Street off-ramp. Go east one mile on Carson Street, which becomes Lincoln Avenue: the cemetery is on the north side of the street between Bloomfield Avenue and Moody Street. Open daily 8:00 A.M.–5:00 P.M. (714) 828-3131.

Karen Carpenter's fame endures not merely because she started her career as a rock 'n' roll curiosity (a girl who could play drums!), nor because of her nineteen hit songs ("We've Only Just Begun," "Top of the World," etc.). Nor is it because her flaccid warbling epitomized for many teens what was wrong with '70s music (with no gusto: "Why . . . do . . . birds . . . suddenly appear . . . ?")—but rather because she starved herself to death at age thirty-two. Suddenly anorexia nervosa, once the precious little secret of a million skinny girls, was on the front page. Tabloid photos of the singer's smiling, skeletal face shocked a nation. Now she rests in the rather chunky Carpenter family tomb. To reach it, enter the park and make your way to the towering Ascension Mosaic (it's hard to miss) northwest of the administration building. Enter the mausoleum to the left of the mosaic; turn left through the first door and go a few yards down the hallway. You'll see the large white Carpenter family tomb under a painting of the Madonna and Child at the end of a small alcove on your left. Her epitaph reads: "A star on earth—a star in heaven."

Karen Carpenter's tomb

Also buried here in Cypress is '50s rock idol Eddie Cochran ("Summertime Blues," "C'mon Everybody"), whose catchy, energetic teen anthems had epitomized the kind of vitality that the Carpenters lacked. His 1960 death in a bloody London car crash after a sold-out tour across England made bigger headlines in Europe than

Buddy Holly's similarly tragic death a year earlier. He is supposedly buried in the Abiding Faith section, near the fence along Lincoln Avenue, though his grave is not easy to find.

Buena Park

Medieval Times
Where the Cable Guy heard hoofbeats.

> 7662 Beach Boulevard, one block north of Knott's Berry Farm. Shows held Mon.–Thurs., 7:00 P.M.; Sat. at 6:00 and 8:15 P.M.; Sun. at 5:00 and 7:15 P.M.; showtimes vary on Fri. Admission: adults, $35; children age 12 and under, $23.95. (714) 521-4740 or (800) 899-6600.

These days you just don't get many opportunities to watch a nice, savage joust. This dinner-theater spectacle is staged inside the kind of fake castle that Orange County does best. One all-inclusive price buys a faux crown and meaty repast sans fork while costumed horses and riders career around a stadium wielding swords, shields, bludgeons, and axes. Viewers got a glimpse of all this in *The Cable Guy,* which was filmed here. A torture museum inside the castle stocked with chastity belts, stretchers, and more whets appetites and provides diversion for ticket holders waiting for the evening to begin.

Movieland Wax Museum
Where Dorothy doesn't move.

> 7711 Beach Boulevard, one block north of Knott's Berry Farm, across the street from Medieval Times. Open Mon.–Fri., 10:00 A.M.–6:00 P.M.; Sat.–Sun., 9:00 A.M.–7:00 P.M. Admission: adults, $12.95; children ages 4–11, $6.95; under age 4, free. (714) 522-1154.

Over three hundred life-size likenesses cast a slightly creepy spell at this wax palace, which has been chiseling replicas since 1962. Detailed dioramas recreating scenes from *The Wizard of Oz, Star Trek, Patton,* and many other productions stay preternaturally still, with some figures looking a lot more realistic than others. A Chamber of Horrors section evokes gory scenes in typical wax museum fashion. The on-site Starprint Gallery features autographs and hand- and footprints put there by flesh-and-blood celebs, including Gloria Estefan and Ed Asner.

Anaheim

Disneyland Disasters
When dreams fall apart.

> *1313 Harbor Boulevard, at Katella Avenue—you can't miss it. Open every day; call for current hours. Admission: adults, $39; children ages 3–11, $29. (714) 781-4565 or (714) 781-4000.*

Once upon a time—actually more than once—things have gone terribly wrong at Disneyland, turning it, for some, into the *unhappiest* place on earth. On opening day in July 1955 dark omens were already under way when actors James Mason and Jeff Chandler scuffled over which of their children would ride first on the carousel. Months later a woman was seriously injured by falling barrels when a cable broke inside Mr. Toad's Wild Ride. Maimings and deaths were to materialize like fairy dust over the passing years. The towering Matterhorn has claimed several victims: In 1964 a boy stood up in his bobsled, tumbled to the tracks below, and was mortally injured. Twenty years later another rider fell off, was struck by a passing bobsled, and died. Two teens were stabbed at the foot of the mountain during a gang fight in 1981; one died. Less idyllic than it looks, Tom Sawyer Island has witnessed two deaths. In 1973, and again in 1983, boys trying to stage Huckleberryish capers of their own drowned in the shallow waters surrounding it. On Christmas Eve in 1998 a passenger aboard one of the park's least exciting rides, a riverboat, died when a mooring anchor broke loose and struck him. Speaking of deceptively dull rides, consider the Monorail. In 1966 it killed a man who was attempting to sneak into the park. In 1967 the pokey and now defunct People Mover crushed a teen when he tried to crawl between cars. The ride had to be taken apart to free his corpse. Many more riders were injured over the next few years, and then in 1980 another teen attempting to climb between cars was dragged a ways, crushed, and killed. Many a visitor has sued Disneyland over injuries sustained while "driving" the Autopia cars; others have fallen from the Big Thunder Mountain Railroad, been hurt riding Dumbo, and faced violence in the parking lot. That's where a teen was killed during a 1987 fracas between Samoan and Tongan gangs.

Those radical Yippies staged a riot here on "Yippie Day"—August 6, 1970, anniversary of the Hiroshima bombing. A few hundred of them stormed the park, flushed tourists out of Fort Wilderness, and ran up a Vietcong flag. Nudity and drug-fueled antics ensued. Since opening day the park has lured a steady stream of crowned heads and celebs. Liz Taylor rented the whole place for her sixtieth birthday celebration; Michael Jackson was spotted one day crawling onto the Peter Pan ride disguised as an invalid. Some pay thousands to join the exclusive Club 33. Watch its door at 33 Royal Street in New Orleans Square for a possible peek at the likes of Arnold, Jack Nicholson, and Kevin Kline.

Garden Grove

Disney's First Garage Workshop

In the Stanley Ranch Museum, 12174 Euclid Street, south of Chapman Avenue, about 2 miles southwest of Disneyland. Tours are given only on the third Sunday of each month at 1:30 P.M. Admission: adults, $2; children, $1. (714) 530-8871.

Walt Disney's first animation workshop was a garage next to the home of his uncle Robert Disney at 4406 Kingswell, in L.A.'s Silverlake district (see page 118). In 1982 the garage was purchased, removed from the property, and put in storage. Eventually it was installed here in the Stanley Ranch Museum, a collection of antique buildings from around Garden Grove that have been rescued from the perils of development. The garage looks out of place among the old barbershops and schoolhouses; the only reason it was brought here was the park's proximity to Disneyland. From 1923 to 1926 Disney created some of his first crude cartoon shorts inside the barnlike garage, which is now festooned with antique filmmaking and animation equipment. Unfortunately, the museum is open only one day a month, and the garage is so far back in the lot that passersby can't see it from the street when the museum is closed.

Crystal Cathedral
Sheer spirituality.

12141 Lewis Street, at Chapman Avenue, Garden Grove. Tours given Mon.–Sat., 9:00 A.M.– 3:30 P.M.; Sun. 12:30–4:00 P.M. (714) 971-4000; memorial park, (714) 971-4138.

If you think TV ministries are evil, then this place will definitely give you the shivers. A shimmery twelve stories high, it's the world's largest glass building. The Reverend Robert Schuller, its helmsman, launched his career in the 1950s as pastor of a "drive-in" church—what could be more Californian? Now he broadcasts his weekly *Hour of Power* TV program from here. Christmas and Easter pageants staged on the premises feature the likes of Glen Campbell, Crystal Gayle, and John Tesh, not to mention live camels. Do *you* have enough faith to visit a glass church in earthquake country? The adjoining memorial park is the permanent home of Marie Cal-

lender, real-life foundress of the eponymous pie restaurant chain. Her remains are in
the Sanctuary of Praise mausoleum room.

Newport Beach

Hard Rock Café
*451 Newport Center Drive, at San Miguel Drive, in the Fashion Island shopping mall, New-
port Beach. Open Sun.–Thurs., 11:30 A.M.–11:00 P.M.; Fri.–Sat., 11:30 A.M.–11:30 P.M. (949)
640-8844.*

A plethora of priceless rock 'n' roll artifacts dangle from the walls while a stylish
vintage Cadillac looks on. Inspect a bunch of original Beatles and Elvis stuff.
Also here are Elton's eyeglasses and lofty platforms and Madonna's leather jacket—
displayed, for laughs, along with her high school yearbook. Also check out the famous *Purple Rain* suit worn by the Artist Once Again Known as Prince.

San Clemente

Nixon's Western White House
*4100 Calle Isabella, San Clemente. Calle Isabella is in a gated community called Cypress
Shores, in the southernmost part of San Clemente: the entrance is on Avenida del Presidente
at Avenida Vista del Oceano, on the west side of Highway 5, below San Clemente State Park.
The Western White House is at the very end of Calle Isabella, overlooking the beach, at the
southernmost tip of Orange County. Note: Casual visitors are barred from Cypress Shores.*

When the pressure of being the most hated president since Herbert Hoover got
too much to bear, Richard Nixon fled to his San Clemente home, which he
called Casa Pacifica but which the world knew as the Western White House. Its location suited the Secret Service: a nearly inaccessible strip of land on a bluff overlooking the ocean, at the back of an exclusive private enclave behind a heavily
guarded gate. Just to the south was a little-used Coast Guard station with buildings
for staff members, to which Nixon was ferried in a golf cart along a private road.
Nixon hated Washington and loved this house, so he spent a lot of time here during
his tenure. Neighbors saw world leaders such as Leonid Brezhnev showing up at all

hours to talk with him. (Odd coincidence number 374: President Franklin D. Roosevelt once stayed in the house back when it was called Cotton's Estate, home of a wealthy Democrat named Hamilton Cotton.) After Watergate, Nixon was often seen walking alone on the beach, mumbling to himself. He moved out in 1980.

The beach below the house is public: access it either from San Clemente State Park to the north or the trail Nixon himself must have used, which runs from the intersection of Avenida del Presidente and Cristianitos Road, right past the back of the house, down to the beach. Look up when you get to the famed surfing spot called Cotton's Point (named after the house itself); you can see the red-and-white adobe-style building on the bluff over the beach. And that's about as close as you can get.

Yorba Linda

Richard Nixon Library and Birthplace
Where they love Dick.

18001 Yorba Linda Boulevard, at Eureka Avenue, Yorba Linda. Open Mon.–Sat., 10:00 A.M.–5:00 P.M.; Sundays, 11:00 A.M.–5:00 P.M. Admission: adults, $5.95; children, $2; under age 8, free; no charge to visit gift shop. (714) 993-5075.

Old Glory flies proudly over a little house where the only U.S. president ever to resign was born. Also on the property are nearly two dozen exhibition galleries and theaters recounting Nixon's life and career. Childhood items, clothes, books, and the disgraced president's fully furnished study are here, along with a big chunk of the Berlin Wall. Don't miss the shiny .45 automatic pistol—a gift to Nixon from the patriotic Elvis Presley. In one gallery, lifelike bronze replicas of world leaders schmooze in armchairs. At another point visitors can don headsets and hear an incriminating tape in which Nixon reveals his impending involvement in the Watergate affair. A touch-screen TV lets you "ask" the president about it and hear his "answer." A gift shop offers Nixonian wares including coffee mugs, yo-yos, golf balls, and more. As an extra bonus, also on the property are the first lady's colorful garden and the graves of Dick and Pat themselves.

Hollywood

(Entries arranged as a tour running east to west.)

Pantages Theatre

6233 Hollywood Boulevard, near Vine. (213) 480-3232.

When it first opened in 1930 impresario Alexander Pantages was in prison for raping a teen (he was later acquitted). This was the nation's first Art Deco cinema, and its entryway is still resplendent in sunshine gold and swimming pool blue, with golden statuary evoking cowboys and Indians. After Howard Hughes acquired the place in 1949 it became the Academy Awards' venue for the next ten years, and it was here that the first televised Oscar ceremony was held. Since 1977 the focus has been on live performances. Hughes's ghost is said to haunt the Pantages, as is that of a young actress who allegedly died of malnutrition in the balcony in the theater's early days. Staffers report ghostly voices singing in the empty theater—"auditioning," they say.

Pantages Theatre

Capitol Records Building

1750 N. Vine Street, just north of Hollywood Boulevard, Hollywood. Lobby usually open during business hours. (323) 462-6252.

Legend has it that Nat "King" Cole and Capitol Records cofounder Johnny Mercer (composer of such hits as "That Old Black Magic" and "Moon River") designed this circular office building to resemble a stack of records. The "stylus" on top has a light that blinks out "H-O-L-L-Y-W-O-O-D" in Morse code. Founded in

1942, Capitol Records has had many of this century's
top stars on its roster, from Frank Sinatra to the Beatles
to Pink Floyd. Though Capitol offers no tours of the
building, visitors can prowl the lobby and admire hundreds of gold records by artists such as the Beach Boys,
Jimi Hendrix, the Beatles *(Rubber Soul, Abbey Road)*, the
Steve Miller Band, Cole himself, and gold CDs from
groups like Megadeth. Many of the Walk of Fame stars
on the sidewalk in front of the building honor Capitol
Records performers. And on the south side of the building, overlooking the parking lot, is a grotesque mural of
Billie Holiday and other famed jazz musicians.

Hollywood Walk of Fame

Capitol Records Building

Stars on the sidewalk.

> Hollywood Boulevard, on both sides of the street, between La Brea and Gower; also on Vine
> Street, between Sunset and Yucca. For information on upcoming unveilings of new stars, call
> the Hollywood Chamber of Commerce: (323) 469-8311.

Forty years ago the Hollywood Chamber of Commerce cooked up this idea as a
publicity stunt. New names in bronze are installed monthly along the seventeen-
block stretch to join over two thousand others. In five categories—movies, radio,
TV, live theater, and recorded music—practically everyone you can think of is here,
from Lucille Ball to Groucho Marx to Fleetwood Mac, not to mention Buster
Keaton, Ronald Reagan, Robin Williams, Red Skelton, Dolly Parton, Lassie, Wesley
Snipes, Greta Garbo, Patrick Swayze, John Lennon, Roy Rogers, David Hasselhoff,
Audrey Hepburn, Ingrid Bergman, and William Shatner. A stroll along these blocks
becomes bizarre as you spot more and more names that seem either completely un-
deserving or totally unfamiliar. Morning unveilings tend to draw a celebrity crowd,
as colleagues hail the guest of honor. New stars installed in 2000 immortalize Don
Knotts, Jim Carrey, KISS, and more.

The L. Ron Hubbard Life Exhibition

Scientologists salute their helmsman.

> 6331 Hollywood Boulevard, at Ivar Avenue, on the north side of the street. Open daily,
> 10:30 A.M.–10:00 P.M. Admission: $5, but sometimes free for skeptics at the cashier's discre-
> tion. (323) 960-3511.

As you wander down disorienting corridors a spunky tour guide describes colorful exhibits recalling the travels, art, and revelations of Scientology's founder,

L. Ron Hubbard. (But Scientology is not even mentioned until well into the tour.) Examine photographs of Hubbard extracting wisdom from spiritual masters in remote lands. View a vast collection of the pulp fiction he wrote for a living. Thrill to life-size dummies in space suits enacting scenes from Hubbard's sci-fi novels. (John Travolta starred in 2000's *Battlefield Earth,* a film based on one of these books.) A series of vivid paintings shows Hubbard wowing scientists with his radical theories regarding illness and health. Enter a room jammed with copies of Hubbard's self-help tomes—originally written, Hubbard later admitted, as a joke. At this point you will hear the *S*-word and its companion, the *D*-word: *Dianetics.* Right before the tour ends, a film with high production values pulls out all the stops, exhorting slack-jawed viewers to join the movement. And finally, an image of Hubbard beams out at you from amid his dozens of awards as his recorded voice thunders above.

The Knickerbocker
Where they couldn't conjure Houdini.

1714 Ivar Avenue, at Hollywood Boulevard, on the east side of the street.

Today this towering structure, with its impressive vintage neon sign, is an all-Russian senior citizens' residence. By the 1960s it had fallen on hard times, but in earlier years this was a glamorous hotel. After Harry Houdini died in 1926 his widow Beatrice conducted a séance here. During his life the escape artist had been a skeptic, but Houdini felt that if any spirit could slip its bonds and speak to the living, it would be his. Though Beatrice staged several séances—the most famous of which was held here—she had no luck. Other sad stories cling to the place; reportedly, the celebrated yet surnameless studio costume designer Irene leaped to her death from an upper floor of the Knickerbocker, and D. W. Griffith died here a disdainful drunk in 1948.

Hollywood Studio Club
Where "Auntie Em" overdosed.

1745 Wilcox Avenue, just north of Hollywood Boulevard, on the west side of the street.

This yellow-and-aqua complex has a heavy-handed faux Art Deco façade that shimmers behind a row of palms. The apartment building formerly on this site, then numbered 1735 Wilcox and now torn down, was home to Clara Blandick, who played Auntie Em in *The Wizard of Oz.* In the spring of 1962 she faced failing eyesight and other health problems. As the story goes, she went to the hairdresser, came home to her modest flat, dressed immaculately, and swallowed an overdose of sleeping pills, slipping a plastic bag over her head to make extra sure. Rumor has it that later tenants in this building have included both Farrah Fawcett and Snoop Dogg.

"You Are the Star" Mural

On the east side of Wilcox Avenue, just a few steps south of Hollywood Boulevard.

Rows and rows of movie greats are painted as if they're sitting in a theater staring fixedly at . . . *you*. Marilyn is there, as are John Wayne, Woody Allen, Joan Crawford, Humphrey Bogart, Lauren Bacall, and Charlie Chaplin. Richard Burton is there, too, dressed as Marc Antony. The muralist obviously struggled with perspective and proportion, and lost. Thus shoulders and noses jut at unlikely angles; Bacall's head seems swollen and about to burst.

Celebrity Lingerie Hall of Fame

Frederick's of Hollywood Lingerie Museum, 6608 Hollywood Boulevard, at Whitley Avenue, on the south side of the street. Open Mon.–Sat., 10:00 A.M.–6:00 P.M.; Sundays, noon–5:00 P.M. (323) 466-8506.

Frederick's has been famous for decades as the store where you can buy peekaboo teddies, push-up bras, marabou tidbits, and crotchless knickknacks. In the store's rear—where else?—is an underwear history museum stocked with pointy torpedo bras and such. The museum's Celebrity Hall of Fame has actual lingerie previously worn by Marilyn Monroe, Cher, Doris Day, Belinda Carlisle, Pamela Anderson, Madonna, and many others. Inspect the stars' bras, slips, panties, bustiers, and other unmentionables. Wow, if that tricot could talk . . . ! Check out

Celebrity Lingerie Hall of Fame

Mae West's feathered robe, Robert Redford's striped boxer shorts, Tom Jones's garters, Phyllis Diller's bra (embroidered "This Side Up"), and a purple lace confection Natalie Wood wore in *Bob and Carol and Ted and Alice*.

Musso & Frank Grill
Hollywood's oldest watering hole.

*6667 Hollywood Boulevard, on the north side of the street. Open Tues.–Sat., 11:00 A.M.–
11:00 P.M. (323) 467-5123 or (323) 467-7788.*

These red vinyl booths, richly paneled walls, and big mirrored bar have soothed
the famous ever since the place opened in 1919. Charlie Chaplin preferred a
booth just to the left of the door. Dorothy Parker, Nathanael West, Erskine Caldwell,
F. Scott Fitzgerald, Aldous Huxley, Lillian Hellman, Dashiell Hammett, William
Saroyan, and William Faulkner would stroll over from the nearby Writers Guild
headquarters. Raymond Chandler is said to have written *The Big Sleep* here—no
wonder Humphrey Bogart was a habitué. They say Keith Richards stops by whenever he's in town; and they say the sauerbraten, Salisbury steak, Welsh rarebit, and
shrimp Louie still attract the likes of Sean Penn, David Lynch, Jonathan Winters,
Madonna, and more.

Les Deux Cafés

*1635 N. Las Palmas Avenue, just south of Hollywood Boulevard, on the east side of the
street. (213) 465-0509.*

Walk right in, it's around the back. But don't expect anything so gauche as a
sign out front to guide you to this hidden garden restaurant. Be bold and
sally forth down an unmarked breezeway on the south side of the house. Madonna
and her pals have been spotted here. And when Nicole Kidman came home from
making *Eyes Wide Shut* in England, this is where she threw herself a welcome-back
party. An olive tree and burbling water tank preside over the patio where foie gras,
confits, frisée, and vol-au-vent are served atop mosaicked tables whose chairs sport
gaily striped cushions. One kitchen here is devoted exclusively to pastry. How *do*
those gals stay so svelte?

Egyptian Theater
Anubis welcomes you.

*6712 Hollywood Boulevard, at Las Palmas Avenue, on the south side of the street. (323)
466-3456.*

The American Cinematheque—a film-loving nonprofit whose headquarters are
now lodged in this historic cinema—screens films here and stages other events
celebrating the moving image. Built with a flourish in 1922 by the same Sid Grauman who brought you the nearby Chinese Theatre, this one has an Egyptian theme
inspired by the discovery of King Tut's tomb that same year. Statuary and exotic

plants created an unforgettable effect: *The Ten Commandments* premiered here. But ironically the beautiful theater that was inspired by a ruin eventually became a near ruin itself. A massive renovation preceded its reopening in 1998. Now the theater's frescoes, hieroglyphics, waterfalls, sphinxes, sculpted deities, and papyrus plants are back in the pink.

Egyptian Theater

Hollywood Wax Museum
Great moments in paraffin.

> 6767 Hollywood Boulevard, at Highland Avenue, on the north side of the street. Open Sun.–Thurs., 10:00 A.M.–midnight; Fri.–Sat., 10:00 A.M.–2:00 A.M. Admission: adults, $9.95; children, $6.95; under age 6, free. (323) 462-8860.

If you're hungry for fun," chortles the museum's rendition of a talking apple tree from *The Wizard of Oz,* stationed near the door, "come in." Over two hundred wax figures portray stars of cinema and TV, and biblical personages, not to mention re-creations of painful torture devices. Facsimiles of the *Phantom Menace* cast are here, as well as Antonio Banderas, the *Titanic* cast, and Mike Myers as Austin Powers. Waxen versions of Elvis, Stallone, and Marilyn share the limelight with waxen apostles, though the artisanry falls far short of perfection.

El Capitan Theatre
> 6838 Hollywood Boulevard on the south side of the street. (323) 467-7674.

Built by the architect who designed Griffith Park Observatory and the Shrine Auditorium, this lush building boasts Spanish Colonial finery inside and out. During the '20s and '30s, stage plays and song-and-dance shows performed here starred Fanny Brice, Rita Hayworth, Will Rogers, Clark Gable, Joan Fontaine, and others. A new era was launched when *Citizen Kane* had its world premiere here in 1941. After Disney acquired the theater a million-dollar restoration got under way and was unveiled in 1991. Today the entryway is palatial, chockablock with sculpted cupids and masks. Fantastic scenes are painted across interior walls in brilliant colors. The enormous stage, soaring ceiling, and costumed ushers will sour you on multiplexes forever. Disney premieres its blockbuster films here, pulling out the stops to accompany them with elaborate live acts—chorus lines, a pipe organ, the works.

Mann's Chinese Theatre

6925 Hollywood Boulevard, at Highland Avenue, on the north side of the street. (323) 461-3331 or (323) 464-8111.

At the world's most famous movie theater, most visitors are content to stay outside. In 1927 then-owner Sid Grauman had the kooky idea of getting stars to step in wet cement out front. The theater changed hands in 1973, but it still sports the faux pagoda front adorned with rampant dragons. In the forecourt are hundreds of footprints—from Shirley Temple, John Wayne, Paul Newman, Liz Taylor, Cary Grant, Marilyn Monroe, the Marx Brothers, Myrna Loy, Fred Astaire, Ginger Rogers, Sophia Loren, Doris Day, Eddie Cantor, Sidney Poitier, Gene Kelly, Natalie Wood, Jean Harlow, Tom Hanks, Denzel Washington, Al Pacino, Meryl Streep, Robin Williams, Steven Seagal, and many more. Crowds roam around thrusting their own feet into the prints. Most won't fit in Mary Pickford's, but Arnold Schwarzenegger's are among the most popular. Alongside them he scrawled,

Mann's Chinese Theatre

"I'll be back." And Clint Eastwood wrote alongside his own prints, "You made my day."

Hollywood Roosevelt Hotel

7000 Hollywood Boulevard, on the south side of the street. (323) 466-7000.

In 1927 this grand Spanish Revival hotel was erected with the express purpose of luring the Hollywood elite. Legends grew apace. A metal plaque in the hotel's Blossom Room records how the first Academy Awards ceremony was held here—allegedly it lasted a scant few minutes. On a still-extant tiled stairway in the back corner of the lobby, little Shirley Temple received a tap-dance lesson from Bill "Bojangles" Robinson. Potted palms and gorgeously painted ceilings maintain the glamour that attracted lovebirds Clark Gable and Carole Lombard. During Prohibition, Errol Flynn cooked up bootleg hooch in the barbershop here. Hemingway, F. Scott Fitzgerald, and even Salvador Dalí loitered in the hotel's Cinegrill, where Liberace and Mary Martin performed, though not at the same time. Marilyn Monroe

Marilyn Monroe mirror, Hollywood Roosevelt Hotel

lounged beside the pool. A mirror that used to be hers now hangs on a wall in the basement, just to the left of the elevators as you step off. A picture of Marilyn is strategically positioned so that her face appears ghostlike in the glass. In fact, her specter is said to manifest hereabouts, as is (on the ninth floor) Montgomery Clift's. Photos, clippings, and memorabilia displayed on the mezzanine trace the hotel's history. One cherished feature of the Roosevelt, now gone for good, was a miasma of curvy lines that artist David Hockney painted on the bottom of the swimming pool. An overeager cleanup job bleached them away.

Hollywood Entertainment Museum

7021 Hollywood Boulevard, at Sycamore Street, downstairs. Open daily July 1–Labor Day, 10:00 A.M.–6:00 P.M.; the rest of the year, Tues.–Sun., 10:00 A.M.–6:00 P.M. Admission: adults, $7.50; students, $4.50; children, $4; under age 5, free. (323) 465-7900.

The main attractions here are real-life famous TV film sets, including the actual bar from *Cheers* and the command bridge from *Star Trek: The Next Generation*. Celebrating cinematic history while offering a glimpse of what goes on behind the scenes, the museum features an editing suite as well as footage, costumes, interactive displays, and artifacts from the Max Factor collection (which formerly comprised a museum of their own, elsewhere). Assorted props include a *Ben-Hur* chariot.

Los Angeles Film Office

7083 Hollywood Boulevard, 5th floor, near La Brea Avenue. Open Mon.–Fri., 8:00 A.M.–6:00 P.M. Each day's shoot sheet costs $10; bring ID. (323) 957-1000.

This no-nonsense government office issues permits to companies wishing to film in Los Angeles. More interestingly, it also publishes a daily list of the exact locations where every movie, TV show, commercial, and video will be shot in the city that day. Show up at this office in the morning, fork over $10 for the list, and you can spend all day rubbernecking amid assistant directors and extras. Don't expect your ten-page list—called a "shoot sheet"—to mention a *Pulp Fiction* or an *L.A. Confidential:* since all the movies are still in the process of being made, you won't have heard of any of them yet. Years ago, yes, there were shoot sheets that listed where *Pulp Fiction* was being shot that day, but the title wouldn't have meant anything to you at the time, so you probably would have gone to see them making *Ninja Vengeance* instead. Thus the shoot sheet is more entertaining when used in conjunction with the weekly newspaper *Daily Variety*, which usually lists the names of actors and directors making movies in production. The day we tried out a shoot sheet, for example, a film then tentatively titled *Coyote Ugly* was being shot all over the place. Will *Coyote Ugly* be considered a classic years from now? Doubtful. Working titles of films-in-progress are often changed before release. TV shows are a little safer, since the same actors come back week after week. As another example, our sheet listed *Martial Law*, so we knew we had a good chance of seeing kung fu maestro Sammo Hung debasing himself for an American audience. Don't expect to meet a star loitering about between takes (they're usually inaccessible), and be warned that filming is 95 percent waiting around and 5 percent action. But once you've tasted what moviemaking is really like, you may get the fever and never want to go home.

Gardner Street School
Home of the Michael Jackson Auditorium.

> 7450 Hawthorn Avenue, at Gardner Street, between Hollywood and Sunset Boulevards; auditorium is visible on the southeast corner. (213) 876-4710.

Michael Jackson Auditorium, Gardner Street School

Jacko only attended this pinkish beige Art Deco elementary school for about a month of his sixth-grade year, yet he later donated money to enhance its music program. In return the campus—now in a largely Russian neighborhood—named its auditorium after him. Ukrainian murderer Mikhail Markhasev—who shot Ennis Cosby (see **Ennis Cosby Murder Site**, page 88)—is also a Gardner alumnus.

Divine Death Site

> Formerly the Regency Plaza Suites, now the Regency Apartments, 7940 Hollywood Boulevard, on the south side of the street, near Fairfax Avenue, at the western edge of Hollywood. (323) 656-4555.

Flamboyant transvestite Divine was the leading "lady" of ten feature films, most of them directed by gross-out king John Waters. The team paired up in the late 1960s and rose from Baltimore's netherworld to national fame as auteurs of some of the most revolting films ever made, including the classic *Pink Flamingos*, in which Divine eats dog doo on camera. The 1980s saw Divine (real name: Glen Milstead) gaining respectability with critically acclaimed performances in *Polyester* and *Hairspray*, but just as s/he teetered on the verge of mainstream stardom, a heart attack in this low-key hotel ended the party. You can't see the inside of the second-story front room where the morbidly obese Divine died in his sleep, but you can stand in front of the pastel green building—recently converted into apartments—and snap pictures of the window where it supposedly happened.

ABOVE HOLLYWOOD BOULEVARD

Hillside Strangler Home

Tamarind Place Apartments, 1950 Tamarind Avenue, at Chula Vista Way, on the east side of the street.

Big and pink and peach, this balconied complex has a tiled roof and a '70s mien. One former tenant is Kenneth Bianchi, now notorious as half of the Hillside Strangler team. After a string of L.A. women turned up murdered in late 1977 and early 1978, Bianchi was caught and led police to his cousin, Glendale upholsterer Angelo Buono. Current residents are aware of their sinister predecessor, though management does not disclose which apartment was Bianchi's. (See also page 149.)

Church of Scientology Celebrity Centre International

5930 Franklin Avenue, at Cheremoya Avenue, three blocks north of Hollywood Boulevard. (323) 960-3100.

Tall, white, charming Chateau Elysée was once a retirement home for aged actors and, before that, a residence for many Hollywood types, including Mary Pickford. Today the Church of Scientology operates a restaurant and hotel inside. Celebrity Scientologists such as John Travolta, Kirstie Alley, Kelly Preston, and Jenna Elfman have a way of popping up here all the time. An authentic replica of founder L. Ron Hubbard's office graces the ground floor near the entrance. As far back as the '50s Hubbard actively sought celebrities as spokespersons for the church, and his dreams have come true. A full schedule of seminars, screenings, and classes—all of which are thinly disguised recruitment sessions—is offered amid elegant furnishings and gardens. But staffers have been known to act a tad skittish toward curious visitors who prowl around uninvited.

Church of Scientology Celebrity Centre International

Don't expect to escape without repeated, insistent offers of a "free tour" that may end up lasting your whole life.

Alto Nido Apartments
Where the Black Dahlia lived.

1851 Ivar Avenue, just north of Franklin Avenue, three blocks north of Hollywood Boulevard, on the west side of the street.

A starstruck wannabe while alive, Elizabeth Short grabbed headlines after death in January 1947 when her mutilated corpse turned up in a vacant lot. Nicknamed "the Black Dahlia" for her dyed hair, she was tortured and killed by a person—or persons—unknown, and remains one of L.A.'s most famous murder victims. A drifter and a good-time girl, Short lived at the time of her death in this tile-roofed white apartment house whose balconies offer a romantic view of the hills. The house also appears in the movie *Sunset Boulevard:* before making his fateful move into Norma Desmond's mansion, William Holden's character lives here. In an early scene we see him through a third-floor window at the house's northwestern corner, overlooking the street. And there's more: Wallace Beery was an early owner, Claudette Colbert lived for a while in the penthouse, and Renee Zellweger was a recent tenant.

Alto Nido Apartments

Day of the Locust House

Parva Sed Apartments, 1817 Ivar Avenue, just north of Franklin Avenue, three blocks north of Hollywood Boulevard, on the west side of the street.

The author Nathanael West (born Nathan Weinstein) lived in a third-floor studio, complete with a Murphy bed, on the northwestern corner of this Tudor-style house. All the striving and conniving in his midst inspired him to write *The Day of the Locust*, a novel that unmasks '30s Hollywood in all its hedonistic madness (and features a protagonist named Homer Simpson). Those wild times would claim him, too: West died young, driving recklessly.

Hollywood Bowl

2301 N. Highland Avenue, just west of the Hollywood Freeway (Highway 101), in the hills directly above Hollywood. Grounds open to visitors during daylight hours. Museum open July–September, Tues.–Sat., 10:00 A.M.–8:30 P.M.; October–June, Tues.–Sat., 10:00 A.M.–4:30 P.M. (323) 850-2000 (events) or (323) 850-2058 (museum).

This world-famous concert venue has seen memorable performances by the Beatles (who were the first rock band to play here, in August 1964), Elton John,

Bob Dylan, Jimi Hendrix (who opened for the Monkees!), and the Doors. Chosen at random, any live album recorded sometime in the last forty years is likely to announce "Live at the Hollywood Bowl!"—and that goes double for bootlegs. Famous bands still play here regularly, and special events usually feature appearances by movie stars. During the day you can prowl the empty outdoor theater, and even climb on the same stage (though this is discouraged) where your favorite band, whichever it was, is likely to have played at one point or another. The on-site museum features, among other things, exhibits on many of the best-known concerts here, including rare video clips, audio recordings, and photos of the greats in action. Several movies also feature scenes shot here, including the original version of *A Star Is Born,* and the disastrous *Xanadu.*

Bobby Fuller Death Site

1776 Sycamore Avenue, at Franklin Avenue, on the east side of the street.

He had a hit in March 1966 with "I Fought the Law." Months later, singer Bobby Fuller was found dead in his fume-filled car in front of this sleek three-story apartment complex whose swimming pool is fringed invitingly with tropical foliage. Officially it was ruled a suicide, though certain details still cloud the story. Why, for example, would young Fuller snuff himself at the peak of his career near the curb of a house where he did not live? Occasional news crews still arrive to probe the mystery.

Highland Gardens Hotel
Where Janis died.

7047 Franklin Avenue, at Sycamore Avenue, on the north side of the street. (323) 850-0536.

Today this modern hotel basks in dappled sunlight as venerable palm trees shield it from the world. Banana plants add yet more lushness, and a row of international flags flutters out front. The management firmly keeps mum about Janis Joplin's death here on an October night in 1970, when this was still called the Landmark Hotel. Staying in room 105, Joplin had a visit from a heroin dealer. After making a purchase, she ventured outside for a while. Later she returned to her room. A quick trip to the lobby for cigarettes was the last time she was seen alive. Her overdose that night was most likely accidental.

Yamashiro
Masquerades as Japan in movies and TV.

> *1999 N. Sycamore Avenue; follow the signs uphill (north) from Franklin Avenue. Open Sun.–Thurs., 5:30–10:00 P.M.; Fri.–Sat., 5:30–11:30 P.M. (323) 466-5125.*

B uilt as a private residence in 1914, this hillside replica of a Kyoto palace was originally landscaped with a private zoo, canals, a large imported pagoda, and an entire miniature Japanese village. Later it was an exclusive club, then, during the depression, a reputed brothel where down-and-out actresses made ends meet. During World War II, accusations flew that it was a secret signal tower for the Japanese. To assuage the prevalent paranoia, Yamashiro was altered beyond recognition. Then it fell into such disrepair that by 1948 it was scheduled for demolition—only to be saved at the eleventh hour. Lovingly restored, it became an exotic restaurant whose Japanese ambience lured a Hollywood crowd. Some, including Richard Pryor, lived in apartments on the property. The lofty "Skyroom" doubled as Japan in such movies as *Sayonara* and *Teahouse of the August Moon.* It also appeared in TV shows including *I Spy, Route 66, Perry Mason,* and *My Three Sons.* These days, celebrity soirees are a staple here—the *Lethal Weapon 4* post-premiere party, for instance.

Ozzie and Harriet House
> *1822 Camino Palmero (a cul-de-sac), at Franklin Avenue, on the east side of the street.*

T he popular '50s TV show starred Ozzie, Harriet, David, and Ricky Nelson playing characters called Ozzie, Harriet, David, and Ricky Nelson. This gray-shingled New England–style home stood in for the TV family's house in exterior shots. Surprise! In a *Truman Show*–esque twist, this was also the actual Nelsons' actual home. (The TV Nelsons lived on "Sycamore Road.") Eager fans are said to have loitered here hoping for a glimpse of Ricky. Today the house hides behind a heavy iron gate and thick hedge.

SUNSET BOULEVARD

(Entries arranged as a tour running east to west.)

KTLA Studios (formerly Warner Bros. Studio)
Where the first talking picture and Looney Tunes were made.

> 5800 Sunset Boulevard, between Van Ness and Bronson Avenues, just west of the Holly-
> wood Freeway (Highway 101). (323) 460-5500.

Other movie sites claim primacy for this or that innovation, but KTLA has the "first" that really counts: it was on this exact location in 1927 that Warner Bros. made *The Jazz Singer,* the world's first talking picture, thus launching the film industry as we know it today. *The Jazz Singer* was actually just the first film with dialogue; *Don Juan,* also made on this site but a year earlier, was the first film with a *soundtrack,* which many believe is the more important breakthrough. Though Warners moved most of its operations to Burbank a short time later, this lot still hosted some productions, including Jimmy Cagney's *Public Enemy,* with its classic grapefruit-in-the-face scene. In the '40s Warners made the immortal Looney Tunes animated shorts here (with Bugs Bunny and the gang), as well as propaganda films for World War II. Later the lot was mostly taken over by KTLA, one of the nation's first television stations and proud claimant to several more broadcasting firsts: the first station to show an atomic bomb explosion; the first station to broadcast live from a helicopter; the first station to broadcast color programs; and the only TV station ever to win an Academy Award. In the '90s KTLA gained more fame as the "All O. J., All the Time" station, the only one in the country to show every single minute of the seemingly endless O. J. Simpson trial. KTLA does not offer tours of the facility, so the only way onto the lot is to pick up free tickets (from Audiences Unlimited, or in front of Mann's Chinese Theatre) to any of the live-audience shows taped here, such as *Judge Judy.*

Sunset-Gower Studios (formerly Columbia Pictures)
> 1438 Gower Street, just south of Sunset Boulevard, on the east side of the street. (323) 467-
> 1001.

The uninspiring sobriquet "Sunset-Gower Studios" hides the true former identity of this property. For fifty years it was the home of Columbia Pictures, a scrappy underdog studio that had to try harder to keep up with its bigger competitors. The extra effort paid off: celebrated films made here over the years include *It Happened One Night, From Here to Eternity, Mr. Smith Goes to Washington, On the*

Waterfront, and *Dr. Strangelove.* In the 1960s Columbia jumped with both feet into the world of television and through its subsidiary Screen Gems made favorites like *I Dream of Jeannie, Bewitched,* and *The Monkees.* In 1971 Columbia absconded, and the property became an un-affiliated rental lot. There's not much for the casual visitor to see here now except a wall-sized photo mural in the lobby showing Sunset Boulevard in the '20s. But you can get on the lot to dream of Peter Tork and Barbara Eden by reserving tickets (through Audiences Unlimited) to some of the live-audience TV shows currently taped here, most notably wet-dream Brandy's *Moesha.*

Sunset-Gower Studios (formerly Columbia Pictures)

The Hollywood Palladium
The mother of all ballrooms.

6215 Sunset Boulevard, at Argyle Avenue. (323) 962-7600.

Opening in 1940 as the world's largest dine-and-dance venue, the 40,700-square-foot Palladium easily accommodated thousands. Throughout World War II the era's top big bands came to play here, and Hollywood notables such as Betty Grable and Tyrone Power mingled with hordes of plebes on the dance floor. Lawrence Welk spent ten years broadcasting his TV show from the streamlined ballroom. Under its sparkling chandeliers the Emmy Awards, Grammy Awards, and Lollapalooza have been staged since. All this Decoesque vastness appeared in *The Blues Brothers, The Bodyguard, Day of the Locust, F.I.S.T., Mr. Saturday Night, What's Love Got to Do with It,* and others. A continuing stream of concerts here includes everyone from James Brown to the Who to Alice in Chains.

The Hollywood Palladium

Hollywood Athletic Club
Where Johnny Weissmuller trained to become Tarzan.

6525 Sunset Boulevard, at Wilcox Avenue, on the north side of the street. (323) 962-6600.

This big white landmark, built in 1924, once housed a private residential club founded by Cecil B. DeMille and popular with actors. Charlie Chaplin was an early habitué. A huge gym that used to be on the premises attracted macho types: Cornel Wilde was a lifeguard at the pool where Weissmuller and Buster Crabbe swam laps and into which, it is said, Errol Flynn took whizzes from two stories above. Stood up by Flynn, Jean Harlow arrived here once wearing only a coat. And on another legendary night John Barrymore was brought here by friends for a final drink—Barrymore was

Hollywood Athletic Club

freshly dead at the time. Departing from his image as an upstanding American, John Wayne was known to stand on the roof, throwing billiard balls at passing vehicles. In 1949 the first Emmy Awards were held here—a bronze plaque recalls the event. The pool has been converted to a ballroom; now the place is a dance hall and restaurant whose patrons include a sampling of the local talent.

Sunset Sound
Studio to the stars.

6650 Sunset Boulevard is the official address, though the entrance is around the corner on Cherokee Avenue, just south of Sunset.

You may never have heard of it, but Sunset Sound is the studio where some of rock's all-time greats recorded their best-known albums and songs. While Janis Joplin was in L.A. to record her album *Pearl* (with "Me and Bobby McGee") here at Sunset Sound, she overdosed just a few blocks away. The Doors made many of their hits here. Led Zeppelin recorded all the songs on their second and fourth albums here, including (yes!) "Stairway to Heaven." Ringo went solo behind these walls. Michael Jackson recorded *Thriller* here, at least in part. Prince—as he is again known —used the facilities to make *Purple Rain* and *1999*. More recently, Sheryl Crow and the Wallflowers recorded albums here. The studio is hard to notice because it has no sign; the owners took it down during the Rodney King riots, fearing looters would mistake the studio for a stereo store. Anticipating future civil unrest, they've never re-installed it. Sadly, no tours are offered. Unless you're a world-famous rock 'n' roller, all you can do is stand on the sidewalk and stare.

Designer Donuts
Doing its best to bloat Leonardo.

6660 Sunset Boulevard, in a strip mall on the south side of the street. (323) 463-7079.

Framed head shots on the wall reveal who adores these greasy, frosted delights: Brad Pitt, Pamela Anderson, Arnold Schwarzenegger, Matt Damon, Steven Spielberg, Sylvester Stallone, Alicia Silverstone, and "Weird Al" Yankovic beam down at the pink vinyl stools. Over the counter a sign reads: "Through extensive research and testing we have developed the ultimate . . . our exotic combination of flavors is designed to arouse." This doughnut hut prides itself on delivering its wares to casts and crews. A younger Steven Spielberg was once a partner in the biz but, as the story goes, it ended ickily. Along with his autograph, Leonardo writes, "Your donuts are unsinkable."

Designer Donuts

Cross Roads of the World
World's first shopping center.

6671 Sunset Boulevard. (213) 463-5611.

A Streamline Moderne tower capped with a globe soars above a building made to look like a ship, complete with portholes. Surrounding this centerpiece are other buildings in a mishmash of styles: Moorish, Tudor, Spanish, Bavarian. Five years after a flashy gangster was murdered on the property in 1931, his widow sought to erase the bad vibes by erecting this architectural fantasy. Originally the winsome structures housed shops, making this the world's first outdoor mall. Scenes from *L.A. Confidential* and *Indecent Proposal* were filmed here. Today it is an office complex, with a metal plaque declaring its landmark status.

Cross Roads of the World

Hollywood High School
Alma mater of the stars.

1521 N. Highland Avenue, at Sunset Boulevard, on the northwest corner. Alumni Museum open by appointment only: (323) 461-3891.

Moderne architecture replete with rounded corners distinguishes this campus, whose students today speak mainly Spanish and Armenian. "Welcome to World Famous Hollywood High School," declares an arrogant greeting painted on the wall of the administration building. Also on this building's "Walls of Fame" names of alums are painted amid jaunty red stars: Jason Robards, Judy Garland, James Garner, Fay Wray, Mickey Rooney, Tuesday Weld, Alan Hale, Ione Skye, Donovan Leitch, Linda Evans, Lana Turner . . . even the controversial spiritualist Bishop Pike. Adorning the building's main office are portraits, magazine covers, clippings, yearbook pages, and other novelties recalling Nanette Fabray, Carole Lombard, Carol Burnett (editor of the school paper), John Ritter (student body president), Warren Christopher (on the debate team), and more. Housed in another building slightly to the north (kept firmly locked unless you have an appointment) is the Alumni Museum: a maze of artifacts; articles,

Hollywood High School Alumni Museum

and mementos recall the aforementioned celebs, as well as Yvette Mimieux, Mike Farrell, Alexis Smith, Gloria Grahame, and the pioneering L.A. deejay "Real Don" Steele.

Chaplin Studios and A&M Records Site
1416–1420 N. La Brea Avenue, at Sunset Boulevard, on the east side of the street.

This area was the boondocks when Charlie Chaplin arrived and built his studios here in 1917. He built a lot of cute English-style cottages, complete with steep roofs and high brick chimneys, surrounded by landscaped greenery. And here he made his classic films, including *City Lights, Modern Times, The Great Dictator,* and *The Gold Rush.* After Chaplin's departure, TV shows were made here in the '50s. Later still, when A&M Records used this as its headquarters, the

Chaplin Studios and A & M Records site

"We Are the World" recording session was staged here. Scenes from 1992's biopic *Chaplin* were shot here, of course. After a series of corporate devourings, the much-shrunken facility was shut down in 1999, leaving its old-time tower, cute bungalows, and Chaplin's cement footprints to languish behind a stark metal fence, awaiting a new master.

Hollywood's Rock Walk
Where pickers put their fingers.

Guitar Center, 7425 Sunset Boulevard, on the north side of the street. Open Mon.–Fri., 10:00 A.M.–9:00 P.M.; Saturdays, 10:00 A.M.–6:00 P.M.; Sundays, 11:00 A.M.–6:00 P.M. (213) 874-1060.

In 1985 this guitar store took up the prints-in-wet-cement tradition. Under the big red awning out front, find your faves' handprints and signatures: Frank Zappa, Ozzy Osbourne, Dick Dale, Stevie Wonder, Smokey Robinson, the Ventures, Jan and Dean, Black Sabbath, Los Lobos, John Mayall, Johnny Cash, George Martin, Johnny Winter, the Ramones, Mötley Crüe, Alice Cooper, and more, are all here. But, axe fans, there's more. Memorabilia fills the storefront windows and display cases in a gift shop just to the left of the Rock Walk and the store's main entrance. Check out Bo Diddley's handmade guitar, a 1957 Les Paul amp, Jeff Beck's Stratocaster, Keith Moon's drums (you can't blame them for not being guitars) from *Tommy,* Peter Criss's platform   *Handprints at the Rock Walk*
boots, and a jacket worn by Nancy Wilson (of your favorite band, Heart). A hand-scribbled lyric sheet for "Garden Party" reveals what a sorry speller Ricky Nelson was.

Hugh Grant Blow Job Zone

The pickup happened at the northeast corner of Sunset Boulevard and Courtney Avenue (which becomes Spaulding Avenue to the south) in front of the Hollywood Church of Religious Science at 7677 Sunset Boulevard, across the street from All-American Burger. The interrupted BJ supposedly went down three blocks away at the intersection of Curson and Hawthorn Avenues.

It's never nice to see your mug shot plastered on the front page. But when the terms "oral sex" and "lewd conduct" appear in the caption, that's gotta hurt. Squeaky-clean and cute-as-an-English-schoolboy Hugh Grant brought this calamity upon himself on June 27, 1995, when he needed something his gorgeous girlfriend Elizabeth Hurley apparently couldn't supply. Hugh "met" Divine Brown on Sunset

Boulevard at Courtney. They drove to a quiet corner a few blocks away for a little business transaction, which—oops!—was interrupted by the cops. The international scandal machinery spun into action, but the sordid details seemed only to boost Hugh's career, banishing a vaguely unsatisfying sexlessness that his sheepish grin and boundless chivalry had previously given him. He got probation and a small fine and was on his way. The peaceful corner of Curson and Hawthorn is trimmed with leafy trees, palms, and bougainvillea—perfect for a midnight rendezvous.

Nightmare on Elm Street House
Your nightmare is real.

> *1428 Genesee Avenue, just south of Sunset Boulevard, three blocks east of Fairfax Avenue.*

D ream-world slasher Freddy Krueger has terrified two generations of moviegoers who have emerged from the theater relieved that "after all, it's just a movie." Or

is it? Walk down Hollywood's residential Genesee Avenue and you might start having second thoughts. The house identified as "1428 Elm Street" in the *Nightmare on Elm Street* horror films is in a fact a real house: Freddy fans will immediately recognize the home's mansard roof, white columns, and arched entryway. It's just that *Nightmare on Genesee Avenue* didn't have quite the same ring to it.

The Nightmare on Elm Street *house*

Halloween Houses
Where baby-sitting turned bad.

> *1534, 1536, and 1537 Orange Grove Avenue, at Sunset Boulevard.*

E xteriors for the original *Halloween* film were shot at the Colonial-style house at number 1534, which has shutters and stately trees. (A "corpse" was tossed off a balcony here at one point.) More were shot at the similarly Colonial number 1537, across the street, which boasts a widow's walk, a big front porch, and smooth white columns. *Halloween 3: Season of the Witch* was partly filmed at the equally lovely number 1536.

One of the houses used in Halloween

Schwab's Pharmacy Site

Former address, 8024 Sunset Boulevard; now a mall with a Virgin Megastore and Wolfgang Puck Café, 8000 Sunset Boulevard, at Crescent Heights Boulevard, on the southeast corner.

As William Holden put it so succinctly in *Sunset Boulevard,* Schwab's Pharmacy was the movie industry's "headquarters" for over three decades. Actors, agents, producers, and screenwriters used Schwab's as an informal office and playground. Over coffee and toothpicks (pharmacies in those days served food and drink) deals were made, careers launched, hopes dashed. Charlie Chaplin whiled away his leisure hours here, playing pinball and making milk shakes. Schwab's neon sign inspired songwriter Harold Arlen to write the melody for "Somewhere over the Rainbow." Legend has it F. Scott Fitzgerald died here of a heart attack while buying cigarettes. In fact, nearly every legend you've ever heard about Schwab's is true, except the most famous one: Lana Turner was *not* discovered here. (That happened at the long-gone Top Hat Malt Shop, across from Hollywood High School, from which she was playing hooky.) Torn down in 1986 and replaced with a mall, Schwab's is not only gone, it seems to be forgotten as well. Employees at Virgin and Wolfgang Puck's seem never to have heard of a place called Schwab's.

Pandora's Box Site

Music club that inspired the song "For What It's Worth" and **Riot on Sunset Strip.**

On a triangular traffic island in the middle of Crescent Heights Boulevard, where it intersects Sunset Boulevard, across the street from the Virgin store and the Wolfgang Puck Café.

Pandora's Box was a miserable little shack of a nightclub that graduated in the late '50s from jazz dive to beatnik hangout. By 1962 rock 'n' roll–crazed teens scared off the bongo-beating hipsters. A trendsetting booking policy made Pandora's Box the center of the Sunset Strip youth scene, and crowds of hormone-rich youth spilled out of the tiny club night after night. What a traffic hazard! By 1966 the police decided to clean up the corner by enforcing a strict curfew on teens attending shows here. The kids would have none of it: inspired by more socially meaningful riots elsewhere, they fought back. A series of nightly melees became a spectator sport for thousands. As punishment, the cops shut down the club for good. It was later demolished and turned into a barren traffic island with a bus stop and shrubbery. But the disturbances at the club made a big impression on L.A. at the time—enough to inspire the 1967 exploitation film *Riot on Sunset Strip.* And the protests glamorized in Buffalo Springfield's biggest hit "For What It's Worth" ("Stop, hey, what's that sound . . ."), were not Vietnam War protests, as everyone assumes, but rather the Pandora's Box riots.

Garden of Allah Site

*Now a shopping complex at the southwest corner of Sunset and Crescent Heights Boule-
vards, anchored by a Washington Mutual Bank at 8150 Sunset Boulevard, at the western
edge of Hollywood.*

The Garden of Allah was a collection of courtyard bungalows owned by silent-era
actress Alla Nazimova, who rented them out by the night or by the year to
movie-industry types. In the '30s and '40s it was essentially a free-form, free-love
commune of actors, writers, humorists, producers, and starlets, where great names
exchanged ideas and bodily fluids. Nearly everyone you ever heard of attended parties here; permanent residents included Errol Flynn, Dorothy Parker, F. Scott
Fitzgerald, Clara Bow, Humphrey Bogart, Greta Garbo, Tallulah Bankhead, Orson
Welles, and hundreds more. The nonstop deal-making, skinny-dipping, and swing-
ing lasted until 1959, when the Edenic complex was razed to make way for a bank
and its parking lot. Joni Mitchell later mythologized this destruction in her 1970 hit
"Big Yellow Taxi"; its lines "Don't it always seem to go, you don't know what you've
got till it's gone? / They paved paradise and put up a parking lot" were written about
the Garden of Allah. A strip mall now lines the back of the lot, featuring El Pollo
Loco, Subway, and McDonald's. The building in the center of the lot was taken over
by predatory megabank Washington Mutual, which had the corporate gall to remove
a miniature model of the Garden that a previous bank had installed.

The Dudley Do-Right Emporium and Former Jay Ward Headquarters

*The Emporium is at 8200 Sunset Boulevard, on the south side of the street, near Havenhurst
Drive, in Hollywood but less than a block from the West Hollywood city limits. Open Tues.,
Thurs., and Sat., 11:00 A.M.–5:00 P.M. (323) 656-6550 or (323) 654-3050. Hollywood
Hounds is a few yards west at 8218 Sunset Boulevard. (323) 650-5551.*

For most of the '60s and '70s Jay Ward's satirical cartoons dominated the afternoon television screens of young America, molding millions of nascent psyches
with aburdist humor and sly social commentary. Rocky and Bullwinkle, Boris and
Natasha, Sherman and Peabody, Dudley Do-Right and Snidely Whiplash, George of
the Jungle and Super Chicken are still going strong in reruns and videos, and especially here at the Dudley Do-Right Emporium, the world's only Jay Ward–themed
souvenir store. Bullwinkle animation cels and Natasha T-shirts are on sale here,
along with refrigerator magnets, slippers, mugs, wrapping paper, dishes, books, and
more, bearing the cartoon characters' images. With the recent release of live-action
film versions of many Ward cartoons, new generations of kids are getting to know
Natasha, et al. Most motorists zipping past on Sunset Boulevard notice not the shop
itself but a fifteen-foot-high statue of Rocky and Bullwinkle a few yards west, in

front of a *different* building that once housed Jay Ward's offices. Before Ward moved in, the house was owned by character actor Fess Parker, best known for playing Davy Crockett. Parker threw big parties, and invited his guests to sign their names in wet cement out front; among those of Fess's colleagues from his TV days with Disney—and still visible—is the autograph of Walt himself. (Ward and Disney, two animation legends at opposite ends of the social spectrum, both immortalized in one spot: coincidence, or cosmic sign?) The property is now occupied by Hollywood Hounds, a celebrity dog-watching service.

Bullwinkle statue in front of Hollywood Hounds

Chateau Marmont
John Belushi checked in, but he didn't check out.

> 8221 Sunset Boulevard, at Laurel Canyon Boulevard, on the north side of the street. (For a peek at the bungalows, which are largely obscured behind canvas and foliage, climb Marmont Lane around the west side of the hotel, then turn right on Monteel Road.) (323) 656-1010 or (800) 242-8328.

Perched on a slope above the Strip, this hotel is modeled after a French castle—complete with gardens and impressive stone archways. Though oozing discretion, it has been the scene of many a scandal since it opened in 1929. In 1939 film mogul Harry Cohn reportedly said, "If you must get in trouble, do it at the Chateau Marmont." In 1965 Liz Taylor brought her bloodied pal Montgomery Clift here, of all places—and not to a hospital—after the actor was injured in an accident. They say Natalie Wood first met James Dean here; that Paul Newman and Joanne Woodward fell in love here; and that Barry Mann and Cynthia Weil penned the hit "You've Lost That Lovin' Feelin'" here. Jim Morrison was hurt during a failed attempt to enter his upstairs room through an outside window. Members of Led Zeppelin are said to have once roared into the lobby astride Harley-Davidsons. Former guests include Greta Garbo, Jean Harlow, Boris Karloff, Marilyn, Mick, Ringo, Janis, John, Yoko, Keanu, and dozens more. In 1982 the hotel made international headlines when John Belushi, staying in bungalow 3 (according to most sources, though a few insist it was bungalow 2) to work on a script, met with a local gal who taught him how to combine coke

Belushi bungalow, Chateau Marmont

and heroin. Overindulging in this novelty, he OD'ed in the bungalow and was carted off to the morgue amid the popping of flashbulbs.

LOWER HOLLYWOOD

Marie Prevost Possible Death Site
She was a winner that became a doggie's dinner.

> 6230 Afton Place, just east of Vine Street, on the south side of the street, between Sunset and Santa Monica Boulevards.

Poor Marie. A successful silent-era actress, Marie Prevost had trouble adjusting to the talkies. In the '30s her aging face and ballooning weight made roles hard to find. (The problem was *not,* as is frequently reported, a New York accent: she was raised in Canada and attended high school in L.A.) Like many before and since, she dieted. It wasn't enough, so she stopped eating and started drinking instead. She died in 1937 of malnutrition and alcoholism. What makes this story the stuff of Hollywood legend is that the cops found Marie's body partially devoured by her dachshund. Trapped in the apartment for days, the little fella had nothing to eat but a stringy corpse.

Where this gruesome discovery took place is still a bit of a mystery. Many sources insist it was in the four-story cream-and-beige Art Deco apartment building at 6230 Afton Place. But neither the current residents nor the current owner nor the previous owner have heard of Prevost, nor was she listed in the 1936 or '37 phone books. So the rumor remains unconfirmed, though this seems the most likely spot. (Although the manager was also unfamiliar with the story, interestingly he noted that in recent years he personally has found three of his elderly residents dead in their rooms, undiscovered for days on end, like Marie.) The gory tale enjoyed a burst of notoriety in the mid-'70s after Kenneth Anger gloated over it in his book *Hollywood Babylon.* Then British New Waver Nick Lowe made Marie a household name with his unforgettable but misspelled hit "Marie Provost." Its

Marie Prevost possible death site

lyrics make a hilarious epitaph: "The cops came in and they looked around, / throwing up everywhere over what they found. / The handiwork of Marie's little dachshund: / that hungry little dachshund. / She was a winner / that became a doggie's dinner. / She never meant that much to me. / Oh, poor Marie."

The Aetherius Society

6202 Afton Place, on the south side of the street at El Centro Avenue, one block east of Vine,
between Sunset and Santa Monica Boulevards, on the same block as the Marie Prevost house
(see above). (323) 465-9652.

It may look like just another modest home in a residential Hollywood neighborhood. But inside you'll find the headquarters for one of the nation's more intriguing UFO religions. The Aetherius Society's theology is a convoluted amalgam of
Hinduism, UFOs, Gaia theory, Christianity, channeling, and various Eastern
philosophies. Krishna, Jesus, Buddha, and most other spiritual leaders, the society
believes, are from outer space. Known as "Cosmic Masters," they visit Earth periodically to help us evolve to a more spiritual plane. Other Cosmic Masters include
Master Aetherius and Mars Sector 6: they contacted the Englishman Sir George
King in 1954 and inspired him to found this new religion a year later. King began to
channel wisdom from more Cosmic Masters, and these channeled teachings form
the society's beliefs. King died in 1997, but the new religion carries on sans its guru.

As far as religions go, Aetherius is amazingly benign: neither apocalyptic (like
Aum Shinrikyo) nor suicidal (like Heaven's Gate or People's Temple), neither selfish
(like Satanism or Scientology) nor condemnatory (like Christianity), neither sexu-
ally libertine (like Bhagwan Shree Rajneesh's followers) nor deceptive (like Moonies),
Aetherians are perfectly frank about what they believe and about their desire to help
everyone on Earth through yoga, prayer, and paving the way for friendly flying
saucers. It's surprising that the Aetherius Society is not better known, given the
Heaven's Gate hubbub. Thursdays at 7:50 P.M. Aetherians gather here for a ritual
called Operation Prayer Power. Psychic energy from the prayers is directed toward
and stored in Spiritual Energy Batteries. Once fully charged, these batteries can be
saved for later use, often to help people in natural disasters. Every July 8, prayers are
directed at the Earth, whom Aetherians see as a wonderful goddess who has suffered
much at our hands. Sunday-morning services begin at 11:00 A.M. (like at a regular
church) and Monday nights are for ritual blessings. Tuesday evenings and Saturday
mornings are set aside for welcoming visitors with individual spiritual healing sessions, but you can show up anytime to browse the little bookstore. Don't be shy.

Hollywood Forever (Hollywood Memorial Park)

6000 Santa Monica Boulevard, between Gower Street and Van Ness Avenue, on the south
side of the street; entrance is opposite Gordon Street. Admission is free, but a useful map to
celebrity graves costs $3 in the flower shop (on the right as you enter). Open Mon.–Fri.,
8:30 A.M.–5:00 P.M.; Sat.–Sun., 10:00 A.M.–3:00 P.M. (323) 469-1181.

With the possible exception of Forest Lawn Glendale, Hollywood Forever cra-
dles more dead celebrities than any other cemetery in the world. Until a few

years ago, the grounds—formerly known as Hollywood Memorial Park—had fallen into total decrepitude. A fast-talking (some would say "visionary") young funeral home operator stepped in with big plans for the old place. Its new name, Hollywood Forever, drew a few howls from preservationists. Broken windows, cracked walls, and desiccated landscaping were nursed back to health. Then computer monitors were installed throughout the cemetery. Input the name of whomever you've come to visit, and *poof!*—a video about his or her life unfolds on the screen. The staff prepares videos about celebrity "residents," but anyone planning to be buried here can make a video. A celebrity grave map helps you explore. (Note: For locations of the following areas within the park, consult the map.)

Mel Blanc's headstone, Holly-wood Forever

Crypts in the Hollywood Cathedral Mausoleum south of the lake include those of Rudolph Valentino, visited for years by a mysterious "woman in black" (enter the mausoleum, take the second corridor to the left, go to the end of it, turn right, go to the back of the short hallway, and Valentino is in crypt number 1205 on your left); Peter Finch, Oscar-winning actor (directly across the hallway from Valentino); William Desmond Taylor, film director and famed murder victim (from the mausoleum entrance, take the second corridor to the right, and look for crypt number 594 [real name: William Deane-Tanner]); and Peter Lorre (across the hall from Taylor/Tanner in the Alcove of Remembrance, in a small niche at shin level). Also in the mausoleum: dancer Eleanor Powell and Hollywood founder H. Wilcox. Douglas Fairbanks Sr. is entombed at the end of the reflecting pool next to the mausoleum. Around the lake north of the mausoleum are Marion Davies (in the freestanding Douras family tomb), Tyrone Power (surrounded by ducks on the lakeshore), Virginia Rappe, a starlet whose shocking death rocked the film industry (at the northeast edge of the lake, near a Celtic cross, under a tall juniper), Jayne Mansfield's memorial cenotaph (near Virginia at the northern tip of the lake, though her actual body is not here), as well as Cecil B. DeMille, John Huston, and Janet Gaynor.

In the Pineland section are Carl Morgan Bigsby, whose Atlas Rocket tombstone is famed as the pinnacle of kitsch (visible from afar), and Mel Blanc, voice of Bugs Bunny and many other cartoon characters (look for the grave that says "That's All, Folks," on Pineland Avenue, one hundred yards south of Maple Avenue). In Beth Olam, the Jewish section at the western edge of the grounds: Benjamin "Bugsy" Siegel, gangster and cofounder of Las Vegas (in the Beth Olam Mausoleum in section M-2, sixteenth row, against the back wall). In the Abbey of the Psalms: *Our*

Gang rascal Darla Hood (in the Sanctuary of Light, second corridor on the left, two-thirds of the way to the end, top row). Also here are noted director Victor Fleming, actress Norma Talmadge, and Charles Chaplin Jr. (Legend has it that a tombstone marked "The Little Mouse," elsewhere in the cemetery, marks the grave of Charlie Chaplin's *other* son, who was born deformed and only lived three days; because his mother was underage, the baby was buried here in secrecy. The Little Mouse's location is unknown.) Other stars buried throughout the park include Carl "Alfalfa" Switzer, Nelson Eddy, Woody Herman, Paul Muni, and hundreds more.

Paramount Studios

5555 Melrose Avenue. The lot occupies the block bounded by Gower Street, Melrose Avenue, and Van Ness Avenue. The Melrose Gate/main entrance is at Melrose and Windsor; the Bronson Gate is at Bronson and Marathon, just off Melrose; the ticket office is on Gower. Tours leave Mon.–Fri., every hour between 9:00 A.M. and 2:00 P.M. (more frequently if it's crowded); the price of the tour is $15. (323) 956-1777 or (323) 956-5575.

Hollywood" is linguistic shorthand for the film industry. But don't be fooled into thinking any movies are actually *made* in Hollywood. Long ago, yes; but the studios have long since moved to Burbank, Culver City, and points afar. All, that is, except one. Paramount is the last major studio to never grow up and leave home, the only back lot remaining in Hollywood. And every inch is soaked in cinematic history. Thousands of classic films were shot here—at least in part—including *Breakfast at Tiffany's*, *The Godfather, Love Story,* and many more, not to mention TV shows ranging from *Mission: Impossible* to *The Brady Bunch*. Part of the lot was once RKO Studios, responsible for hundreds more classic films. After passing through the hands of Joseph Kennedy, Howard Hughes, and Lucille Ball, RKO was eventually absorbed into Paramount.

Today, aside from working here, there are only three ways to see the lot: (1) Take the $15 walking tour (described below). (2) Get free tickets to one of the live-audience TV shows taped here; nab some at Paramount's ticket office or call (323) 956-1777. Or, easiest of all, (3) show up at the main Melrose gate and say you want to shop in the Paramount souvenir store. The guards will give you a visitor's pass and find someone to escort you to the store. Often you'll get a free mini–tour narration along the way, and a good view of the astounding "blue sky" mural used to great effect in *The Truman Show*'s climactic scene.

Paramount Studios' famous Bronson Gate

Once they drop you off, you're pretty much on your own, though nosing around the lot is discouraged. The actual tour also leaves from the main gate every hour or so—no reservations allowed. Tour guides narrate the studio's history as they lead you from one soundstage to the next. If you're lucky, you'll watch part of a rehearsal. And you'll likely see props, unused sets, and, of course, the souvenir shop.

To merely admire the studio from the outside, examine its famous Bronson Gate, a short ways east of the main gate. You might recognize it from numerous films, most famously *Sunset Boulevard*. Legend has it that aspiring actors and actresses hug the gate's bars for good luck, quoting that film's final line: "All right, Mr. DeMille, I'm ready for my close-up." One such struggling young actor named Charles Buchinsky went so far as to adopt the gate's name as his own: now he's Charles Bronson. The iron filigree topping the gate was supposedly put there to keep out frenzied female fans desperate to touch a crowd-shy Rudolph Valentino.

Raleigh Studios
5300 Melrose Avenue, on the south side of the street at Bronson Avenue, across from Paramount Studios. (323) 466-3111.

Despite what we said about Paramount (across the street) being the only studio left in Hollywood, Raleigh Studios has been here since 1914 and is still going strong. It's just that Raleigh is not a studio in the sense that anybody recognizes the name: it has no identifiable brand or logo. Raleigh is more of a "rent-a-lot," and has been such for its entire history. But what a history. Hundreds of Oscar-winning pictures have come out of Raleigh, including *In the Heat of the Night* (1967's Best Picture), and hundreds of classics: *What Ever Happened to Baby Jane?*; screwball comedies and films noirs with Cary Grant and Barbara Stanwyck; most of the *Beach Party* series; and recent special-effects extravaganzas like *Species*. Future president Ronald Reagan spent a lot of time here at Raleigh, making his TV show *Death Valley Days;* many other early TV shows were made here as well, including *Gunsmoke, Have Gun Will Travel,* and *Superman*. Unfortunately, no tours are offered.

Lucy's Café El Adobe
Where the elite meet to eat enchiladas.

5536 Melrose Avenue, at Plymouth Boulevard, on the south side of the street. (323) 462-9421.

They say Linda Ronstadt met California governor Jerry Brown at this Mexican restaurant across the street from Paramount Studios—its *arroz con pollo* is still called the "Jerry Brown Special." A certain divey-ness hardly matches its hefty prices, but photos of famous diners deck the walls. While you dip into your $10 tacos, keep an eye peeled for the likenesses of Jackson Browne, Dolly Parton, Burt Bacharach, Linda Blair, Connie Chung, Edward James Olmos, Faith No More, and both Teds: Kennedy and Nugent.

Hollygrove Children's Home
The orphanage where Marilyn Monroe lived as a child.

> 815 N. El Centro Avenue, at Waring Avenue, on the west side of the street. (323) 463-2219.

Pretty little Norma Jeane Baker—the future Marilyn Monroe—lived in this low-profile facility from 1935 to 1937. It was then called the Los Angeles Orphans Home, and Norma Jeane ended up here when her beautiful but unstable mother entered an asylum. Framed photos along one hallway include one of blond Norma Jeane posing chummily with another child. Other pictures reveal stars of that era (such as Clara Bow, Jean Harlow, and Shirley Temple) visiting the orphanage's young residents. The Paramount film lot is visible from the orphanage, and legend has it that an unhappy Norma Jeane gazed out at the studio lights and vowed to become a star.

Vine Street Elementary School
Marilyn Monroe's alma mater.

> 955 N. Vine Street, at Barton Avenue, on the west side of the street. (213) 469-0877.

When she was still a lonesome little girl named Norma Jeane who lived in a nearby orphanage because her mother was in an asylum, the future star attended this school. No trace of that ten-year-old remains today, however.

Gold Star Recording Studio Location
> At the southeast corner of Santa Monica Boulevard and Vine Street, Hollywood. A mini-mall now occupies the site.

Pioneering producer Phil Spector perfected his "Wall of Sound" recording technique in this grungy Hollywood studio, where he crammed dozens of pianists, bassists, guitarists, and singers into a small room to create a distinctive style that sounds as fresh today as it did in the early '60s. Legend has it that hundreds of immortal classics were created here, including the Ronettes' "Be My Baby," the Righteous Brothers' "You've Lost That Lovin' Feelin'," the Beach Boys' "Good Vibrations," and a substantial percentage of most oldies stations' playlists. The era's greatest musical geniuses would loiter outside between takes, and in-the-know fans would sneak by for a peek. As with so many other historic locations in Los Angeles, it was torn down to make way for a splendid mini-mall, with a much-needed Philly Steak Depo.

Mae West House
Come up and see it sometime.

The Ravenswood Apartments, 570 N. Rossmore Avenue, at Clinton Avenue.

Her stage and screen persona was as steeped in sexuality as baklava is in honey. And Mae West was as much a self-parody as a mystery: older and heftier than your average love goddess, she spouted *wink-wink nudge-nudge* quotations incessantly. One rumor that surfaced during her lifetime, and still persists long after her 1980 death, suggests that Mae West was, of all things, a man. Hmm. All records of her birth have apparently vanished. In 1927 she authored a play about gay men, *Drag*—a follow-up to her 1926 play, *Sex*. And what about that husky voice? Consider, too, the swagger, the hands, the absent cleavage. *Hmm.* West lived in this imposing white Deco apartment house for nearly fifty years—from the 1930s to her death.

Happy Days House
565 N. Cahuenga Avenue, at Clinton Avenue.

Ever bemused by the antics of his pals Fonzie, Potsie, and Ralph, *Happy Days'* Richie Cunningham inhabited a gentle world that scarcely resembled the real '50s, if survivors are to be believed. Used in the show's exterior shots to represent the Cunninghams' all-American house, this imposing white two-story is an actual home on a graceful, leafy street. Gables and impossibly green grass and a widow's walk produce the desired effect. But there's more. Long before its '70s stint as *chez* Cunningham, this was the home of Lupe Velez, cinema's "Mexican Spitfire." Not at this house, but at another in faraway Beverly Hills, Velez killed herself in 1944.

Happy Days *house*

Patina
A celebrity favorite.

5955 Melrose Avenue, between Highland Avenue and Vine Street. (323) 467-1108.

Zagat rated this the most popular restaurant in Los Angeles. But how will you ever know for sure, when a morsel of tenderloin costs nearly $35? Celebrity patrons seen here enjoying private booths and plebe-repellent prices include Tom Cruise, Kevin Costner, and Kareem Abdul-Jabbar.

Citrus
Another celebrity favorite.

> *6703 Melrose Avenue. Open Mon.–Thurs., noon–2:30 P.M. and 6:30–10:30 P.M.; Fri., noon–2:30 P.M. and 6:00–10:30 P.M.; Sat., 6:00–10:30 P.M.; Sun., 6:00–10:00 P.M. (323) 857-0034.*

Attracting a celebrity clientele, this trendy Frenchish eatery with its pebbly floor has also been top-rated by Zagat. So many stars come here seeking solitude that the management won't list them by name.

Pink's
Where winners eat wieners.

> *711 N. La Brea Avenue, off Melrose Avenue, on the west side of the street. Open Sun.–Thurs., 9:30 A.M.–2:00 A.M.; Fri.–Sat., 9:30 A.M.–3:00 A.M. (323) 931-4223.*

Paul Pink started selling 10¢ chili dogs from a pushcart in the weedy, wide-open spaces near Paramount Studios in 1939. Struggling actors liked the low prices. Lodged in an actual building since 1946, Pink's has fed generations of stars. One legend tells how Orson Welles ate eighteen dogs in one sitting. Yet another tells how Bruce Willis proposed to Demi Moore here amid the sizzling Guadalajara Dogs, Fajita Dogs, and Pastrami Burrito Dogs. Satisfied customers whose photos line the walls include Leonardo DiCaprio, Ricky Martin, Eddie Murphy, the Backstreet Boys, Jason Alexander, James Woods, Jerry Lewis, Courteney Cox, Bette Midler, Alex Trebek, Michael J. Fox, Carl Reiner, and Roseanne Barr.

Pink's

Howard Hughes Building
Where the millionaire worked for a living.

> *7000 and 7050 Romaine Street, at Sycamore Avenue, one block south of Santa Monica Boulevard, on the south side of the street.*

Occupying nearly an entire block, this white-on-cream Art Deco wonderland abounds in squiggles and zigzags. Howard Hughes employed the best materials and designers of his day when building the place in 1929. He used it as a color film-processing plant. But since his then lucrative but now obsolete recipe contained nitrate, which is potentially volatile, Hughes installed an explosion-proof set of vaults along with other superstrong fittings. During Prohibition, Hughes's father cached a huge amount of liquor in the vaults. (The eccentric recluse did not drink, and the stuff was uncovered untouched during a late-'80s revamp.) As Hughes's paranoia grew, he maintained a heated correspondence with government leaders, bribing top politicians to stop Nevada's atomic testing, because he felt poisoned by the radiation. He also financed the raising of a downed Russian sub off the Florida coast. Hughes's documents regarding these projects were the object of a high-profile heist here. Today the building's long pale corridors still sport forbidding metal doors, monuments to a nervous genius.

Hollywood Center Studios
Where Harry met Sally.

   1040 N. Las Palmas Avenue, at Santa Monica Boulevard. (323) 469-5000.

S ince this studio was built in 1919, hundreds of movies have been made here. They range from classic silents such as *The Freshman* to Golden Age confections including *The Moon and Sixpence* and *Pennies from Heaven*. As if that weren't enough, the prolific studio behind its pink façade has also brought you *Johnny One Eye, Frances, The Karate Kid,* and *Shampoo,* not to mention *When Harry Met Sally, Misery,* and *Spawn.* A substantial percentage of history's greatest TV shows were filmed on soundstages here as well: *The Addams Family, The Beverly Hillbillies, I Love Lucy,* and *Pee Wee's Playhouse,* to name but a few.

Los Angeles City College
Illustrious alumni.

   855 N. Vermont Avenue, between Melrose Avenue and Santa Monica Boulevard. (323) 953-4000.

I t's not UCLA, but its alumni include Donna Reed, Robert Vaughn, Gene Roddenberry, James Coburn, Clint Eastwood, Morgan Freeman, Alexis Smith, Cindy Williams, and Mark Hamill. Is it any wonder that its theater department is nationally known and respected? Clint, by the way, was not a drama major.

West Hollywood

SUNSET STRIP

(Entries arranged as a tour running east to west.)

The Cajun Bistro
Site of the Source.

8301 Sunset Boulevard, at Sweetzer Avenue, on the north side of the street. (323) 656-6388.

Woody Allen's character in *Annie Hall* is appalled at the glaring L.A.-ness of a health food restaurant where Annie dines blithely. Thus tolls the death knell of their affair. That scene was filmed at the Source, a Sunset Strip standby where Allen liked to eat in real life. It is now defunct, and in its place is a bustling seafood grill whose patrons include Fabio. What was once the Source's famous outdoor seating area is now mostly enclosed.

The Cajun Bistro

The Argyle
Where John Wayne had a cow.

8358 Sunset Boulevard, at Olive Drive, on the south side of the street. (323) 654-7100.

During Hollywood's Golden Age it was named the Sunset Tower, and later it was a private club. Over the years, having housed many of the high and mighty, this fifteen-story Art Deco palace has racked up its share of madcap anecdotes. Misbehavin' mobster Bugsy Siegel was asked to move out. Howard Hughes is said to have buzzed back and forth from room to room here between multiple lovers. John Wayne, craving fresh milk, kept a live cow outside his penthouse suite. Marilyn Monroe lived here; later, Oprah and Whoopi. Rick James reportedly imprisoned his unfortunate girlfriend on the premises. The place lay fallow for a few years before a major

The Argyle

renovation. Today the Argyle is a luxury hotel, a dazzling landmark whose ornamental friezes depict animals, Adam and Eve, and a blimp. Framed photographs recall guests gone by, including Harpo Marx, Charles Laughton, Elsa Lanchester, Greta Garbo, Bob Hope, and Alfred Hitchcock. *Get Shorty* was partly filmed here, as were *The Player, Strange Days, Wayne's World II,* and more.

Hyatt West Hollywood
Yet another place where Jim Morrison dangled from a balcony.

8401 Sunset Boulevard, on the north side of the street. (323) 656-1234.

Rock stars' hijinks throughout the 1970s gave this Hyatt Hotel its rhyming nickname: "the *Riot* Hotel." Occupying several floors during an extended stay, Led Zeppelin held orgies, acted wild, and angered the management with their penchant for riding motorcycles up and down the hall. In those dissolute days that many would rather forget, John Lennon used to hang out here with his pal Harry Nilsson; Jim Morrison dangled off a balcony; Axl Rose held a barbecue on another balcony; Keith Richards tossed a TV out a window. Commanding lovely vistas, the hotel is a traditional fave among performers doing shows at the Hollywood Bowl and the Forum. Other celebrity guests have included the Who, Joan Baez, Gregg Allman, Gordon Lightfoot, R.E.M., and Blondie. Appropriately enough, the rock parody *This Is Spinal Tap* was partly filmed here.

House of Blues
8430 Sunset Boulevard, on the south side of the street. (323) 848-5100.

A corrugated tin roof and round tower lend authenticity to this Mississippi-inspired nightclub and restaurant. (One of its original owners was Blues Brother Dan Aykroyd.) Spooky folk art entailing multiple bottle caps crowds the covered porch and bar. Bas-reliefs of blues greats adorn the ceiling. And actual Mississippi mud lies under the stage and elsewhere around the place—"voodoo dirt," it is said, gathered from the crossroads where bluesman Robert Johnson allegedly sold his soul to Satan. Performers here range from Al Green to Eminem to Air Supply, drawing celebrity-studded crowds. You never know who will pop up: Rod Stewart, Robert Plant, Jimmy Page, Tori Spelling, George Michael, Kevin Costner, Sheila E., Paul McCartney, and Steven Tyler have been spotted here. Dustin Hoffman is said to have held his son's bar mitzvah reception in the place, and stories are told of one night in 1995 when Bill Clinton and Al Gore joined Jim Belushi onstage.

Ciro's/The Comedy Store
Where Sinatra drowned his sorrows.

8433 Sunset Boulevard, on the north side of the street. Open nightly, 8:00 P.M.–2:00 A.M. (323) 656-6225.

Since the '70s this premier stand-up venue has hosted Robin Williams, Billy Crystal, David Letterman, and Roseanne, among others. A distinctive awning is adorned with comics' autographs, and photos in the Comedy Store's entrance hall comprise a virtual who's who. But the building's history goes way back. In the '40s and '50s it was Ciro's, a perpetually crowded nightclub where big names came to drink, dance, make headlines, make out, break up, and cut up. Among its regulars were Frank Sinatra, Judy Garland, Clark Gable, Ginger Rogers, Marilyn Monroe, Bogart and Bacall, Lena Horne, and more, including the insatiable Howard Hughes—noted for his habit of slipping out to Ciro's parking lot for a bit of the old "in-out, in-out." Performers onstage ran the gamut from Xavier Cugat to Nat "King" Cole. But by 1959 that era was over.

Mondrian Hotel
Probably too cool for you.

8440 Sunset Boulevard, at Olive Drive, on the south side of the street. (323) 650-8999 or (800) 525-8029.

Vast expanses of polished wooden floor are punctuated with abstract objets d'art. Its implacably pale and postmodern surroundings make this hotel a fave with touring rock stars such as Smashing Pumpkins, the Cranberries, Guns N' Roses, Public Enemy, and a lot more. It was here that Milli Vanilli's Rob Pilatus slashed his wrists and tried to jump out a window after the duo, caught lip-synching, was stripped of its Grammy. Cindy Crawford's husband created the hotel's lofty Sky Bar, where a drink will cost you nearly twenty clams *if* you can get past the notoriously choosy doorman. Once inside, lucky tipplers can inspect a panoramic view that just might include the likes of Elle Macpherson, Quincy Jones, Jacqueline Bisset, or Anna Nicole Smith.

77 Sunset Strip Location
8524 Sunset Boulevard, on the south side of the street, next door to the Tiffany Theater.

During the popular TV program's 1958–64 run, its key characters had their office at the titular 77 Sunset. Its awninged entrance was next door to "Dino's Lodge," where the hair-obsessed Kookie parked cars. The actual building used in those shots is long gone. But anyone making the ginchy pilgrimage will find a series of sidewalk tiles here solemnly decreeing that, yes, *77 Sunset Strip* was filmed on this site.

Ben Frank's Site
Where the Monkees stayed up late.

> Mels Drive-in, 8585 Sunset Boulevard, on the north side of the street. Open daily, 24 hours. (310) 854-7200.

During the wee hours when the clubs shut down, the in-crowd beat a path to Ben Frank's. Like Canter's in Fairfax, this twenty-four-hour coffee shop was, in the '60s, a popular late-night spot for musicians and those who dug them. Legend has it that the casting call for what would later become *The Monkees* specifically requested "Ben Frank's types." Sure enough, the four who eventually became the band were Ben Frank's habitués. Today the original building still stands, but it houses a link in the retro Mels chain. One wall at the back of the restaurant has a photo exhibit recalling the old days.

Kenneth Cole Walk of Fame
Footprints of the famous.

> 8752 Sunset Boulevard, on the south side of the street. (310) 289-5085.

As part of an AIDS fund-raising campaign, stars were solicited to step barefoot into the wet cement fronting this chichi shoe shop where Tori Spelling, for one, is said to lay down major dough. Amid numerous footprints, Rosie O'Donnell's are deep; Matthew Modine's could pass for just anybody's; Liz Taylor, whose little dog left its prints alongside hers, evinces a certain flatness of foot (Liz also poured White Diamonds perfume into the wet cement which,

Elizabeth Taylor's footprints, Kenneth Cole Walk of Fame

after rain or a hosing, remains faintly fragrant years later). As for Richard Gere—is it true what they say about guys with small feet?

Book Soup
Hip lit on the Strip.

> 8818 Sunset Boulevard, on the south side of the street.
> Open daily, 9:00 A.M.–midnight. (310) 659-3110.

After a long hard day on the set or in the studio, what could be more fun than curling up with a good book? Reputed regulars in these aisles include David Bowie, Drew Barrymore, and Madonna. And when celebs pen books of their own, this is where they show up to autograph 'em. Authors including Wes Craven, Mia Farrow, Patti Smith, John Waters, and Oliver Stone attract huge crowds. When Howard Stern came to town, his fans got so out of hand that Book Soup had to shut down and shoo them away.

Book Soup

The Viper Room
Where River Phoenix died.

> 8852 Sunset Boulevard, at Larrabee Street, on the south side of the street. (310) 358-1880.

It was here that Tommy Lee attacked a paparazzo who wanted a snap of him with his occasional wife Pamela. Lee was later convicted of assault. (Later still, he assaulted Pamela and served time in prison—oops!) Mick Jagger, Uma Thurman, and others have reportedly been involved in melees at the Viper Room, whose list of performers—from Johnny Cash to Iggy Pop to Oasis— is no less illustrious than its clientele. (Johnny Depp is a co-owner.) The club made headlines in 1993 when River Phoenix, lodging nearby at the Nikko Hotel, arrived here and began puking all over himself amid the striking black surroundings. His companions' attempts to refresh him failed. Phoenix was brought outside, and on the sidewalk in front he had fatal seizures brought on by too many drugs. Shortly afterward he was pronounced dead at Cedars-Sinai.

The Viper Room

Whisky A Go-Go
The Doors were its house band.

> 8901 Sunset Boulevard, at San Vincente Boulevard, on the north side of the street. Open daily, 8:00 P.M.–2:00 A.M. (310) 652-4202.

S oon after it opened in 1964, "Secret Agent Man" singer Johnny Rivers was the house act. A female deejay would play records in a little suspended cage between sets. When the deejay bopped to the beat in her cage, the crowd couldn't get enough. The "go-go girl" was born. By 1966 the Doors were performing here almost nightly. (Naturally, the club later appeared in *The Doors,* the biopic about the band.) Back when it was *the* Sunset Strip hot spot, the Whisky hosted the Who, the Byrds, Buffalo Springfield, the Kinks, Jimi Hendrix, Love, and more. Another legend has it that during the Beatles'

Whisky A Go-Go

first L.A. trip, Jayne Mansfield, of all people, invited them to spend an evening with her here. Later years saw shows by Led Zeppelin, X, the Cramps, the Go-Go's, Gun Club, Van Halen, the Germs, and others whose sound helped shape the '70s and '80s, and beyond. After various closures and reopenings, it still draws live acts.

Duke's
Where the elite meet to eat egg-salad sandwiches.

> 8909 Sunset Boulevard, at San Vicente Boulevard, on the north side of the street. Open Mon.–Fri., 7:30 A.M.–8:45 P.M.; Sat.–Sun., 8:00 A.M.–3:45 P.M. (310) 652-3100.

O ld-fashioned meals are served at this old-fashioned pine-paneled coffee shop snuggled up close to the Whisky A Go-Go. Autographed photos adorning the wall attest to a celebrity-studded crowd of diners, including Tom Hanks, Chris Rock, Sharon Stone, Mike Myers, Robert Downey Jr., Sandra Bullock, Bill Pullman, and more.

Roxy Theatre
Where rock 'n' roll memories were made.

9009 Sunset Boulevard, near Doheny Drive, on the north side of the street. (310) 278-9457.

After it opened in 1973 this humble club helped shape post-1960s music in all its dubious glory. Many performers now known as the era's biggest stars entertained audiences at the relatively intimate Roxy before graduating to stadiums. Too bad you missed those shows by Bruce Springsteen, Bob Marley, Boz Scaggs, Cheech and Chong, Jimmy Buffett, and others. John Belushi allegedly ate his last meal at a private dining room upstairs here before his date with death at the nearby Chateau Marmont. Alternative and hard-rock bands now play behind the club's moody bluish purple façade several nights a week.

Rainbow Bar & Grill/Villa Nova
Where Marilyn and Joe had their first date.

9015 Sunset Boulevard, at Hammond Street, on the north side of the street. (310) 278-4232.

This used to be the Villa Nova restaurant, where Vincente Minnelli asked Judy Garland to marry him, and where Marilyn Monroe had her first date with future husband Joe DiMaggio. (The name Villa Nova is still spelled out in holes across the ceiling.) Conveniently located next door to the Roxy, the Rainbow became a 1970s rock 'n' roll hangout, luring the likes of John Lennon and Led Zeppelin. More recent clients are said to include Jack Nicholson and Nicolas Cage. Adorning the walls over its vinyl booths and long low bar are gold and platinum records as well as guitars once played by Van Halen, Motörhead, James Brown, Guns N' Roses, and more. Among many snapshots taken in the club and now lining the foyer is one of the doomed John Belushi in a party mood.

NEAR THE SUNSET STRIP

Dorothy Dandridge Death Apartment
El Palacio Apartments, 8491–8499 Fountain Avenue, at La Cienega Boulevard, on the north side of the street.

Set back behind a deep and lushly landscaped courtyard, this romantic Spanish-style complex sports grillwork and a peacock motif. James Mason bought the place from its original owner; Marilyn Monroe is said to have once rented a unit. Amid the architectural splendor lived *Carmen Jones* star Dorothy Dandridge. Having made inroads rare for an African American actress of her time, she faced a career slump in the early '60s. Her health declining, her affair with Peter Lawford over, Dandridge joined an investment scheme that bankrupted her. When she turned up dead (naked, save a scarf) on the floor of her apartment, and leaving a cryptic will, many concluded that the forty-one-year-old had killed herself with barbiturates. Others say an embolism resulting from a recent toe fracture is actually what killed her. The mystery persists.

Sal Mineo Death Site
Where James Dean's costar met a tragic end.

> 8569 Holloway Drive, on the north side of the street, near Alta Loma Road, between Sunset and Santa Monica Boulevards. See the entry below for precise location.

Returning home from a play rehearsal one evening, screen legend Sal Mineo encountered a burglar in his ground-floor apartment. The thief chased him from the building and stabbed Mineo in the heart as he was running back toward his car in the alleyway behind the apartment. Mineo died on the spot. It was February 12, 1976, twenty years after he rocketed to stardom in his role opposite James Dean in *Rebel without a Cause.* The killer escaped from the scene, but was later caught and convicted after bragging to others about the crime. The senseless murder was the third link in what many now see as the *Rebel* curse: all four young stars in the movie (Dean, Mineo, Nick Adams, and Natalie Wood) died young under tragic circumstances. Famous for Oscar-nominated roles in *Rebel* and *Exodus,* Mineo made plenty of clunkers, too, like *Escape from the Planet of the Apes* and *Who Killed Teddy Bear?*

Here's exactly where the crime happened: This block of Holloway Drive has a series of identical apartment complexes pressed up against each other, but walkways extend between the buildings, and each has a separate address. Take the walkway between 8567 and 8569 Holloway and go between the buildings until it emerges into the alleyway behind the apartments. Mineo died between the carports for 8567 and 8569, just where the pedestrian walkway connects to the alley, next to a water faucet, a brick planter, and a drainpipe on the eastern side of the walkway. There is sometimes a garden hose curled up on the spot. It's also possible to reach the site by coming directly down the alleyway from Alta Loma Road along the back of the buildings until you see the addresses mentioned above, between the two carports. Apartment 1, where he lived and discovered the burglar, is on the west side of the walkway just a few yards south of the death site. (Note: You may find other guidebooks that say Mineo was killed at 8563 Holloway. They're all copying this incorrect address from each other. Residents of the building and police reports agree it was 8569 Holloway.)

Marilyn Monroe–Shelley Winters Apartment
Where the two were roommates.

8575¼ Holloway Drive, on the north side of the street.

In her autobiography Shelley Winters recalls a stint as Marilyn's roommate. The two actresses lived in what was then a nearly new and rather elegant courtyard apartment house. Shelley treasures wild memories of their antics at that time, circa 1951, in the two-bedroom upstairs unit. Both actresses supposedly spent so much time out on dates that they only saw each other when they stopped home to change clothes or reapply makeup.

Diane Linkletter Plunge House

Shoreham Towers, 8787 Shoreham Drive, at Horn Avenue, on the northeast corner.

Marilyn Monroe–Shelley Winters apartment

Kids do the darnedest things. That's what people said after Art Linkletter's daughter Diane leaped to her death from a sixth-floor window at this fortresslike complex in 1969. Art's fatherly face comforted millions; imagine the widespread despair when Diane's plunge was linked with LSD. Today the ambience here is forbidding, despite the lanais. Ominous eucalypti heighten the effect.

SANTA MONICA BOULEVARD AND NEARBY

Formosa Café
Where the elite meet to eat egg foo yung.

7156 Santa Monica Boulevard, at La Brea Avenue, on the south side of the street. Open Mon.–Fri., 4:00 P.M.–2:00 A.M.; Sat.–Sun., 6:00 P.M.–2:00 A.M. (323) 850-9050.

Paper lanterns swing at this historic cocktail bar and Chinese restaurant. Occupying a disused trolley, it is strategically poised across the road from a major studio. Since 1934 its shadowy ambience has launched

Formosa Café

many a legend. Elvis Presley, for instance, is said to have left his waitress a Cadillac in lieu of a tip. Stenciled names in the parking lot whimsically "reserve" spaces for John Wayne, Lucille Ball, and Bette Davis. A key scene in *L.A. Confidential,* in which a detective mistakes Lana Turner for a whore, was filmed here. The real Lana is said to have dined here frequently with doomed boyfriend Johnny Stompanato, whose gangland pal Bugsy Siegel liked the place as well. In another legend, mobster Mickey Cohen stashed cash here in his own private safe. Scads of autographed photos reveal a clientele ranging from Grace Kelly to Gary Coleman, not to mention Emilio Estevez, Christian Slater, Jodie Foster, and dozens more. As of 2000, a multiplex theater was slated to be built surrounding the café, which will remain in business.

Warner Hollywood Studios

1041 N. Formosa Avenue, at Santa Monica Boulevard, on the west side of the street. (323) 850-2600.

I n 1919 Mary and Douglas established Pickford-Fairbanks Studios here and turned out classic silent films. Fairbanks installed his own gym in one of the buildings. D. W. Griffith and Charlie Chaplin signed on in 1922. Samuel Goldwyn took over in 1924. Later, as the United Artists studio, this was the filming location for *Casablanca, Wuthering Heights, Some Like It Hot, Foreign Correspondent, The Best Years of Our Lives,* and many others. Private bungalows on the property once lodged the likes of Frank Sinatra and Marlon Brando. F. Scott Fitzgerald and the Gershwin brothers penned masterpieces here. After Warner Bros. bought the place in 1980, *Basic Instinct* and *L.A. Confidential* were made on-site. Although the grounds are closed to the public, a

Warner Hollywood Studios

black-and-white photo exhibit recalling bygone days hangs in the receptionist's office, open weekdays from 8:30 A.M. to 5:30 P.M.

The Sex Walk of Fame

Tomkat Theatre, 7734 Santa Monica Boulevard, at Spaulding Avenue, on the west side of the street. (213) 650-9551.

W hen this theater was called the Pussycat, *Deep Throat* played here a long time. (Yes . . . oh . . . really *long*.) To celebrate their dawning Golden Age, porn stars took up the Hollywood tradition of pressing body parts into wet cement out front. (Hands and feet only, of course.) Linda Lovelace offered hers in 1973, Marilyn Chambers in 1980. (Cutely, she dotted the *i* in her name with a heart.) Harry Reems and John Holmes are here, too, though their hand- and footprints merely tease. These days, the theater is the all-gay Tomkat. Under a purplish façade, flanked by unpleasant carpeting, cement squares signed by gay porn stars lie to the west of those imprinted by hets of yore.

The Sex Walk of Fame

Judith Campbell Exner's Apartment
Love nest of JFK's controversial mistress.

1200 N. Flores Street, half a block north of Santa Monica Boulevard, on the east side of the street.

Monica, step aside. What presidential peccadillo could compare to JFK's affair with Judith Campbell? Born Judith Immoor, the striking blue-eyed brunette married young to actor Bill Campbell, and socialized with Hollywood jet-setters. After Frank Sinatra learned that the good-looking Campbell had gotten divorced, he flirted with her a bit himself before introducing her to his pal John F. Kennedy. Judith Campbell was smitten. Her intense affair with the married Kennedy began in March 1960. It continued even after he won the election; Kennedy broke it off in early 1963 after J. Edgar Hoover discovered the relationship and reportedly threatened Kennedy with exposure.

Hoover didn't know the half of it: Kennedy was also using Campbell as a go-between, ferrying White House payoffs to underworld mafiosi whom JFK had hired to assassinate Fidel Castro. During this period, in 1961, Campbell was living here in an upscale West Hollywood apartment building, now landscaped with palms and banana trees. It's not recorded whether Kennedy ever came to these premises for a bit of the old in-out, but it's quite likely. Campbell was embroiled in the Kennedy administration's murkiest intrigues, yet the nation knew nothing of her. It's hard to imagine, post-Clinton, but newspapers at that time would never dare break such a story.

It was not until 1975, when she was called to testify before the Senate about anti-Castro plots, that the public first heard this woman's amazing tale. Even then, they refused to believe that their beloved JFK could have been such a cad. Campbell Exner (having remarried by then) was vilified and disbelieved by Democrats and Republicans alike. But in the years since, her story has held up under intense scrutiny and is now accepted as fact. When she died in September 1999, she took a lot of secrets with her. (She had, for example, recently revealed that after making her pregnant in 1962, Kennedy arranged for a then-illegal abortion.)

But wait, there's more: in one of those cosmic coincidences, another would-be presidential mistress, Donna Rice (linked with front-runner Gary Hart), allegedly lived here two decades later.

Jack Cassidy Death Site
Where the actor ignited.

1221 N..Kings Road, #401, at Santa Monica Boulevard, on the west side of the street.

A song-and-dance man who performed in chorus lines, Jack Cassidy is perhaps (if sadly) best remembered as the husband of Shirley Jones and the father of both Shaun and David Cassidy. One December night in 1976 he threw a party in his roomy flat overlooking Kings Road. Cassidy fell asleep on a couch, and no one is sure whether the lit cigarette that started the ensuing fire was in his hand or was merely dropped by a guest and left to smolder. When it was all over, the place was such a wreck that no corpse was immediately apparent. Loved ones hoped against hope that Cassidy had left the house before the fire started. Some even speculated that he was in Palm Springs. But charred teeth and jewelry found in the ruins revealed his fate. Today the fully restored and airy apartment is an interior-design studio, which, unfortunately, is generally not open to the public.

Barney's Beanery
Where the Lizard King peed on the bar.

8447 Santa Monica Boulevard, at Croft Avenue, where Santa Monica Boulevard becomes Holloway Drive, on the north side of the street. Open daily, 6:00 A.M.–2:00 A.M. (323) 654-2287.

D ishing out chili since 1925 amid an anti-chic ambience, this roomy restaurant has sparked many a legend. Early patrons included Bette Davis, Errol Flynn, Ronald Reagan, and Jane Wyman. Later its hominess and vast beer selection endeared it to Jim Morrison, who in an unfettered moment took a whiz on the bar, in front of assorted diners. Janis Joplin used to drink Jack Daniel's at Barney's, and had her last meal here. Neither Jim nor Janis was daunted by the sign out front, now gone, that said "Fagots—stay out." The old circus-colored vinyl seats, license plate–studded ceiling, Coors lamps, and rampant neon signs remain in place, though new owners took over in 1999. Unsurprisingly, scenes from the Oliver Stone film *The Doors* were filmed here, not to mention *About Last Night*. Latter-day habitués include Vanna White. And a recent anecdote involves Johnny Depp, who allegedly marched out in a huff when told he couldn't smoke here.

Alta Cienega Motel
Where the Lizard King liked to crash.

1005 N. La Cienega Boulevard, at Santa Monica Boulevard, on the west side of the street. (310) 652-5797.

O verlooking an intersection where the traffic never ends, room 32 on the upper level of this motel is where Jim Morrison lodged, on and off, in 1969. At that time his office and recording studio were across the street. Behind a green-and-orange exterior with Astroturf stairs, the corner room now gets special treatment from the current owners, who bought the place un- awares and learned its history when a Doors cover band made the pilgrimage from Poland, of all places. Posted on one wall in the motel's office is part of a published inter- view conducted with Jim in room 32. The reporter makes no bones about Jim's ill- treatment of a nubile groupie of whom he has just acquired carnal knowledge. Fans from every corner of the world show up at the motel all the time to marvel at what the owners now call "The Jim Morrison Room."

The Jim Morrison Room, Alta Cienega Motel

Benvenuto Caffé
The Doors' former headquarters.

8512 Santa Monica Boulevard, at La Cienega. Open Mon.–Thurs., 11:30 A.M.–2:30 P.M. and 5:30–10:30 P.M.; Fri., 11:30 A.M.–2:30 P.M. and 5:30–11:00 P.M.; Sat., 5:30–11:00 P.M.; Sun., 5:30–10:30 P.M. (310) 659-8635.

I n what is now an Italian restaurant, Jim and his minions performed those dull tasks that kept the band in business. It was here that, in the winter of 1970–71, the Doors rehearsed and recorded *L.A. Woman,* their last album before Jim's putative death in a Paris bathtub. Office work went on upstairs. Since the band's departure, the building has been through various incarnations, including a stint as a gay and les- bian community center. On the corner at 8500 Santa Monica Boulevard, what is now a mobile-electronics shop was once the Extension, a topless bar where Jim liked to go. And around the corner at 962 La Cienega Boulevard was Elektra Studio, where the Doors recorded their albums *Soft Parade* and *Morrison Hotel.*

Doug Weston's Troubador
Where John Lennon put a Kotex on his head.

> 9081 Santa Monica Boulevard, at Doheny Drive, on the north side of the street: (301) 276-6168.

Since the late '50s this club has hosted a steady stream of greats: Joan Baez, the Smothers Brothers, Steve Martin, Van Morrison, Linda Ronstadt, John Denver, Willie Nelson, Mötley Crüe, and more. In its early days, folk acts and "hootenanny nights" drew enthusiastic crowds. Comedy venues were scarce in L.A. then, and Lenny Bruce got busted here. Later the club was a proving ground for fledgling artists including Cheech and Chong, Elton John, and Randy Newman. And it was here that John Lennon, separated from Yoko at what was arguably his lowest ebb, heckled performers while drunk and wearing a Kotex on his head. A wood-paneled Victorian-style tavern adjacent to the concert hall has a photo exhibit dubbed the "Troubador Hall of Fame."

Doug Weston's Troubador

ELSEWHERE IN WEST HOLLYWOOD

Tail o' the Pup
Hot dog–shaped hot dog stand.

> 329 N. San Vicente Boulevard. Open Mon.–Sat., 6:00 A.M.–5:00 P.M.; Sun., 8:00 A.M.–5:00 P.M. (310) 652-4517.

This historic hot dog stand is a seventeen-foot, stucco-and-steel frankfurter, bun and all. Southern California used to have lots of buildings shaped like hats, tepees, and such; today this is one of the few that remain. Slated for demolition in 1987, the stand was declared a landmark just in time and moved to its current address. Perhaps you've glimpsed it in such films as *L.A. Story, Ruthless People, Volcano, Body Double,* and *My Girl II.* Items

Tail o' the Pup

on the menu include the Boston Celtic, the Mexican Olé, and other dogs. Photos on display reveal celebrity carnivores including Magic Johnson, Richard Dreyfuss, Ice Cube, Lou Rawls, Barbra Streisand, and Pamela Anderson.

Jerry's Famous Deli

8701 Beverly Boulevard, at Sherbourne Drive, on the north side of the street. Open Sun.– Thurs., 6:00 A.M.–3:00 A.M.; Fri.–Sat., 6:00 A.M.–4:30 A.M. (310) 289-1811.

Knishes, kishka, beef brisket, and banana blintzes are on a seven hundred–item menu, served amid glaring "stage" lights, theater posters, and other Broadway-themed effects whose presence feels absurd in the middle of L.A. Garth Brooks, Shaquille O'Neal, Pete Rose, Jon Lovitz, Jerry Seinfeld, and a string of soap opera actors have been spotted at this branch of the deli chain.

The Colonial House
Apartments of the stars.

1416 N. Havenhurst Drive, off Sunset Boulevard, on the east side of the street.

Now listed in the National Register of Historic Places, this creamy brick 1927 high-rise was erected in the French Colonial Revival style specifically to lure film industry types fresh from points east, including Europe. Over the years Bette Davis, Clark Gable, and Nicholas Ray have all been tenants in its luxury apartments.

Fairfax/Melrose Area

The Groundling Theatre
Where Pee-wee Herman was born.

7307 Melrose Avenue, at Poinsettia Place, on the north side of the street. (323) 934-9700.

Since 1974 this constantly evolving comedy and improv troupe has spawned some seriously funny alumni, including Jon Lovitz, Lisa Kudrow, Laraine Newman, Julia Sweeney, Cassandra "Elvira" Peterson, Paul Reubens (better known to the world as Pee-wee Herman, the character he developed while onstage here), and the late Phil Hartman. Photos decorating the lobby recall these and more. A plaque declares that the theater is now dedicated to Hartman's memory. Catch rising stars at a live performance here.

Audience Associates
Frolic in a studio audience for free.

7471 Melrose Avenue (suite 10). Open Mon.–Fri., 10:00 A.M.–5:00 P.M. (323) 653-4105.

When sitcom actors and game show contestants get up to their hilarious antics, who does all that yukking and clapping in the background? *You* do. This office dispenses free tickets to live tapings, since major studios such as CBS, NBC, Fox, and Universal need to fill the seats. Get up close and personal with *Hollywood Squares, 3rd Rock from the Sun, Everybody Loves Raymond, Veronica's Closet, Family Feud,* and more. You also have the option of signing up as a crowd-scene extra for the filming of a major motion picture. They prefer that you call to reserve tickets rather than show up at their office in person.

Canter's
Where Pearl Jam ponders potato pancakes.

419 N. Fairfax Avenue, at Oakwood Avenue, on the west side of the street. Open Sun.–Fri., 24 hours. (323) 651–2030.

The decor has a '50s flair and brisket is king in this round-the-clock deli. An L.A. institution, Canter's has sold more than two million pounds of lox. Oy, to whom? To regulars like Bugsy Siegel, Jack Benny, Elvis, and Marilyn Monroe. (For her marriage to Arthur Miller, Marilyn converted to Judaism. Canter's named a tomato-cheese sandwich after her.) During the '60s rockers like Frank Zappa, Joni Mitchell, and even the Beatles flocked here after hours. (Rumor has it that Keith Moon once came in clad as a Nazi—and quickly left.) Punk bands hung here in the '70s; their tattooed descendants uphold the tradition. Others spotted schmoozing in the restaurant and its bar, the Kibitz Room, include Johnny Depp, Lenny Kravitz, Pearl Jam, Guns N' Roses, and Madonna.

Canter's

CBS Television City
Join a live studio audience.

7800 Beverly Boulevard, at Fairfax Avenue, on the east side of the street, just north of Farmers Market. (323) 575-2458 or (24-hour recording) (323) 575-2624.

You've heard it countless times: "Filmed before a live studio audience." Just where do they get those audiences? Right here! Show up, get your free ticket, and studio lackeys will show you how to respond on cue. This is the studio where Elvis taped his first appearance on *The Ed Sullivan Show.* Later it launched *The Sonny and Cher Show* and many more. These days you never know exactly what will be on offer: could be tickets to *The Martin Short Show, Hollywood Squares, Politically Incorrect, The Price Is Right,* or *Family Feud.* Call ahead to reserve if you're choosy. An on-site gift shop sells products with logos.

Petersen Automotive Museum
Where Notorious B.I.G. was gunned down.

6060 Wilshire Boulevard, at Fairfax Avenue, on the east side of the street. Open Tues.–Sun., 10:00 A.M.–6:00 P.M. Admission: adults, $7; seniors and students, $5; children, $3; under age 5, free. (323) 930-2277.

Just as he was leaving a 1997 awards program at this car-culture museum, rap star Notorious B.I.G. was killed by a drive-by shooter. Those fatal shots struck the plump rapper when he was—where else?—in his car. It's a sad story and true, but whimsical surprises await inside. Celebrated autos on display include Herbie the Love Bug. Also here are the *Dukes of Hazzard* car and *The Flinstones'* Flintmobile. Stars' cars on exhibit include those of Clark Gable, Lucille Ball, and Joan Crawford. Watch vehicularly themed TV shows such as *My Mother the Car* in special screening rooms.

Monster truck, Petersen Automotive Museum

Rebecca Schaeffer House
Where fandom proved fatal.

120 N. Sweetzer Avenue.

Rebecca Schaeffer had once considered becoming a rabbi. The young actress's Hollywood career was gathering steam in the summer of 1989 when, on the morning of July 18, Schaeffer answered her doorbell. Hurriedly preparing for an audition, she greeted the young male fan who appeared at the door, but then she politely excused herself and began to retreat. He shot her and fled. Caught soon after, the killer proved to be a schizophrenic; eventually he was convicted of murder and sentenced to life without parole. He had been seen in the days before the murder carrying Schaeffer's picture around the area, asking neighbors where she lived.

Hard Rock Café

8600 Beverly Boulevard, at the northern tip of Beverly Center. (310) 276-7605.

This is America's first Hard Rock Café, and the second in the world. Most prominently displayed is Elvis's Harley-Davidson. On the walls are guitars once belonging to Jerry Garcia, Todd Rundgren, Iggy Pop (along with a pair of Iggy's sandals), Frank Zappa (along with an original painting Zappa did in 1958), and John Lennon (along with his jacket and his original, hastily scrawled lyrics for "Help!"). Buddy Holly's high school yearbook is here, as are Elvis's cowboy shirt, rare posters, gold records by numerous artists, and a sequinned suit worn by Paul Revere of the Raiders. A pair of Elton John's glasses spell out "Elton" in lights. Diners munch burgers, quaff pilsner, and browse in the gift shop hoping for live stars to materialize amid the relics. Michelle Pfeiffer and KISS's Gene Simmons have been known to turn up.

John Lennon's scrawled lyrics to "Help!"

Cedars-Sinai Medical Center

Where the elite meet to give birth, die, and have appendectomies.

8700 Beverly Boulevard, between San Vicente and Robertson Boulevards. (George Burns Road runs between Beverly and Third; Gracie Allen Drive runs between George Burns and San Vicente, within the medical-center grounds.)
(310) 855-5000.

Stars regularly undergo profound rites of passage here. But, confidentiality being what it is, staffers tend to keep mum. River Phoenix, Lucille Ball, Michael Landon, Eva Gabor, Danny Kaye, and Sammy Davis Jr. are among those who have reportedly died here. But buck up! Happy things happen here, too! Jodie Foster and Annette Bening

The corner of George Burns Road and Gracie Allen Drive , Cedars-Sinai Medical Center

allegedly gave birth here, as did Debbie Rowe (she was married to Michael Jackson at the time). And celebrities like Steven Spielberg regularly drop in for emergency surgery. George Burns was such a staunch Cedars-Sinai supporter that today a pair of intersecting roads on hospital grounds are named for him and his beloved wife, Gracie Allen.

Beverly Hills

RODEO DRIVE DISTRICT AND THE FLATS

Rodeo Drive
We don't need no stinking price tags.

Between Wilshire and Santa Monica Boulevards.

This is rumored to be the world's most expensive three-block shopping strip. And it's the sort of place where you definitely don't ask what stuff costs. Legendary designer boutiques (Giorgio, Gucci, Vuitton, Escada, Dior, Chanel, and such) share the tree-lined thoroughfare with legendary jewelers (Cartier, Tiffany, etc.). Hilariously costly hair salons here inspired the one in *Shampoo*. Stars are habitually spotted tossing away small fortunes in these emporia. The tiny pedestrian mall dubbed "Two Rodeo," starting at Wilshire, has brick, marble, and wrought-iron detailing. The fakey European effect thrills many a non-European visitor. A scene from *The Muse* was shot here, as was a scene in *A Civil Action,* in which Travolta tries on a suit at Sulka.

Regent Beverly Wilshire Hotel
Where crowned heads hang their hats.

9500 Wilshire Boulevard, at Rodeo Drive. (310) 275-5200.

Overflowing with hand-carved balustrades, wrought-iron balconies, Carrara marble, mirrored arches, chandeliers, inlaid floors, and gaslights a-poppin', this bit o' Versailles has appeared in such films as *Clueless, Beverly Hills Cop, American Gigolo,* and *Escape from the Planet of the Apes.* In real life its suites are tagged at $5,000 and $7,500 per night. This has not hindered princes Charles and Andrew, the emperor and empress of Japan, the Dalai Lama, Prime Minister Benazir Bhutto, Denmark's Princess Margarethe, and Jordan's King Hussein and Queen Noor. Other guests have included Jimmy Stewart, Steve McQueen, Roger Moore, the Beatles, Elton John, Mick Jagger, and more. Elvis Presley enjoyed the Presidential Suite, which has its own dining room and two sunken tubs. Perhaps you saw it in *Pretty Woman* or *Wag the Dog*.

Planet Hollywood Beverly Hills

9560 Wilshire Boulevard, between Camden and Rodeo Drives. Open Sun.–Thurs., 11:00 A.M.–midnight; Fri.–Sat., 11:00 A.M.–1:00 A.M. (310) 275-7828.

Headliners attended a glittering block party when this link in the PH chain opened in 1995. Stars such as Arnold Schwarzenegger, Sylvester Stallone, Bruce Willis, and Demi Moore received stock in exchange for promoting the place. Though the firm faced bankruptcy in 1999, this restaurant remained open, displaying enough Hollywood memorabilia to unman King Kong. Examine the *Clockwork Orange* switchblade, *Titanic* dishware, *Coneheads* cone, Dustin Hoffman's *Tootsie* glasses, David Carradine's *Kung Fu* flute, and Patrick Swayze's *Dirty Dancing* shoes. View costumes worn by Susan Sarandon in *Thelma and Louise*, Ben Affleck in *Good Will Hunting*, Julie Andrews in *The Sound of Music*, Judy Garland in *The Wizard of Oz*, James Dean in *Giant*, Brad Pitt in *Interview with a Vampire*, Jet Li in *Lethal Weapon 4*, Jim Carrey in *The Mask*, and many more. Don't miss Barbara Eden's *I Dream of Jeannie* harem pants.

Schwarzenegger costume, Planet Hollywood

House of Winston

Where the stars borrow their Oscar-night jewels.

371 N. Rodeo Drive, at Brighton Way, on the southwestern corner. (310) 271-8554.

Stay outside if you know what's good for ya. Doormen pose intimidatingly by the front door, while in the windows some of the world's most expensive jewelry glitters and winks. Seated at lamp-lit tables inside, customers sample the wares. Proprietor Harry Winston, having acquired the Hope Diamond, gave it to the Smithsonian. In the 1940s, as a perverse form of publicity, Winston started loaning his merchandise to stars for Oscar night. It was he who supplied Gloria Stewart's $20 million blue diamond the night *Titanic* swept the awards. Hosting the show in 1999, Whoopi Goldberg wore a record-breaking Winston array worth more than $40 million.

Nate 'n' Al
Where the glamorous get chopped liver.

414 N. Beverly Drive, on the east side of the street. Open daily, 7:00 A.M.–9:00 P.M. (310) 274-0101.

Corned beef perfumes this sprawling deli that has been luring the local talent since it opened in the 1940s. Groucho Marx, Ava Gardner, and Rita Hayworth adored it. Doris Day is said to have arrived daily, once upon a time, to enjoy breakfast clad in a bathrobe. Later patrons included Johnny Carson, Paul Newman, Joanne Woodward, and Cher. Today comics such as Larry King and Roseanne are regulars, as is the Lewinsky family. When Chelsea Clinton arrived (legend has it she ordered *matzah brei*), a team of Secret Service agents stood vigil over every entrance; they'd cased the joint first.

Museum of Television and Radio

465 N. Beverly Drive, at Little Santa Monica Boulevard. Open Wed. and Fri.–Sun., noon–5:00 P.M.; Thur., noon–9:00 P.M. Suggested contribution: adults, $6; students, $4; children age 12 and under, $3. (310) 786-1000.

Housed in a modern white marble edifice flanked by the Barbara and Garry Marshall Pool, this is the western branch of a New York institution seeking to prove that *Maude* and *Magnum, P.I.* are artworks in their own right. Visitors have access to dozens of screens and headsets that offer cherished moments from TV and radio—drawn from an archive more than 100,000 programs strong. This collection includes comedies, cartoons, commercials, sporting events, serials, sci-fi—every type of program, from fireside chats to *King of the Hill* and beyond. Also on the premises is a working radio studio. Special programs staged here include screenings and live appearances, and the museum hosts a popular annual festival.

Chasen's
Sixty-plus years as the screen stars' favorite.

246 N. Cañon Drive, on the east side of the street. (310) 858-1200.

In its original Beverly Boulevard location, Chasen's was beloved by Bogart, Barbara Stanwyck, Errol Flynn, W. C. Fields, Joan Crawford, and others. The restaurant was founded in 1937; Golden Age legends abound. Orson Welles allegedly threw a burning can of Sterno at John Houseman there. The entertainment at Jimmy Stewart's bachelor party, held there, included midgets wearing diapers. Elizabeth Taylor had Chasen's chili jetted to her table when she was filming *Cleopatra* in Rome. Ronald Reagan, who counted the place as a favorite, is said to have proposed to Nancy in

one of its booths. After shutting down in 1995, the restaurant moved two years later
to this new location. Regulars are said to include Quentin Tarantino, Sharon Stone,
and John Travolta. A paneled dining room is augmented with soft, ambient music;
jackets are required after 6:00 P.M.

Edelweiss Chocolates

444 N. Cañon Drive, on the east side of the street. (310) 275-0341.

R anked at the top of its class in Zagat, this tiny slot of a shop has been in business for more than fifty years, and it still uses its original recipes for chocolate-
covered marshmallows, glacéed fruits, and other treats. Chocolates are hand-dipped
in a kitchen out back. Steven Spielberg, Lauren Bacall, Kirk Douglas, David Geffen,
and sundry royals have been linked with the place. A romantic story is still told of
how comedian Marty Ingels bought the whole store as a Valentine's Day present for
his wife Shirley Jones a few years back. (It's under different ownership now.) Hungry? These babies will set you back more than twenty bucks a pound.

Beverly Hills City Hall

*455 N. Rexford Drive, occupying the block between Rex-
ford and Crescent Drive, at Santa Monica Boulevard. (310)
285-1000.*

T his phallic tower has starred in a number of films
over the years, sometimes as a symbol of Beverly
Hills, sometimes anonymously. Most famously, it stood
in for the Beverly Hills Police Station in *Beverly Hills
Cop 1* and *2;* you can see a brash Eddie Murphy strut-
ting in and out of the Art Deco Spanish Baroque building several times throughout the movie. Scenes in *Six
Days, Seven Nights* were filmed here as well.

Beverly Hills City Hall

Slimmons
Richard Simmons's gym.

*9306 Civic Center Drive, which is also known as Little Santa Monica Boulevard. Open
Mon.–Thurs., 9:00 A.M.–1:00 P.M. and 5:00–8:00 P.M.; Fri., 9:00 A.M.–1:00 P.M. and 4:30–6:30
P.M.; Sat., 9:00 A.M.–12:30 P.M.; Sun., 9:00–11:00 A.M. (310) 275-4663.*

F or $10 visitors can take a Tuesday- or Thursday-night class led by Simmons
himself in the very gym where his national TV show was filmed. Beyond its
pink-and-green awning, twist and grunt alongside some of the world's wealthiest cel-
lulite. Classes here include Sweat!, Sweat Plus!, Tone!, and Shape and Tone! Sou-

venirs on sale at the counter include Simmons's *Farewell to Fat* cookbook and his "Love to Stretch" stretch strap.

Beverly Hills High School
An all-star student body.

241 Moreno Drive, at Heath Avenue. (310) 229-3685.

G uess what its zip code is. Wrong! It's 90212. Alumni include Rob Reiner, Albert Brooks, Marlo Thomas, Nicolas Cage, Joel Grey, Richard Dreyfuss, Betty White, Shaun Cassidy, Crispin Glover, Julie Kavner, Alicia Silverstone, David Schwimmer, Richard Chamberlain, Laraine Newman, Carrie Fisher, Monica Lewinsky, and the murderin' Menendez brothers, Erik and Lyle. Though the TV show about BHHS isn't filmed here, the dance-floor scene from *It's a Wonderful Life* was. In that scene, the actor Carl Switzer (*Our Gang's* ill-fated "Alfalfa") plays a man who pushes a button that makes the floor recede, revealing a swimming pool beneath, into which the revelers fall.

Academy of Motion Picture Arts and Sciences
Where winners pick up their Oscars.

8949 Wilshire Boulevard, on the north side of the street. Gallery open Tues.–Fri., 10:00 A.M.–5:00 P.M.; Sat.–Sun., noon–6:00 P.M. Free. (310) 247-3600.

T he statuettes they hand out on Oscar night are anonymous and unmarked. Upstairs in these Academy offices, the real Oscars are fitted with plaques bearing the winners' names. During the weeks following the show, these permanent Oscars wait here, packaged in pretty purple bags, for the winners to come and pick them up—just like a pizza. (Some winners reportedly send servants.) Gaze up at the huge golden Oscar statue guarding the elevator on your way to the fourth-floor gallery, where changing exhibits celebrate film and filmmakers. Another gallery is on the ground floor. Classes, screenings, and other events are also held here regularly.

Zsa Zsa Gabor Arrest Site
The parking spot in front of 8551 Olympic Boulevard, at LeDoux Road, on the northwest corner, just west of La Cienega Boulevard.

M ore famous for her jewels and sharp ripostes than for her stage and screen antics, the former beauty queen has for decades been an object of mockery. In June 1989 a Beverly Hills cop tried to pull her over for speeding at Olympic and Fairfax. But the flashy Hungarian fled, and it was another three blocks before the cop caught up with her. Here on this busy corner lined with stucco homes, Gabor slapped the policeman as he attempted to write her a ticket. The assault got her into hotter water than mere speeding would have done. Zsa Zsa went to jail, the tabloids went wild, and the spot of the famous "slappening" became another stop on the rubbernecking tour.

> ABOVE SANTA MONICA BOULEVARD

The "Witch House"
516 Walden Drive, at Carmelita Avenue, on the southeast corner.

The "Witch House"

Built in 1921 as a movie set at Culver City's Willat Studios, this cottage is crooked on purpose. Faux Bavarianisms and deliberately creepy touches include motley shingles, warped pickets, dangling shutters, and a hilariously steep roof. After appearing in several silent films, the house was moved to this location and became a private home. Now the Witch House (officially named the Spadena House) stands out on this street of elegant mansions. You may have seen it in *The Loved One* (John Gielgud's character lives there), and in *Clueless,* where Alicia Silverstone's character meanders past. A rose garden, lampposts, mini-waterwheel, and wooden bridge out front enhance its nutty appeal. Reportedly, the place sold for well over a million in 1998.

Clara Bow House
512 N. Bedford Drive, at Santa Monica Boulevard, on the east side of the street.

According to a hot rumor that helped sink her career, the "It Girl" may or may not have slept with the entire 1927 USC football team here (including a tackle called Marion Morrison, the future John Wayne). Bow's secretary, Daisy DeVoe, published an exposé claiming that in this relatively modest one-story house her boss banged not only the team, but also Eddie Cantor, Gary Cooper, Bela Lugosi, and others. The room of choice, DeVoe claimed, was a Chinese-themed den. Bow denied it, but the damage was done. DeVoe was later arrested for stealing from the actress. Another legend links Bow with a married doctor. In the Chinese den he allegedly gave the actress "nerves therapy," applying a "love balm" which, of course, came directly from his dingdong.

Marilyn Monroe–Joe DiMaggio Home
508 N. Palm Drive, at Santa Monica Boulevard, on the east side of the street.

If it wasn't in Beverly Hills, this would look like an ordinary middle-class home. But it *is* in Beverly Hills, and into this house moved newlyweds Marilyn and Joe. Their marriage did not last long, and the house with its neat green lawn has outlasted them both.

Marilyn Monroe–Joe DiMaggio Home

Menendez Murder House
Where bad seeds grew.

722 N. Elm Drive.

Erik Menendez was nineteen and his brother Lyle was twenty-two when, on the night of August 20, 1989, they crept into their own home and murdered their parents. José and Kitty Menendez had been watching TV and eating ice cream before their sons appeared in the semidarkness, toting shotguns. When the bloodbath was over, the boys had blown off part of their father's head. Their mother had been shot ten times. The brothers subsequently alleged in court that they had suffered unbearable abuse on the part of entertainment mogul José. Prison awaited them. The wide pale house with its heavy gate and arched doorways (said to have sold for more than $3 million in 1991) is also said to be a former home of Elton John's and Michael Jackson's—though not together.

Lupe Velez House
Where death quenched the Mexican Spitfire.

732 N. Rodeo Drive.

Her career started on the Mexican stage, then skyrocketed as she starred in films opposite the likes of Douglas Fairbanks and Gary Cooper. By the '30s she had been linked romantically with Fairbanks and Cooper as well as with Charlie Chaplin and, of all people, Jimmy Durante. Cooper's eventual dumping of the "Mexican Spitfire" was a media event. After her five-year marriage to Johnny Weissmuller ended with a stormy divorce, Velez faced loneliness and depression. Her career sagged. In 1944, pregnant with the child of an uninterested actor, the thirty-five-year-old actress overdosed on Seconal here at her sprawling Spanish-style home. Less-than-literary suicide notes were part of her elaborate preparations; she had dressed up specially for the occasion, and decorated the house. Newspapers reported that she died in bed, but tales have circulated since of a messier death: e.g., that a vomiting Velez drowned in a toilet.

Lana Turner House
730 N. Bedford Drive.

In the spring of 1958 the "Sweater Girl" was having a torrid affair with small-time gangster Johnny Stompanato. He abused her, and flew into a rage after she attended that year's Academy Awards ceremony without him. On April 4, days after moving into this extra-wide white mansion, Turner tried to break up with him. By night's end he lay mortally wounded in a plush, pink-carpeted upstairs bedroom. Turner's fourteen-year-old daughter Cheryl Crane, charged with stabbing Stompanato, maintained she had done it to defend her mother's life. Turner mourned dramatically. The crime was ruled to be justifiable homicide, and Turner abruptly moved out of the mansion. Some believe the actress killed Stompanato herself, then persuaded young Crane to take the blame.

Bugsy Siegel Death House
Where karma caught up with him.

810 N. Linden Drive, at Whittier Drive.

Starstruck mobster Benjamin "Bugsy" Siegel was linked not only with hard-core gangsters "Lucky" Luciano and Meyer Lansky, but also with Cary Grant, Jean Harlow, and George Raft. Siegel's Flamingo casino helped put Las Vegas on the map. On the night of June 20, 1947, he was relaxing here in the home of his girlfriend, Virginia Hill, who was out of town at the time. An assassin crept up on the usually hypercautious Siegel and fired through a window. Part of Siegel's head was blasted away. The gunman slipped into the night and was never seen again.

The Other Dead Man's Curve
Where Jan crashed.

Sunset Boulevard, just west of Whittier Boulevard.

Teen idols Jan Berry and Dean Torrence had a 1964 hit with "Dead Man's Curve." The melodramatic song recounts a catastrophic car crash on a busy L.A. road. Two years later Berry was speeding in a Corvette Stingray when he hit a stationary truck near where Whittier intersects Sunset. The accident killed his passengers and landed Berry in a coma. He came out of the coma but was permanently disabled. They say it was three years before he could remember the words to his own songs. Afterward, many presumed that *this* was the curve the boys had sung about. Ironically, it wasn't. The actual Dead Man's Curve is on Sunset opposite UCLA's football field.

ROXBURY DRIVE HOMES
OF THE STARS

⌐f you've never been to Beverly Hills, you might think its streets are paved with
⌐ gold and lined with stars' homes. Well, the part about the gold isn't true. The
other part isn't, either—*except* for a certain street called Roxbury Drive. More
superstars have lived along three short blocks of Roxbury than on any other
three blocks in the world. In the early 1950s Roxbury Drive became de rigueur
for tour buses. That tradition continues to this day, so as you follow this little itinerary you might have a lot of company.

Here's where to begin: from Santa Monica Boulevard, turn north up Roxbury Drive, and go three blocks. Our tour starts at Lomitas Avenue and continues north along Roxbury to Benedict Canyon Drive.

- **809 N. Roxbury: Maureen O'Sullivan and Mia Farrow.** On the set of
1936's *Tarzan Escapes,* Maureen O'Sullivan, who was playing Jane, hooked up
with screenwriter John Farrow. Eventually they married. The Catholic couple
had a lot of babies, one of whom they nicknamed Mia. Struck with polio at age
nine, the child remained pale and fragile thenceforth. This would prove a magnet for men. Little Mia's life has been fraught with scandal. Despite a Catholic-
school education and a youth spent here in a house where priests were
frequent guests, she has enjoyed a love life that is anything but ordinary. From
a grotesque mismatch with the nightmarish Frank Sinatra she went on to
homewrecker status, breaking up the Previn family. An ensuing relationship
with Woody Allen yielded eventual heartache. And it all started with Tarzan.
- **905 N. Roxbury: Oscar Levant.** Brilliant pianist, talented composer, hilarious comedian, and miserable misanthrope, Oscar Levant was a complex human being. He reportedly drank forty cups of coffee and smoked five packs
of cigarettes a day. He was bosom buddies with George Gershwin (see **1019
Roxbury**). After George died in 1937 Oscar refused ever again to pass his
late pal's house. When visiting Ira Gershwin he drove blocks out of his way so
as to approach Ira's home at 1021 from the other direction. Levant was way
ahead of his time, revealing his neuroses to shocked TV talk-show audiences
during the 1950s. In later years he became addicted to prescription drugs.
Doctors would pull up in front of this house in the middle of the night and in-
ject him with phenobarbital as he sat in their cars.
- **918 N. Roxbury: Jimmy Stewart.** America's favorite actor lived here in a
Tudor-style mansion, where he played with his dogs and grew corn in the yard,
just like the down-home sorta fella he often portrayed. He also killed thousands
of people as a bomber pilot in World War II, making him the one Oscar-

winning actor who caused more deaths than any other. (Reagan never won an Oscar.) He liked clowning around with neighbor Lucille Ball but valued his privacy. One day when a family of tourists had the gall to lay out a picnic on his front lawn, Stewart walked outside and wordlessly turned on the sprinklers. After he died on the premises in 1997 his heirs sold the house to a businessman who tore it down to build a house more to his taste in its place.

- **1000 N. Roxbury: Lucille Ball and Desi Arnaz.** Even before Lucy moved in, this house was famous because a former owner, exasperated with tourists mistaking his residence for neighbor Jack Benny's, had posted a sign out front. It read, "JACK BENNY DOES NOT LIVE HERE. HE LIVES THERE." When Lucy and Desi took up residence, tourists started arriving in droves. For a while the duo had a grand old time, dressing up and handing out candy on Halloween, letting little Desi Jr. bilk tourists out of cash, inviting all their famous neighbors to parties. But then Lucy tired of Desi's incessant extramarital fornicatin'. She kicked him out in 1960; new husband Gary Morton moved in later. Her rise from sexy '30s glamour girl to beloved TV comedienne to empire-building media mogul is one of the great Hollywood success stories. After Lucy died here in 1989 new owners built an Italianate façade to disguise the house and confuse fans, to little effect.

- **1002 N. Roxbury: Jack Benny.** In the early 1950s Jack Benny's Colonial home was the most famous on the street. So many tour buses pulled up outside his house every day that he made a classic gag out of it on his popular TV show, riding one of the buses home as if it were public transit. Ever gracious, he often opened his front door to the tourists who knocked on it day and night. He even kept a stack of publicity photos near the door to hand out as souvenirs. Though for laughs he portrayed himself as a selfish miser, in private he was generous and thoughtful; even the nastiest Hollywood gossips can say nothing bad about him. His only equal in perfect comedic timing was Lucille Ball, who, strangely, lived next door. Celebrity-studded parties he held here drew not just neighbors but all the era's top stars. Failing health forced him to move out in 1965, despite his being only thirty-nine years old. (According to Benny, he'd been thirty-nine for decades.)

- **1004 N. Roxbury: Peter Falk.** The danger of being a good actor is that if you master a role too well, you become forever identified with the fictional character you brought to life. So it was for Peter Falk, better known to most Americans as Columbo. The show's success spelled doom for his career, as he was typecast as the eccentric detective. (Imagine this horror: the part was originally written for warbler Bing Crosby, who decided he'd rather play golf.) At last report, the one-eyed actor still lives here.

- **1019 N. Roxbury: George and Ira Gershwin, José Ferrer, and Rosemary Clooney.** Speaking of Bing Crosby and the name Columbo: Bing's main rival in the early 1930s was talented crooner Russ Columbo, who was accidentally shot to death with an antique dueling pistol here at 1019 Roxbury in 1934. Songwriting superstars George and Ira Gershwin moved in two years later and wrote some of their best-loved songs here, for the film *Shall We Dance:* "They Can't Take That Away from Me," "Let's Call the Whole Thing Off," and "Nice Work If You Can Get It." But the magic was short-lived: George died young of a brain tumor in 1937. A despondent Ira moved next door. In 1953 singer Rosemary Clooney and husband José Ferrer moved in, turning the house into the Roxbury village social center. Rosemary's only real claim to fame was the atrocious hit "Come-on-a-My-House"; José had recently won the Best Actor Oscar for *Cyrano de Bergerac.* While their kids made a pretty penny selling lemonade to tourists, Rosemary's young nephew George Clooney got his first show-business job here, helping out during radio shows that Rosemary broadcast from the house. Whenever she invited Bing Crosby on the air as a guest star, he studiously avoided the den where Russ Columbo met his maker, lest he, too, be smitten by some kind of "crooner curse." After José left in 1964 Rosemary lost her marbles and for a time was locked up in a psycho ward; her memories of that time became the basis for a TV movie. She emerged with her sanity intact and returned to this house, where she still lives.
- **1021 N. Roxbury: Ira Gershwin.** After George Gershwin's tragic death Ira couldn't bring himself to stay in the house where it happened. Their next-door neighbor at 1021 was an elderly woman who for over a year had listened enraptured as the brothers composed wonderful melodies on the piano late into the night. Sympathetic to Ira's plight, she offered to sell him her house so he could escape the memories but stay in the neighborhood. Ira accepted and spent the rest of his life here, writing the lyrics to such classics as "I Got Rhythm" and "Old Man River."
- **1023 N. Roxbury: Agnes Moorehead.** Best known to post–baby boomers as magical mother-in-law Endora on *Bewitched,* Agnes Moorehead had an illustrious career that is now largely forgotten. Not only was she nominated for five Academy Awards, she also had a Ph.D. in literature. Though she died of lung cancer long ago, she still makes headlines: recent books hail her as a not-completely-closeted lesbian.
- Other stars who lived or live on Roxbury: **Nanette Fabray (708 N. Roxbury), Lionel Barrymore (802 N. Roxbury),** and **Polly Bergen (1025 N. Roxbury).**

Beverly Hills Hotel
9641 Sunset Boulevard. (310) 276-2251.

Room rates here start at nearly $300. But what do you expect from a twelve-acre, five-star, pink stucco fantasyland that has housed Greta Garbo, Katharine Hepburn, JFK, LBJ, Liz Taylor, Richard Burton, Jean Harlow, Charlie Chaplin, John and Yoko, Clark Gable, Marilyn Monroe, and Howard Hughes (who used to reserve dozens of rooms at one time)? Built in 1912, this hotel predates the town whose name it bears and which more or less grew up around it. Among other wonders, Zsa Zsa Gabor is said to have signed her first film contract at its Polo Lounge restaurant. They say Joan Crawford learned to swim freestyle in its pool. They say John Mitchell was a guest here when he first learned the Watergate cat was out of the bag. The Eagles album *Hotel California* had this hotel's picture on the cover; the place also appears in *The Way We Were, American Gigolo, Shampoo,* and a string of other films. If you feel outclassed amid the banana trees and cabanas, don't say you weren't warned.

George Michael Arrest Site
Will Rogers Memorial Park, 9650 Sunset Boulevard, across from the Beverly Hills Hotel. (310) 285-2536.

In April 1998 pop star George Michael was arrested for engaging in what cops deemed a "lewd act." At the time the singer was all by himself in this park's restroom minding his own business—apparently a bit *too* enthusiastically. He was booked under his real name, Georgios Panayiotou. This leafy retreat is named after Will Rogers; the much-loved raconteur was Beverly Hills' first honorary mayor. Don't confuse it with the much larger Will Rogers State Park a few miles west.

Charlie Chaplin House
1085 Summit Drive, at Cove Way.

Set designers and studio carpenters built Chaplin a graceful forty-room home here in 1922. But they didn't know how to make things that would last. Thus their lovely but fragile creation earned the nickname "Breakaway House," as bits were always snapping off. It was here that the superstar lived in 1925–26 with his nubile bride, Lita Gray. Her lowbrow kin moved in as well. When the pair divorced, Gray published a best-selling booklet claiming Chaplin was a pervert. Among other shockeroos, she claimed he had requested fellatio and suggested a three-way. The ensuing scandal dealt his career a major, as it were, blow.

Pickfair
Legendary home of Mary Pickford and Douglas Fairbanks.

1143 Summit Drive. From Benedict Canyon Drive, turn east up Summit Drive and stay on Summit until you reach 1143, which will be on your left.

O nce the most famous building in America, surpassing even the White House, Pickfair was for fifteen years the epicenter of Hollywood's glamour. Silent-film greats Mary Pickford and Douglas Fairbanks moved into the converted hunting lodge in 1920. It started a fad, and other actors began building homes in the countrified woodlands known as Beverly Hills. A nation watched enthralled as the world's most famous couple held court over a procession of movie stars, politicians, and royals. Throughout the '20s every prince, beauty queen, and millionaire angled for an invitation to Pickfair's fabulous parties. A reporter coined the name Pickfair from the owners' surnames, and in short order the word itself came to symbolize all the wonder that was Hollywood. But by the mid-'30s, both their careers were faltering. The couple split up. When Fairbanks left, a depressed Pickford retreated from the public eye as new generations of stars came and went. Several years after Pickford died here in Pickfair, talentless woman-child Pia Zadora and her zillionaire husband bought the sprawling mansion. If you didn't already have enough reasons to hate Pia Zadora, you can add this one to your list: the pair gutted Pickfair and built a new façade, interior, and garage, all in ineffably bad taste. Less than a year later, bored with the monstrous new creation, they moved out, leaving a mutilated Pickfair in their wake. You can still see the ugly new garage and entrance area, though only those who remember how the building used to look will appreciate how little is left.

Greystone Park and Mansion
Frequently filmed splendor.

905 Loma Vista Drive, at Doheny Road. Grounds open daily in summer, 10:00 A.M.–6:00 P.M.; the rest of the year, 10:00 A.M.–5:00 P.M.; mansion closed to the public. (310) 550-4796 or 550-4654.

S ome call it California's second-best palace, trailing San Simeon. Oil tycoon and Teapot Dome scandal participant Edward Doheny built this Tudor enormity in 1928 for his son. Soon afterward the younger Doheny was shot and killed in his bedroom here by his secretary, Hugh Plunkett, who then killed himself. Rumors of a lovers' quarrel between the two sprang up immediately. Later the fifty-five-room mansion—with its three-foot-thick walls, hand-carved rafters, on-site bowling alley, and acres of landscaped grounds—would change hands and appear in dozens of movies and TV shows—more than forty between 1955 and 1965 alone. To date, those productions include *The Loved One, Ghostbusters II, The Witches of Eastwick, All of Me, Batman and Robin, The Golden Child, Death Becomes Her, Indecent Pro-*

posal, Nixon, The Fabulous Baker Boys, The Big Lebowski, Clueless, Rush Hour, Dynasty, Falcon Crest, and dozens more. Browse the gardens, but you can only admire the stone-bedecked house from outside.

Hollywood Hills

GRIFFITH PARK AND NEARBY

Griffith Park Observatory

2800 E. Observatory Road, atop Mount Hollywood; take Vermont Avenue or Fern Dell Drive (which turns into Western Canyon Road) to its northernmost end. (323) 664-1191.

Inside the big pale hilltop dome is, um, some astronomy stuff. Outside the building is where that crucial knife-fight scene was filmed for *Rebel without a Cause.* According to one legend, the director stopped shooting when he saw that James Dean had accidentally been sliced on the ear during one take, but Dean threw a hissy fit at being interrupted. A bronze bust of the late actor now stands atop a column outside the building. An accompanying plaque commemorates the filming of *Rebel.* Numerous other movies shot around Griffith Park—which stands in for the wilds more often than you realize—include *Jurassic Park, Bowfinger, Austin Powers,* and *The Rocketeer.* In *The Terminator* a nude Arnold Schwarzenegger arrives from the future; near the observatory he stares down at the incomparable view.

Bronson Caves
Where Batman went.

At the northernmost end of Bronson Avenue (Canyon Drive), on the southwestern side of Griffith Park.

In both the TV and movie versions of *Batman,* this natural formation is where our heroes hid their Batmobile. It has also appeared in countless other shows, doubling for the Wild West in *Gunsmoke, Bonanza,* and *The Lone Ranger;* as a jungle in *King Kong;* as a last-resort hideout in *Invasion of the Body Snatchers;* and much more.

Invasion of the Body Snatchers Stairs

Near the intersection of Beachwood and Belden Drives, in the Hollywoodland neighborhood in the hills between Griffith Park and the Hollywood Reservoir. See below for exact location. From Hollywood, take Gower Street north to Franklin Avenue, turn right on Franklin, and after one short block turn left up Beachwood Drive. Follow Beachwood until you reach Belden.

I n 1956's paranoiac masterpiece *Invasion of the Body Snatchers,* the climactic chase scene starts in Sierra Madre's town square and ends in Bronson Canyon. But the shank of the action happens here. When our heroes (portrayed by Kevin McCarthy and Dana Wynter) are discovered by the "pod people" who have taken over their town, they run for their lives. From the town square they are shown fleeing through a wooded neighborhood and up a long flight of stairs. The scene was shot on location in the Hollywood Hills, and most sources agree this was their route: from Beachwood and Belden eastward up to Westshire Drive, to a flight of stairs that starts next to 2744 Westshire; desperate and panting (these stairs are *steep*), they emerge near the intersection of Hollyridge Drive and Pelham Place. (Some sources say they ran in the other direction from Beachwood and Belden, but this seems wrong.) To learn the stirring conclusion, rent the film.

HOLLYWOOD Sign

On top of Mount Lee at the edge of Griffith Park, overlooking the eastern part of Hollywood. The best views of the sign are from around Gower Street (and the blocks on either side of it), between Melrose and Franklin. Getting close to the sign is more problematic: most access points have been gated, and walking to the sign is discouraged. If you want to try, here are a few suggestions for starting points for your attempted hike, all of which can be reached by taking Beachwood Drive north all the way to the top: the end of Innsdale Drive; the end of Deronda Drive; or the eastern end of Mulholland Highway. In all cases you will be wrangling with gates, fences, and possibly alarm systems—unless you find a way around them.

T his eternal symbol of L.A., the movie industry, and California itself was erected in 1923 as an ad for a Beachwood Drive housing development called Hollywoodland. The temporary sign started falling apart and by the late 1940s was in sorry shape. Local boosters got the idea to remove the -LAND part, spruce up the rest, and turn it into an ad for Hollywood. It worked. (See the cover of this very book, for example!) But it's more than a symbol—it's a real place where people have lived and died. Each letter has a story all its own. Struggling actress Peg Entwistle jumped to her death in 1932 from either the second D in HOLLYWOODLAND (now long gone) or, some say, the H or maybe even the first O. (The D seems most likely.) Her death supposedly sparked a rash of suicides by failed starlets. The sign was at one time illuminated by thousands of lightbulbs, maintained by a caretaker who lived in a shack behind one of the two Ls. Songwriter Eden Ahbez, who penned the hit "Nature Boy" for Nat "King" Cole, was one of Hollywood's most colorful characters, a proto-hippie known for his long beard, flowing robes, and the wild look in his eyes. When not writing autobiographical songs like "I'm a Gone Yogi," Ahbez is said to have dozed under the first L in a sleeping bag. In the 1998 version of *Mighty Joe Young,* the giant ape climbs atop an O—with the aid of special effects. A recent restoration of the entire sign was financed by an unlikely coalition of stars including Hugh Hefner and Alice Cooper.

Forest Lawn Hollywood Hills

6300 Forest Lawn Drive. Open daily, 8:00 A.M.–4:00 P.M. (323) 254-7251 or (800) 204-3131.

A replica of the Old North Church (yes, of Paul Revere fame) puzzlingly stands guard over four hundred landscaped acres stuffed chock-full of stars. Ask for a map at the front gate. Attendants will generally not disclose the locations of celebrities' graves, claiming the relatives prefer it that way, though the location of Andy Gibb's, for some reason, is yours for the asking. It's in the Courts of Remembrance area, west of the main entrance. So are those of Bette Davis, Lucille Ball, Charles Laughton, Liberace, and cartoonist Walter Lantz. Freddie Prinze's crypt is next to George Raft's. In the grass out front is the grave of Ernie Kovacs. Just north of the Old North Church, in the Courts of Liberty section, lie Buster Keaton, Stan Laurel, Telly Savalas, and Marty Feldman (who died while filming a death scene). In the adjacent Lincoln Terrace lie William Conrad and Scatman Crothers. Elsewhere on the expansive property are Jack Webb, Gene Autry (in the Sheltering Hills section), Marjorie Main (in the Enduring Faith section), Morey Amsterdam, Dorothy Lamour, Bobby Fuller, Forrest Tucker, Sabu, *The Mickey Mouse Club*'s Jimmie Dodd, and Ozzie, Harriet, and Ricky Nelson. Ricky's marker bears his actual name: Eric.

Mt. Sinai Memorial Park

Say nighty-night to Mama Cass.

5950 Forest Lawn Drive, at Beachwood Drive, just south of the Ventura Freeway, just east of Forest Lawn Hollywood Hills, just outside the northwestern corner of Griffith Park. Open Sun.–Fri., 8:00 A.M.–5:00 P.M. (818) 905-7600.

C ass Elliot's birth name was Ellen Naomi Cohen. Both names appear on the marker over her ashes. Also in these landscaped grounds with their large mosaic recounting Jewish history are TV's Phil Silvers and Norman Fell, and film star Lee J. Cobb (birth name: Leo Jacob, the son of a *Jewish Daily Forward* staffer). Also here are Ross Martin (birth name: Martin Rosenblatt), who portrayed inventive Artemus Gordon on TV's *Wild Wild West,* and 1960s-era stand-up comedienne Totie Fields, who pathetically poked fun at her own weight. For directions to any or all of these graves, ask at the front gate, where staffers will be happy to assist you.

Jack Nicholson House
Where Polanski was very naughty.

12850 Mulholland Drive.

High security protects the home where Jack Nicholson, having snagged more Oscar nominations than any other actor in history, indulges a passion for collecting fine art. Allegedly, he also has a wall-size TV and leaps into his pool from an upstairs balcony. It was to this house that Roman Polanski allegedly brought a thirteen-year-old girl in March 1977, on the pretext of photographing her for the French edition of *Vogue*. Nicholson, whom his pal Polanski had recently directed in *Chinatown*, was not home at the time. The girl told authorities Polanski probed not just one orifice down there, but two. The director, Sharon Tate's widower, was subsequently charged with drugging and raping a minor. Tests showed that the girl had had intercourse but revealed no evidence that it had been forced. But sex with minors is a crime. Polanski denied the charge at first, then admitted partial guilt, then jumped bail and fled the country for an extended exile from which he has yet to return.

Marlon Brando Compound
Money can't buy happiness.

12900 Mulholland Drive.

In his heyday he was a celebrated hunk. But these days Marlon Brando raises eyebrows as a tubby anti-Semite who ditched his career and bought real estate in the South Pacific. Here in L.A. his home is a rambling and very private compound. It was here in May 1990 that Brando's son Christian shot to death Dag Drollet, the Tahitian playboy lover of Christian's half-sister, Cheyenne. Earlier the siblings had discussed Drollet over drinks at Musso & Frank Grill on Hollywood Boulevard (see page 25). Christian later claimed the shooting was an accident, that the men had scuffled because of a misunderstanding in which Christian thought he'd heard Cheyenne say Drollet beat her. The young killer was sentenced to ten years. Cheyenne committed suicide in Tahiti.

Ennis Cosby Murder Site

On Skirball Center Drive, in the hills above Brentwood. To reach the site, take the San Diego Freeway (Highway 405) north from L.A. and exit at the Skirball Center Drive off-ramp. Cosby pulled over on the right shoulder just where the off-ramp ends.

Ennis Cosby, son of comedian Bill Cosby, was driving north from L.A. early in the morning on January 16, 1997, when his car got a flat tire. After Cosby pulled over to fix the flat, Ukrainian immigrant Mikhail Markhasev pulled up in his own car, got out to rob him, and shot him dead when the robbery went sour. The eighteen-year-old Markhasev was convicted and sentenced to life in prison. Hollywood is a small town: when Markhasev was a child newly arrived from the Ukraine, he attended the same grammar school (Gardner Street School) that Michael Jackson had attended years earlier.

Rock Hudson House
Where he lived and died.

9402 Beverlycrest Drive, near Lindacrest Drive, just east of Coldwater Canyon Drive.

Rock Hudson was renting this Spanish-style mansion when, in 1962, Universal offered to give it to him as a contract-renewal gift. Complete with a forty-foot pool and its own steam room, "the Castle"—as it was nicknamed—boasts not one but two living rooms. Hudson threw many a party here and worked on the house for the rest of his life. Struck with AIDS, the actor made waves and broke Hollywood tradition by announcing publicly that he was gay. It was here in his beloved Castle that Hudson died on October 2, 1985. (Pat Boone reportedly laid a Bible on the actor's chest in hopes of a miracle, but to no avail.)

Bluejay Way
As in the Beatles song of the same name.

From Sunset, take Doheny Drive north to Oriole Drive; go east on Oriole to Tanager Way and then to Bluejay.

In 1968 George Harrison was renting a house on this street in a neighborhood where all the streets have bird names. As the story goes, the Beatle was expecting a visit one night from his publicist. But the visitor lost his way on these tiny winding lanes in thick fog. While Harrison waited at home, inspiration struck. The result is his spacy song "Blue Jay Way." Its lyrics beg, "Please don't be long / Please don't you be very long." Rumor has it that the street signs have a funny propensity for getting swiped.

Lenny Bruce OD House
8825 Hollywood Boulevard.

H is edgy commentaries made audiences roar with laughter. But the hypocrisy and social injustice that Lenny Bruce savaged in his shtick were anything but a joke. His offstage life was fraught with trouble. America watched as the daring comedian underwent repeated arrests on drug and obscenity charges. He was residing here in 1966 when he died of an overdose in the bathroom—an ignoble but all-too-common end for a man who history would prove was way ahead of his time.

Bel Air and Nearby

HOLMBY HILLS

Jayne Mansfield/Engelbert Humperdinck Home
10100 Sunset Boulevard, at Carolwood Drive, a cul-de-sac heading south off Sunset Boulevard, just north of the Los Angeles Country Club. The house's entrance gate faces Carolwood, on the southwestern corner with Sunset.

T he busty star had her huge villa painted pink and she installed a heart-shaped swimming pool to suit her image as a squealing sex bomb. In 1967 she died horribly in an auto smashup, though rumors of her decapitation were untrue. The "Pink Palace" is framed with towering palm trees and guarded by dogs who fling themselves at the pink brick wall and white metal gate that surround it. Its current owner is singer Engelbert Humperdinck, who faithfully maintains its pinkness. His initials adorn the mailbox out front.

Tony Curtis and Janet Leigh/Sonny and Cher House
141 Carolwood Drive, at the end of the cul-de-sac heading south off Sunset Boulevard, just north of the Los Angeles Country Club, next to the Pink Palace.

S tone gates topped with sculpted fruit bowls guard a sweeping front lawn bigger than certain city parks. A three-tiered fountain adorns the driveway leading up and up and up to a white Mediterranean-style mansion so rife with windows and so big you can imagine getting lost in it while trying to find a spare roll of paper towels. Dubbed "Owlwood," this was once the home of Janet Leigh and Tony Curtis, the parents of Jamie Lee Curtis (Tony left Janet soon after Jamie's 1958 birth). Years earlier, the mansion belonged to United Artists magnate Joseph Schenk. Marilyn

Monroe reportedly lived in Schenk's guest house here and was compelled to dole out sexual services to the old guy. Years later Sonny and Cher moved in, belying the "Who needs money? We've got love!" ethos of their music.

HOLMBY HILLS STAR HOMES

There's gold in them thar hills. Gold-plated bathroom fixtures. Gold cards. Acapulco Gold. Some of the world's best-known entertainers have lived along these slopes and hollows. Big metal gates along these sedate curving streets near Beverly Hills guard the sort of unspeakable splendor that only an Elvis Presley or a Walt Disney could indulge in and still keep a straight face. **Mick Jagger** once rented the house at **135 Carolwood Drive,** for starters. Over the years, folks from Gregory Peck to Neil Diamond to George Harrison have lived in this extra-special 'hood. *Knock, knock!*—"Avon calling."

- Does size matter? **Aaron Spelling**'s megahouse at **594 S. Mapleton Drive,** near Club View, is legendary even in these parts. They say one dressing room occupies an entire wing, that the house measures 56,000 square feet, has 123 rooms, and is bigger than the Taj Mahal. And just think of the fun that daughter Tori has had in the estate's private gym, bowling alley, tennis court, and skating rink. A former occupant at this address was Bing Crosby.
- **Humphrey Bogart** lived with **Lauren Bacall** at **232 S. Mapleton** and then died here painfully of cancer in 1957. Smoking looks glamorous on-screen, but see what can happen?
- When **Barbra Streisand** was living at at **301 Carolwood,** did she sing in the shower? The house stays safe from trick-or-treaters behind a metal gate hiding absolutely everything.
- **Walt Disney** lived at **355 Carolwood** until he died in 1966. Pilgrimage-bent *Pinocchio* fans will be shocked to learn that the house has been razed.
- **Rod Stewart,** a former gravedigger, lived in the mansion at **391 Carolwood** behind a white stone wall whose climbing vines lend it an English air. Recently the place went up for sale. Ten-million-dollar mansion, anyone?
- **Frank Sinatra** and **Mia Farrow,** one of the most unsettling matches in entertainment history, lived at **120 Monovale** when they were married.
- **Elvis Presley**'s last L.A. home was the imposing steep-roofed one behind a stone gate at **144 Monovale.** He lived here with **Priscilla** for several years before selling it in 1975; legend has it the buyer was **Telly Savalas.**

The Playboy Mansion
Feminists need not apply.

10236 Charing Cross Road, near Mapleton Drive.

I f these walls could talk . . . ! For decades Hollywood's rich and famous hetero-
sexual males have been hankering after invitations to this home of *Playboy* founder
Hugh Hefner. So many fallopian tubes, so little time. When blond Playmate of the
Year Dorothy Stratten schmoozed at soirees here circa 1980, her manager-turned-
husband Paul Snider would seethe with jealousy. His status as a persona more or less
non grata here was one of the factors that whipped him into a murderous frenzy. The
1983 movie *Star 80*, starring Mariel Hemingway and Eric Roberts, and partly filmed
at this address, tells the true story of what Snider did to poor Dorothy.

BENEDICT CANYON

Sharon Tate House
Where Manson's minions attacked.

*10048 Cielo Drive. Take Benedict Canyon Drive north from Sunset Boulevard; Cielo will be
on your left (heading west).*

A ctress Sharon Tate and her husband Roman Polanski lived in a house on this site
in the summer of 1969. Polanski was away that August night when Tate had
some friends over: celebrity hairstylist Jay Sebring, heiress Abigail Folger, and Folger's boyfriend Voytek Frykowski. Susan Atkins, Leslie Van Houten, Patricia Kren-
winkel, and Tex Watson crept up on Tate and her friends and slaughtered all four,
along with the groundskeeper's pal Steven Parent. It was a bungled revenge crime.
Tate's house—10050 Cielo—was the former home of Terry Melcher. And Melcher,
a record producer who is the son of Doris Day, had once considered recording the
music of a fella called Charles Manson. Beach Boy Dennis Wilson had introduced
the two. But Melcher changed his mind. A furious Manson sent his acolytes to
10050 Cielo on a killing mission. . . . Oops! Years later, new owners tore down the
death house, built a Mediterranean-style villa in its place, and changed its address to
10048. (See also **La Bianca House,** page 120.)

Rudolph Valentino House
Where "the Great Lover" lived.

1436 Bella Drive, at Cielo Drive.

The young Italian wasn't all *that* cute. But his role as a would-be rapist in the 1921 film *The Sheik* launched a craze that Valentino himself could hardly cope with. It is said the heartthrob chose this lofty house, dramatically dubbed "Falcon Lair," to escape hordes of slavering females. (Part of his distress may have sprung from his own sexual preference; reporters liked to call him "the Pink Powder Puff.") They say Valentino painted the house's rooms black and stocked them with black furniture. He lived here for a year until his sudden death from peritonitis in 1926— a demise that sparked massive mourning, even suicides. Later the house was bought by doomed heiress Doris Duke.

George Reeves House
Where Superman fell.

1579 Benedict Canyon Drive.

He was in the films *Gone with the Wind* and *From Here to Eternity*. But George Reeves reached the height of fame starring in TV's *Adventures of Superman* during the '50s. He was so skilled in the role, however, that he wound up typecast. Maybe this was weighing heavily on his mind when, on June 6, 1959, he killed himself here at his home, in an upstairs bedroom. . . . Or *did* he kill himself? It was officially ruled a suicide. Reeves had been shot in the head. His relatives maintained it was murder. Reportedly, his ghost still haunts the house.

BEL AIR

Ronald Reagan Home
668 St. Cloud Road.

He joked about bombing Russia. Now the ex-president lurks, demented, behind the huge wall and chain-link fence that hides this house. Thick foliage further repels the curious, though a cozy lamp attached to the gate offers a perfidious sense of welcome. When the Reagans bought the house, its address was 666 St. Cloud; fretting about rumors that her husband was the Antichrist, Nancy changed the number. Needless to stay, guard stations and round-the-clock Secret Service protection scare off fans and stalkers alike.

Beverly Hillbillies Mansion
Escape from Bugtussle.

> 750 Bel Air Road.

"So they loaded up the car," the theme song goes, "and moved to Beverly—Hills, that is." Well, the joke's on you! The house is in Bel Air! A stone's throw from Reagan's retirement home, the splendid mansion at this address was regularly seen on TV as the Clampetts' spread. (In real life it was known as the Kirkeby estate.) In 1986 a rich guy bought it for more than $13 million. Deconstruction, construction, and reconstruction ensued. If Jethro could see the place today, he wouldn't recognize it.

Hotel Bel-Air
The royals' retreat.

> 701 Stone Canyon Road, on the west side of the street, near Tortuoso Road, just north of the Bel-Air Country Club. (310) 472-1211 or (800) 648-4097.

Cross a bridge over a waterway where white swans glide. Roam the shady pathways and colonnades that make this look more like an upper-crust village than a hotel. Cottages fitted with French doors open onto cobblestoned courtyards. Fountains burble amid sheaves of bougainvillea and begonia. Ha ha! Lodgings range from $450 to $2,500 per night. These pastel walls enclose knockdown, drag-out luxury. Portraits near the entrance reveal European crowned heads for whom the Bel-Air has been a home-away-from-castle. Other famous guests over the years have ranged from the Kennedys to Elizabeth Taylor to Oprah. A cottage named after Marilyn Monroe now houses the hotel's gym.

Brentwood

O. J. Simpson House Site
Former home of the world's most famous murder suspect.

> 360 N. Rockingham Avenue, at Ashford Street, on the southeast corner.

This was it, "the Rockingham estate," the 1990s' premier rubbernecking spot. Not so very long ago you could scarcely escape images of O. J. Simpson's sprawling Tudor mansion, viewed from a helicopter or a newscam. Here is where the low-speed chase ended on that June day. Here is where cops arrested O. J., where they found traces of Nicole's blood and Ron Goldman's. Hmm, how did *that* get here?! This is where the Juice was practicing his golf swing in the middle of the night

before fleeing to Chicago for reasons never explained. . . .
Ah, *not* guilty. Circa the summer of 1997 this house
where O. J. once lived with wife and kids was razed. Not
that the new owner was squeamish—he just didn't like
the house and wanted to put a brand-new one in its
place. And the enormous lot was just the right size.
Found not guilty in his first, criminal trial, O. J. lost a
civil suit filed by the victims' kin, so this estate was put
up for sale.

While the wheels of justice spun, yahoos and media
types thronged this posh 'hood, eventually forcing local
authorities to close the surrounding streets. Now that
the current owner has put up a new house where the old
one once stood, the streets are open again. Just across the *The new house where O. J.'s*
street is the site that was sometimes called "Camp O. J.," *once stood*
where hundreds of reporters and satellite trucks invaded
a neighbor's yard and stayed for months. As of late 1999, landscapers were trying to
revive the ravaged property. (See also **Nicole Brown Simpson and Ron Goldman
Murder Site,** page 96.)

Tyrone Power House
407 Rockingham Avenue, on the west side of the street.

A hop, skip, and a jump north of O. J. Simpson's vanished glory, this rambling,
gabled home behind its white picket fence speaks of gentler times. Pinup boy
Tyrone Power was one of Hollywood's most popular products in the 1930s and '40s.
Married more than once, the actor was, by many accounts, bisexual.

Mommie Dearest House
426 N. Bristol Avenue, just north of Ashford Street, on the east side of the street.

After Joan Crawford adopted two kids,
the world hailed her as a paragon of
motherhood. But then adoptive daughter
Christina grew up and published a shocking
memoir, telling tales of abandonment and
abuse. Her memoir, *Mommie Dearest,* and a
subsequent film (starring Faye Dunaway)
showed the late superstar in a shocking light.

Mommie Dearest *house*

Who knows whether the closets in this sprawling, terraced Italianate mansion now contain wire hangers?

Shirley Temple House
209 Rockingham Avenue, at Highwood Street, on the west side of the street.

The talented tap dancer and her grown-ups used to occupy a huge estate that has since been subdivided into three still-large lots. Set back from the road, behind walkways and trees and a playhouse, Shirley's old home resembles a tasteful theme park. In 1936 its architects created a fairy-tale pastiche of medieval chimneys, shuttered windows, a round stone tower, a weathervane—perfect for a child star.

Marilyn Monroe's Death House
Good-bye, Norma Jeane.

12305 5th Helena Drive, just north of the Brentwood Country Club. From Sunset Boulevard, go south on Carmelina Avenue. A series of cul-de-sacs, named 1st Helena Drive, 2nd Helena Drive, etc., leads westward off Carmelina.

This is where the candle burned out long before the legend ever did. Its address numerals may have been removed, but behind a big metal fence and a white brick wall at the end of a quiet cul-de-sac is the low-slung hacienda-style house shaded by bougainvillea and bamboo where, on August 5, 1962, Marilyn was found dead with nearly fifty Nembutals inside her. The official ruling was "probable suicide." Yet some suspect a sinister plot involving Marilyn's romantic links with men in high places. Some say that she was murdered to teach JFK a lesson and that dead girls tell no tales. We may never know.

Brentwood Science Magnet
Where James Dean learned his CBAs.

740 Gretna Green Way, at San Vicente Boulevard. (310) 826-5631.

Rambling bungalows flank a campus done up in cheery fleshtone and green. Legend has it that a young James Dean, fresh from Indiana, was a dyslexic student when the school's name was still Brentwood Elementary. Given the location, it's no surprise that Brentwood-dwelling celebrities send their kids here. Alumni reportedly include offspring of Judy Garland, Vic Damone, and Barbra Streisand, not to mention a grandchild of Lorne Greene.

Westside Vicente Foods and Pharmacy
Where the elite meet to buy ibuprofen.

> *12025 San Vicente Boulevard, at Bundy Drive, on the northeast corner. Open Mon.–Fri., 9:00 A.M.–9:00 P.M.; Sat.–Sun., 9:00 A.M.–8:00 P.M. (310) 476-1237.*

L iquors, bakery, pharmacy," promises the sign. Legend has it this is where Marilyn Monroe bought the pills that killed her. After all, she was living nearby. The surrounding hills and valleys are still crawling with celebrities, so you never know just who might pop into this market for a box of Dexatrim or frozen waffles.

Nicole Brown Simpson and Ron Goldman Murder Site
Former address: 875 S. Bundy Drive. New address: 879 S. Bundy Drive, a few steps north of Dorothy Street, in lower Brentwood.

T hose newly arrived from another galaxy may not have heard that on June 12, 1994, Nicole Brown Simpson and Ron Goldman were stabbed to death at this address. Football star O. J. Simpson's ex-wife had left her glasses at the nearby Mezzaluna restaurant. Waiter Ron Goldman obligingly brought them over. But someone large, holding a very large knife, showed up at the condo and killed them both. All evidence (*all* evidence) pointed firmly at O. J.—he had the motive, the means, the opportunity, and a history of domestic abuse. His blood was found here at the scene. The victims' blood was found on his clothing. His rare shoeprints and a bloody glove resembling half of a pair Nicole had given him were found near the bodies. His hand was cut deeply. He lived nearby and was seen arriving home minutes after the murder (see **O. J. Simpson House Site,** page 93). He threatened suicide when the cops came to arrest him. His alibi seemed an obvious fabrication. Yet he was acquitted.

The new gate of the Nicole Brown Simpson condo

During the trial and for years afterward, Bundy Drive was thronged with rubberneckers seeking the scene of the crime, so the new owners cleverly disguised the building. First of all, the pink two-condo duplex is now surrounded by a wall and tropical landscaping with a terra-cotta entryway and is scarcely recognizable. And the owners not only changed the addresses, they reversed their order as well. The new address of Nicole's condo is 879 South Bundy; as you face the building from Bundy, 879 is the one on your right (to the north of the other one). Walk down to Dorothy Street and turn right to see the back of the building from an access road leading to the garages; from this angle, the side gate of the *other* condo at 877 looks like an exact mirror image of the famous blood-spattered gate from the trial. But don't be fooled. The actual gate where it happened was on the building's north side and has been replaced with a different structure. O. J. now searches for "the real killers" on Florida's golf courses.

Peet's Coffee
Former location of Mezzaluna restaurant.

> 11750 San Vicente Boulevard, at Gorham Avenue.

This café occupies a corner that juts sharply into the middle of a busy intersection, bearing a chilling resemblance to a knife. The premises were still occupied by Mezzaluna on the afternoon of June 12, 1994, when Nicole Brown Simpson arrived here for a meal. Unfortunately, she left her sunglasses behind. The kindly waiter Ron Goldman offered to return them. After stopping off at his nearby apartment to change clothes, he brought the glasses to Nicole's Bundy Drive condo a few blocks away. *Gosh.* For a while Camp O. J. types made Mezzaluna a mecca. But locals avoided it, and after the trial the restaurant went out of business. In the fall of 1999 a branch of the Berkeley-based coffee chain opened here.

Pacific Palisades

Thelma Todd Death Site
> The garage is at 17531 Posetano Road, which is on the hill above Thelma Todd's Sidewalk Café, 17575 Pacific Coast Highway, in the Castellammare district of Pacific Palisades, just west of the intersection of Sunset Boulevard and Pacific Coast Highway.

Wisecracking comedienne Thelma Todd was popular in the early '30s but never made a big splash in feature films. Her most notable performances were in the Marx Brothers films *Monkey Business* and *Horse Feathers*. By 1935 she had settled down to run a coastside diner called Thelma Todd's Sidewalk Café, with washed-up silent-era actor and producer Roland West as a partner. On December 16, 1935, Todd was found dead inside West's garage on the hillside above the café, having suffocated on exhaust fumes from the engine of her car. Though there were signs of a struggle, the death was ruled a suicide. The press had a field day. One suspect was "Lucky" Luciano, a mobster and sometime lover of Todd's who was pressuring her to install an illegal casino above the restaurant. Another was partner West, who was heard arguing with Todd the night before her death. Yet another was a crooked employee whom Todd was getting ready to fire. Not only that, but a number of obsessed creeps had been barraging Todd with death threats for years. A hit man hired by Luciano seemed the most likely killer, but no one was ever charged with the crime. The striking café building still stands after sixty-five years, though it is now an office complex. The death garage is above the café on Posetano Road, which can only be reached indirectly by going back up Sunset Boulevard one block and turning left onto the first side street overlooking Pacific Coast Highway.

Self-Realization Fellowship Lake Shrine
They've got Gandhi's cremains.

> 17190 Sunset Boulevard. Open Tues.–Sat., 9:00 A.M.–4:30 P.M.; Sundays, 12:30–4:30 P.M.
> (310) 454-4114.

Formerly a movie set, these sylvan hills now belong to followers of the Indian spiritual leader Paramahansa Yogananda. In 1950 his Self-Realization Fellowship took over the property with its picturesque spring-fed lake. Now it sports a golden-lotus archway, a houseboat, a floating-island bird refuge, sunken gardens, and a Yogananda museum. Legend has it that Elvis Presley developed a long-term interest in the Fellowship after touring the grounds. Symbols of major religions pop up everywhere, reflecting the group's belief in world unity. One startling landmark is an authentic replica of a sixteenth-century Dutch windmill—it was already here when the group arrived. Now it is open as a chapel Tuesdays through Sundays, 1:00 to 4:30 P.M. Across the lake a marble statue of the goddess Kwan Yin guards a Chinese stone sarcophagus. This is the Gandhi World Peace Memorial, and it contains some of the mahatma's ashes. Yogananda installed them in 1950, having taught the doomed pacifist yoga. Following Yogananda's wish, the Fellowship began the building of a four thousand–square-foot hilltop temple on the property in 1996.

Patrick's Roadhouse
Home-style meals for millionaires.

> 106 Entrada Drive, at Pacific Coast Highway (no number on building; look for the shacklike
> structure just above PCH). Open Mon.–Fri., 8:00 A.M.–3:00 P.M.; Sat.–Sun., 9:00 A.M.–4:00
> P.M. (310) 459-4544.

Arnold Schwarzenegger lives right nearby, and many a morn his ludicrous Humvee is parked outside this restaurant while he eats here. Regarding its star-studded clientele, this place keeps its lips more tightly zipped than some. Nevertheless, you never know whom you'll see here tackling breakfast or a burger: Sylvester Stallone, Tom Cruise, Nicole Kidman, Fran Drescher, Johnny Carson, Sean Penn, and Julia Roberts have all been spotted. Legend has it that Patrick's banana-cream pies were delivered to the karmically challenged O. J. Simpson in jail while he was awaiting trial.

Canyon Service
The mother of all L.A. gas stations.

507 Entrada Drive, off Pacific Coast Highway. (310) 454-2619.

Nostalgic for the days before self-serve? *Lawnmower Man* and much else has been filmed amid the shiny pumps, vintage Coke machine, and nostalgic orange-and-white fixtures of L.A.'s oldest operating gas station. Imported from Oklahoma in an effort to make this place more attractive to moviemakers, the actual 1937 pumps really work.

Canyon Service

Uplifters Club Site
Busby Berkeley drank here.

Rustic Canyon Recreation Center, 601 Latimer Road, off Upper Mesa, in the southern part of Pacific Palisades. (310) 454-5734.

A sign reading "Uplifters Ranch" still marks the entrance to what is now a recreation center. Art and athletic classes are now held here in a woodsy setting. But when Sunset Boulevard was still a dirt road, during Prohibition, this was a private club where Hollywood notables spent their weekends. Harold Lloyd, Will Rogers, Busby Berkeley, and *Wizard of Oz* author L. Frank Baum are known to have "uplifted" their spirits here, with spirits. The club attracted thinkers, as did the surrounding neighborhood: residents then included Christopher Isherwood, Edward Weston, Thomas Mann, and Bertolt Brecht. On the wall in the recre-

Johnny Weissmuller statue

ation center's office are original cartoons by *Krazy Kat* artist George Herriman—he was a member of the club. If a statue outside in the courtyard looks familiar, that's because Johnny Weissmuller, a club member who lived across the street, posed for the sculptor.

AMALFI DRIVE CELEBRITY TOUR

Let's take a leisurely drive along Pacific Palisades' posh Amalfi Drive. Left and right, every house you see is a sparkling mansion. And so many of them have a checkered past or a celebrity lurking inside—or both. This tour follows Amalfi northeastward from Upper Mesa Road to Sorrento Drive, through the heart of Pacific Palisades.

- **719 Amalfi. Eddie Albert** lives—or lived—in this white stucco estate bursting with trees and foliage. He once worked as a circus trapeze artist but found real success onscreen. How appropriate that the *Green Acres* star now has corn growing in his front yard.

- **788 Amalfi.** Director **James Whale** once called this palace home, its expansive lawn and looong balcony protected by a well-trimmed hedge. After making *Frankenstein* and other artful horror flicks, Whale retired here and eventually committed suicide in the swimming pool out back. The 1998 film *Gods and Monsters* was based on the life of the gay director. Decades later **Goldie Hawn** and mate **Kurt Russell** moved in for a while, though from all appearances they don't live here anymore.

James Whale house

- **797 Amalfi.** This former home of **Richard Rosson** has a white picket fence and a driveway crammed full of SUVs. The Rosson brothers—Arthur, Hal, and Richard—were a family success story in Hollywood's early days. Arthur directed dozens of successful silent films before fading into obscurity when talkies arrived. Hal won an Academy Award for cinematography and made headlines as Jean Harlow's last husband. Richard could never live up to his siblings' triumphs and had a comparatively disappointing career as an actor and director in a series of forgotten films during the 1920s and 1930s. He killed himself in this house in 1953, just four years before fellow '30s director James Whale killed himself across the street. Coincidence—or curse?

- **933 Amalfi** (former address: 14000 Sunset Boulevard). This unwieldy white mansion at the intersection of Amalfi and Sunset once belonged to Beach Boy **Dennis Wilson.** One day he picked up some hitchhiking hippie chicks and brought them home. He let them stay for a while and, once ensconced, they brought over their "friend," **Charles Manson.** Before long, the whole Manson Family had moved into the house, and Dennis joined their "free love" orgies and LSD weekends. While Dennis was away or distracted, Family members like Lynette "Squeaky" Fromme handed out his gold records and other pos-sessions to strangers on the street. It was here that Manson met record

Dennis Wilson–Charles Manson house

producer Terry Melcher, whose later indifference to Manson's musical ambi-tions would lead to disaster (see **Sharon Tate House,** page 91). After Dennis moved out in the late 1960s Manson and the gang moved up to Spahn Ranch and began the final chapter of their saga. The house's new owners changed the address to throw rubberneckers off the trail.

- **1258 Amalfi. Ronald and Nancy Reagan** are reputed to have lived in this unprepossessing ranch-style house during the first happy years of their mar-riage in the mid-1950s. His movie career had by then slowed to a relaxing crawl and he had not yet entered the wild world of politics. So while they lived here he made a comfortable living as a TV host and Commie hunter, as Nancy tended house.

- **1515 Amalfi.** This storied mansion supposedly has never been owned by anyone other than a superstar. Its first tenant is said to have been legendary producer **David O. Selznick,** who lived here while making *Gone with the Wind.* He then sold it to **Douglas Fairbanks,** who is said to have passed it on to **Cary Grant,** who then deeded it to teen idol **Bobby Vinton.** Smitten with the home's history, modern mogul **Steven Spielberg** moved in to ab-sorb Selznick's vibes. Rumor has it Spielberg still lives here, though nothing is visible now except a massive gate and a sign that reads, "GUARD DOG—CAUTION. Please remain in car until escort arrives."

- **1570 Amalfi.** From all accounts, this shingled faux castle is the current home of **Sylvester Stallone,** star of *Rocky, Rambo,* and a thousand other gung-ho exercises in machismo (including the arguably homoerotic cop comedy *Tango and Cash,* with down-the-hill Amalfi neighbor Kurt Russell). Speaking of erotic: Hollywood gossips claim Stallone got his start in show business as a porn stud later dubbed "the Italian Stallion." The "Italian" part is pretty clear. As for "Stallion" . . .

Lee Marvin/Johnny Weissmuller House
2 Haldeman Road, across from Rustic Canyon Park.

This shingle-roofed, shady retreat has a swimming pool out front that fits right in with its sylvan landscaping. The house was home to both the athletic *Tarzan* star and the rough-and-tumble *Dirty Dozen* star—though certainly not at the same time. (How could you even contemplate such a thing?)

Arnold Schwarzenegger–Maria Shriver Home
They'll be back.

Evans Road (no number); entrance at 14209 Sunset.

The wealthy couple spent millions buying three neighboring mansions. That way they could have a whole huge swath of property to themselves. Mission accomplished. Thus there is no way you can get onto the private Evans Road, which leads off Will Rogers State Park Road, which in turn leads off Sunset. No way at all.

Tom Cruise–Nicole Kidman Home
1525 Sorrento Drive, Pacific Palisades. From Sunset Boulevard, take Amalfi Drive north for six blocks until it comes to a Y-intersection with Sorrento Drive; bear right onto Sorrento.

It's tough being Hollywood's most popular couple. For some reason the entire nation seems obsessed with the angel-faced Method actor and the Australian beauty. Their match seems made in heaven, and the two smile gamely for the cameras. Yet, naturally, the duo don't like people nosing around their exclusive estate. So much so that sentinels in shiny new SUVs are parked across the street. Wander too near the gated driveway and they're on your heels with handheld video cameras, filming your face, your clothing, and (as you scuttle away in terror) your license plate. It's meant to frighten, and it does, but the guards' ominous presence is almost like a neon sign reading "Tom Cruise Lives Here."

Malibu

Malibu Colony

It's true what they say about Malibu. Close enough to Hollywood for commuting, but far away and exclusive enough to discourage the feeble rubbernecker, this sunny strip is home to more celebs than there are peanuts in a Payday bar. If *you* were a zillionaire, wouldn't *you* want a beach house? In a private enclave? Flanked by the homes of other zillionaires? Of course you would. Nonresidents and uninvited guests are turned away at the colony's guarded gate on Malibu Colony Drive just off Pacific Coast Highway, one-half mile west of Malibu Pier. But this row of lovely homes faces the beach and, hey, the beach is public. Not that you are particularly welcome or anything. Find the little walkways leading to the beach off PCH around the 19900, 20300, and 22700 blocks, not to mention a few between the 24300 and 25100 blocks. Once you hit the sand in this lawful manner, you are allowed to stroll around, but *only* below the high-tide line. *(Back! Back, I say!)* Keep an eye peeled for the likes of Tatum O'Neal, Rob Reiner, Sting, and Bill Murray. And before their deaths, Michael Landon and Brian Keith called the Colony home. No guarantees, but here's a sampling of who, at last report, lived along Malibu Colony Drive: Tom Hanks (23414); Larry Hagman (23730); Bruce Dern (23430); Jack Warden (23604); Jackie Collins (26829); Linda Ronstadt (38 Malibu Colony Rd.); and Dyan Cannon (98 Malibu Colony Rd.).

Malibu Broad Beach

What *is* it about Malibu? Why not Redondo Beach, or Torrance? Yet in Malibu the stars are, and in Malibu they will stay—at least, they might maintain a beach house here until the next divorce. Broad Beach Road is where you might see Danny DeVito (at number 31020); Goldie Hawn and Kurt Russell (30804); Dustin Hoffman (31045); Eddie Van Halen and Valerie Bertinelli (31736); Pierce Brosnan (31663); and Ali MacGraw (31108). Naturally, it's exclusive as all get-out. But a public accessway to the beach is near 31346 Broad Beach Road, and you can walk around below the high-tide line as much as you like. Others you might see here, especially in summer, include Jack Lemmon, Sylvester Stallone, Mel Gibson, Emilio Estevez, Charlie Sheen, Robert Redford, and Carroll O'Connor.

POINT DUME STAR HOMES

Are there more stars in the skies above Malibu than on the ground below? You decide. The Point Dume Area is and/or has been home to Bob Dylan (29400 Bluewater Drive); Johnny Carson (6962 Wildlife Road); Malibu's honorary mayor Martin Sheen (6916 Dume Drive); and many others. In 1985 Malibu resident Sean Penn married Madonna at 6970 Wildlife Road, which was neither his house nor hers. Paparazzi flew over in helicopters; a furious Penn inscribed "FUCK OFF" in the sand for all to see.

Santa Monica

Peter Lawford House
Johnny, we knew ye in the biblical sense.

625 Palisades Beach Road.

P als in Frank Sinatra's famous Rat Pack would later shun Peter Lawford. But the
British-born actor was incomparably well connected, at least for a while. In the
early 1960s he was married to Patricia Kennedy, which rendered JFK and RFK his
brothers-in-law. When they were in town, the dashing politicos could be found here
at Lawford's beachfront home, where they developed a reputation for fornication. It
was here, according to later reports, that they fraternized extramaritally with the local talent. Most famous among these, of course, was Marilyn Monroe. Today a sign
posted on the graceful cream-colored home signals the presence of attack dogs.

Cary Grant House
1038 Palisades Beach Road.

H ere amid sunshine, sand, and salt air, the debonair Brit is said to have swung
both ways. After buying this Norman-style beach house from original owner
Norma Talmadge, Grant shared it with movie cowboy Randolph Scott. The pair
were reportedly more than mere bosom buddies. Yet Grant would later live here with
his bride, heiress Barbara Hutton. She in turn once recalled that she had spent her
happiest moments in this house. Legend has it that during World War II a nostalgic
Hutton refashioned the living room to look like Maxim's, complete with purple carpet. Later still, Randolph Scott moved back in. Brian Aherne bought the house and
began renting it out. Howard Hughes was among his tenants, then Roman Polanski
and Sharon Tate.

Santa Monica Pier
Where many movies have been filmed.

Ocean Avenue at Colorado Boulevard. (310) 458-8900.

N early a hundred years old, the West Coast's oldest pleasure pier has a checkered history. The terminus of Route 66, it was studded with thrill rides and
popular for decades but fell into disrepair by the '70s. Now fully restored, it boasts a
carousel, arcade, solar-powered Ferris wheel, and other amusements. In its various
states of degradation and repair, the pier has appeared in many films, including *Inside Daisy Clover, The Sting, Beverly Hills Cop, Down and Out in Beverly Hills,* and
The Net. It has also been featured on TV shows including *Charlie's Angels; Marcus*

Welby, M.D.; Murder, She Wrote; Three's Company; and, not surprisingly, *Baywatch.* Tales are told of how celebrity madam Heidi Fleiss, here for a meal, once helped rescue a would-be suicide.

Muscle Beach
Where the fitness boom was born.

On the sand, just south of Santa Monica Pier.

Starting in 1934 this stretch of beach served as an open-air gym where local body-builders, movie stuntmen, and others showed off their pecs. Fitted with exhibition platforms and exercise equipment, it grew over the next twenty years into an actual fitness club whose hundreds of members flexed and crunched for wildly applauding crowds. Jack LaLanne was a habitué at these shows before the club shut down in 1958. In 1999, with new equipment and a new set of bleachers spread over nearly three acres of sand, Muscle Beach reopened.

Margaux Hemingway Suicide Studio
139 Fraser Avenue, between Ocean Avenue and Nielson Way, on the north side of the street; studio is up a wooden stairway at the top of the driveway.

In the '70s supermodel Margaux Heming-way launched a film career with the daring revenge flick *Lipstick.* But the ensuing years showed diminishing returns for the striking brunette. In her studio apartment behind a glassed-in porch just steps from the beach, she took too many pills on July 2, 1996. It was the anniversary of the day her famous grandfather, Ernest Hemingway, had committed suicide. Her body was found after neighbors realized they hadn't seen her in a while.

Margaux Hemingway suicide studio

Schatzi on Main
Arnold's restaurant.

3110 Main Street, at Marine Street. Open daily, 9:00 A.M.–11:00 P.M. (310) 399-4800.

Husband and wife Arnold Schwarzenegger and Maria Shriver own this chichi eatery. They are occasionally spotted on its airy terrace, joining their Hollywood pals over a plate of Muscovy duck, sushi, or steak tartare. The menu's Onassis Salad is a nod to the Kennedys, while Arnold honors his Austrian roots with Wiener schnitzel, spaetzle, and other fatteners. Annual Oktoberfests and monthly "cigar nights" are held here to bring out the *oompah* and the emphysema victim in everyone. The restaurant's motto is "You'll be back!"

William Holden Apartment
Where the superstar died all alone.

Shorecliff Towers, 535 Ocean Avenue, on the east side of the street.

H is seventy-plus films include such classics as *Born Yesterday, Sunset Boulevard, The Bridges at Toko-Ri, Sabrina,* and *Network.* Yet in November 1981 William Holden tripped on a throw rug while drunk and struck his head on a nightstand in his fifth-floor apartment here. He bled to death and lay undiscovered for days while his maid was away on vacation. They say Holden was too intoxicated to realize how badly he was hurt. Despite a brilliant career and real estate holdings all over the world, the actor was a serious alcoholic whose drunk driving had once killed a pedestrian.

William Holden apartment

Jane Fonda–Tom Hayden House
139 Alta Avenue, near Ocean Avenue, on the south side of the street.

A vigorous hedge and a chain-link fence shield this home where Fonda spent part of her girlhood, then held court with her spunky husband. Though the palm-fringed beach lies right nearby, the house, with its curving brick walkway and soaring brick chimney, looks as if it would prefer to be in a British fen.

Venice and Marina del Rey

VENICE

Ocean Front Walk

A stone's throw from the sand, this scene-making thoroughfare is popular with scantily clad Rollerbladers. You may have glimpsed it in such movies and TV shows as *Jerry Maguire, L.A. Story, Falling Down, Mixed Nuts, White Men Can't Jump, Xanadu, Shasta McNasty,* or *Pacific Blue.*

Aimee Semple McPherson Disappearance Site
Oceanview Apartments (formerly the Oceanview Hotel), 5 Rose Avenue, at Ocean Front Walk, on the beach.

R ivaling her era's film stars in popularity, evangelist Aimee Semple McPherson was one of the top celebrities of the '20s. Her L.A. sermons attracted thousands. Dazzled by her charisma and (for an evangelist) beauty, fans followed her everywhere she went. On May 16, 1926, McPherson was staying at what was then a beachside hotel. She checked in with her secretary, went to her room and changed clothes, then walked down to the sea for a swim—and disappeared. It is said that a lifeguard drowned while searching for her and that a distraught fan committed suicide. Followers thronged on the sand to pray for her. It was a major media event, and McPherson's funeral was held a few weeks later, though no trace of her had ever been found. Imagine the public's surprise when, at the end of June, McPherson popped up safe and sound in Arizona. Though she never offered a reasonable explanation and her allusions to a bungled kidnap attempt were unconvincing, she returned in triumph to adoring crowds in L.A. Historians speculate she escaped the media glare to have an affair with a secret lover. The six-story white hotel where the mystery began is now an apartment house.

Gold's Gym
Where Arnold pumped iron.

360 Hampton Drive (which is also 2nd Street), at Rose Avenue. Open Mon.–Fri., 4:00 A.M.–midnight; Sat.–Sun., 5:00 A.M.–11:00 P.M. (310) 392-6004.

I n its original location two blocks away, this mother of all Gold's Gyms is where they filmed 1977's *Pumping Iron,* in which Arnold's abs were unveiled for all to see. Before and since, the club has boasted a star-studded membership. You never know who's going to pop up on these StairMasters. Could be Dennis Rodman, Sylvester Stallone, Magic Johnson, Jean-Claude Van Damme, Geena Davis, Keanu Reeves, Ted Danson, Wesley Snipes, Fred Ward, Dennis Hopper, Kevin Sorbo, or Arnold, of course.

Venice Canals
As seen in Touch of Evil.

In his downbeat 1958 film *Touch of Evil*, Orson Welles plays a crooked police chief wrestling with moral dilemmas in a Mexican border town. But that's not really the land of *mañana*—it's Venice. Those moonlit waterways you see in the film are actually the ones that crisscross Venice, forming a network east of Pacific Avenue and encompassing Carroll, Linnie, Sherman, and Grand canals.

Venice Canals

Venice High School
Where alumna Myrna Loy is immortalized in a statue.

13000 Venice Boulevard, on the south side of the street. (310) 306-7981.

In the movie musical *Grease*, actors too old for their roles capered around fictional Rydell High School. The actual campus you saw was this one. Venice High has appeared in other films and in a popular Britney Spears video: she dances amid its lockers. Famous alumni are honored periodically with display-case exhibits: they include singer Gogi Grant and astronaut Walter Cunningham, who also has a school building named after him; and before vaulting to stardom, Myrna Loy (née Williams) was a student here. Outside in the foreyard just before you enter the administration building is a statue in which several chalk-white figures pose around a stone pedestal. Atop the pedestal, towering above them all, is a gowned female figure said to represent Virtue. A very young Loy posed for the sculptor. Though time and vandals have not been kind, the likeness is unmistakable.

Myrna Loy statue

MARINA DEL REY

Dennis Wilson Death Site

In Basin C at dock C-1100, on Marquesas Way, in Marina Del Rey. From Washington Street turn south on Via Marina and then east on Marquesas Way. Dock C-1100 is about two-thirds of the way up Marquesas, on the north side of the condos lining the street. The dock is clearly numbered and visible from shore, but its gate is locked and open only to boat owners.

You'd think that, as the Beach Boys' only actual surfer, Dennis Wilson would be the least likely to drown. He was an expert swimmer. But drugs and alcohol make it hard to swim. Wilson attended a party on a friend's boat here in Marina Del Rey's Basin C on December 28, 1983. After drinking way, way too much, Wilson (who years before had been pals with Charles Manson) decided to go for a dip. He slipped beneath the

Dennis Wilson death site

surface and drowned, inhaling the chilly water. The friend's boat is by now long gone, but the dock where it was moored remains basically unchanged. Small pleasure craft with names like *Volare* and *Half Fast* bob cheerily, making this indistiguishable from many other docks on either side.

Aunt Kizzy's Back Porch

Where the elite meet to eat okra.

4325 Glencoe Avenue, just south of Maxella Avenue, in the Villa Marina Marketplace shopping center, between Panini Café and KooKooRoo. Open Mon.–Thurs., 11:00 A.M.–10:00 P.M.; Fri.–Sat., 11:00 A.M.–11:00 P.M.; Sun., 11:00 A.M.–3:00 P.M. and 4:00–10:00 P.M. (310) 578-1005.

Its old-timey Southern decor includes a real tin roof and a genuine back porch. As diners work their way through hot links, pork chops, and jambalaya, autographed pictures of satisfied patrons smile down from the walls. Among them are Stevie Wonder, Eddie Murphy, Bill Cosby, the Reverend Jesse Jackson, Nancy Wilson, Richard Pryor, Salt-N-Pepa, Pearl Bailey, Sinbad, Gregory Hines, Mr. T, Vikki Carr, the Pointer Sisters, Martin Lawrence, Willie Nelson, the Fifth Dimension, and Al Gore.

Culver City

Culver City Walk of Fame
Memorializing movies made here.

On Washington Boulevard, starting at National Boulevard
and continuing northeast for several blocks, on both sides
of the street.

B right yellow metal wraparounds were fitted around
palm trees to immortalize famous films made at
nearby studios, and their stars. Each wraparound bears
the name and cast of a different film—*Singin' in the
Rain, Spellbound, Treasure Island,* and many more that
were made in this town. This is Culver City's answer to
Hollywood's Walk of Fame, but it occupies a rather un-
inviting semi-industrial stretch of road.

Culver City Walk of Fame

Hal Roach Studios Site
Marked by a plaque under a tree in a small park at the southwest corner of National and
Washington Boulevards, adjacent to a car dealership called C.C. Mazda-Subaru, in the
northern part of Culver City.

M any people first heard of Hal Roach in 1992 when the legendary producer appeared at the Academy Awards on his one hundredth birthday; yet his work
is world-renowned. Roach is the man behind the *Our Gang* series (shown on TV as
The Little Rascals), the Laurel and Hardy shorts, Harold Lloyd, Thelma Todd, Zasu
Pitts, and Will Rogers. During the 1920s and 1930s Roach made more people laugh
than anyone else on earth. Almost all his films were made here at National and
Washington, on a site now rendered unrecognizable by the presence of a large car
dealership. Roach bought a small diner next to the studio, which he named the Our
Gang Café, where the real-life Darla, Farina, Wheezer, and Alfalfa would eat down-
home cooking alongside fans. During World War II, Roach churned out propaganda
like *Tanks a Million* and *The Devil with Hitler,* some featuring B-movie workhorse
and patriot Ronald Reagan. Years after the studio and diner were torn down, the city
put up a plaque marking what was once called, as the plaque declares, "Laugh factory to the world. 1919–1963."

Culver Studios
Frankly, Scarlett, he didn't give a damn.

9336 W. Washington Boulevard, on the east side of the street at Ince Boulevard.

Fans of classic movies will recognize this grand old studio from afar: the Colonial-style mansion that faces the street not only once housed the offices of studio chief

David O. Selznick but was also featured during the opening credits of all Selznick's films. For example, a little B-movie called *Gone with the Wind* was made here at Culver Studios. For the legendary "burning of Atlanta" scene, Selznick torched all the old sets from previous films made on the lot, claiming he needed to make space for new *Gone with the Wind* sets anyway. Over the decades Culver Studios has had many names—RKO, Pathé, and Desilu, among others. So it's not

The Selznick mansion at Culver Studios

especially well known, even though many of Hollywood's greatest creations were filmed here: *King Kong, Gone with the Wind, Citizen Kane,* most of Hitchcock's American films, and even *E.T.: The Extraterrestrial.* Now the lot is owned by Sony, which has its main studio just a couple blocks away on the site of the old MGM lot. Alas, Sony does not offer tours of Culver Studios, so visitors will have to content themselves with gazing wistfully across the lawn at Selznick's mansion. A small plaque on Washington just south of Ince memorializes the site.

The Culver Hotel
The Munchkins slept here.

9400 Culver Boulevard, on an island in the middle of the intersection of Washington and Culver Boulevards. (310) 838-7963.

Former owner John Wayne is remembered with a photo mounted near the entrance. This stolid brick hotel, built in 1924 with Europe in mind, looks like a slice of London. Over the years it has been home to Ronald Reagan, Joan Crawford, Clark Gable, and Greta Garbo. When *The Wizard of Oz* was being filmed nearby, some 120 midgets cast as Munchkins stayed here. Wild tales surfaced later of their debauchery and vandalism. (Did they *really* sing, "Ding dong, the bitch

The Culver Hotel

is dead"?) These tales inspired Chevy Chase's 1981 film *Under the Rainbow*. Yet former Munchkins who held a reunion here in 1998 insist it was all lies, mostly invented by Judy Garland.

Sony Pictures Studios
Where Dorothy followed the Yellow Brick Road.

On the block bounded by Washington Boulevard, Madison Avenue, Culver Boulevard, and Overland Avenue. One entrance is at 10202 W. Washington Boulevard, another is on Overland. Tours given Mon.–Fri., 9:30 A.M., 11:00 A.M., noon, and 3:00 P.M. Admission: adults, $20; children under 12 not permitted. Call in advance for tour reservations: (323) 520-8687.

This is part of the humongous property that became Metro-Goldwyn-Mayer in 1924 and spawned dozens of the world's favorite movies. (Its mascot was Leo the Lion, who roared to accompany the Latin motto *Ars Gratia Artis*, "Art for Art's Sake.") During its peak years in the '30s and '40s, this was Hollywood's biggest and richest studio. For decades its moguls Irving Thalberg and Louis B. Mayer were able to spend unprecedented fortunes on films like *The Wizard of Oz, The Good Earth, Ben-Hur, Grand Hotel, Mrs. Miniver, Singin' in the Rain, Ninotchka, Meet Me in St. Louis, An American in Paris, Gigi*, and the *Thin Man* series. A powerful stable of actors included Jean Harlow, Judy Garland, Bette Davis, the Marx Brothers, Gene Kelly, James Stewart, Lana Turner, Rosalind Russell, Mickey Rooney, Elizabeth Taylor, Spencer Tracy, and Katharine Hepburn. During World War II, the studio churned out some fifty films a year—classics as well as *Tarzan*-type stuff. In the '60s MGM made the era's best musicals. But by the '70s the studio was auctioning off hundreds of thousands of historic props to the highest bidder. Fortunes change swiftly in Hollywood. Recently, under the Sony banner, *Men in Black* was made here, as are TV's *Jeopardy!* and *Wheel of Fortune*. On the two-hour walking tour you can see historic sets and ongoing productions. A high point is the soundstage where Judy Garland marched down the Yellow Brick Road—though the road itself is apparently long gone.

Culver City Star Streets

In a residential neighborhood south of Sony Studios, in the area bounded by Washington Boulevard, Overland Avenue, Culver Boulevard, and Elenda Street.

This subdivision is rumored to have been built on the former back lot of MGM Studios (now Sony), just across Overland to the north. In tribute the developers named most of the streets after stars who made films here: Hepburn Circle, Garland Drive, Astaire Avenue, Skelton Circle, Coogan Circle, and Lamarr Avenue. Now the faux homes of the back lot have been replaced by real, tile-roofed tract homes. Surprisingly, these are about the only streets in all of L.A. that have been named after movie stars. Pickford Way and Fairbanks Way lie about a half mile to the south.

The corner of Garland Drive and Astaire Avenue, Culver City

Holy Cross Cemetery
Bela Lugosi's dead.

> 5835 W. Slauson Avenue, just off the San Diego Freeway (Highway 405). Open daily 7:00 A.M.–5:00 P.M. (310) 670-7697.

Wow, did someone say, "Ave Maria"? Bing Crosby and Bela Lugosi are just south of the Grotto. Rita Hayworth is just east of the Grotto. Sharon Tate and her unborn child are just west of the Grotto. Mario Lanza (D2, B46); Ray Bolger (F2, B35); Spike Jones (A7, B70); John Candy (B1, room 7); and Fred MacMurray (D1, room 7) are all in the mausoleum. Charles Boyer (5, L186) is in the St. Anne section. Jimmy Durante (6, T96) is in Section Y, near a reproduction of the *Pietà*. Lawrence Welk (110, T9) is in Section Y. Also here are Rosalind Russell, Jackie Coogan, John Ford, Mary Astor, Jack Haley, James and Marian Jordan ("Fibber McGee and Molly"), Zasu Pitts, Mack Sennett, and Dennis Day.

Hillside Memorial Park
Hello, Muddah, hello, Faddah . . .

> 6001 Centinela Avenue, at the San Diego Freeway (Highway 405). Open Sun.–Fri., 8:30 A.M.–4:30 P.M. (310) 641-0707 or (800) 576-1994.

Visible from far and wide, a dramatic multitiered waterfall descending from a tall white-columned monument marks the tomb of Al Jolson. Beside it is a bronze replica of Jolson on his knees, in his "Mammy" pose. In the mausoleum of this Jewish cemetery are David Janssen (Memorial Court 516), as well as Eddie Cantor and

Jack Benny (Hall of Graciousness 207 and Sarcophagus F, respectively). The Garden of Memories is permanent home to mobster Mickey Cohen (Alcove of Love A-217) and the Three Stooges' Moe Howard (Alcove of Love C-233). Allan Sherman is in the Columbarium of Hope (niche 513). Actor Vic Morrow and 1960s radical Jerry Rubin are in the Mount of Olives section (5-80-1 and 14-466-3, respectively). In the Courts of the Book are Dinah Shore (Isaiah V-247), Max Factor (Isaiah U-314), and Lorne Greene (lawn crypt 5-800-8B)—that's funny . . . Ben Cartwright doesn't *look* Jewish.

West Los Angeles

WEST L.A. AND CENTURY CITY

20th Century–Fox Studios

10201 Pico Boulevard, at Avenue of the Stars, at the southern edge of Century City. (310) 369-1000.

This land used to be cowboy star Tom Mix's private ranch; but since becoming a studio in 1935, it has launched hundreds of films and TV productions, including *Song of Bernadette, The Razor's Edge, All about Eve, Gentlemen Prefer Blondes, The King and I, The Poseidon Adventure, Patton, True Lies, Die Hard, The X-Files, Fight Club,* and many more. A big winner was *Star Wars.* A big loser was *Cleopatra,* which was, at its time, the most expensive movie ever made and devastated the studio financially. Sadly, no tours are offered to the public. It is possible, however, to see from outside part of the famed "New York Street" set where the Big Apple was re-created for *Hello, Dolly!* and a thousand other productions.

Fox Plaza
It didn't explode, really.

2121 Avenue of the Stars. (310) 282-0047.

The shiny skyscraper where all that mischief happened in *Die Hard* was this one. But see? It didn't explode. Standing more than thirty stories tall, it boasts several other movie credits as well, not to mention the offices of O. J. Simpson's attorney Robert Shapiro and former president Ronald Reagan (though he no longer stops by personally).

Century Plaza Hotel and Tower
Another Western White House.

2025 Avenue of the Stars, at Constellation Boulevard. (310) 277-2000.

Inside, tons of shiny pale marble and priceless panoramas make it elegant. Outside, the thirty-floor structure shows its 1966 vintage: a soaring but soulless grid, like a hive built by robot bees. That doesn't bother the presidents, every one of whom, from LBJ onward, has stayed here. Thus the hotel is one of several places that have been dubbed "the Western White House." Richard Nixon held a "welcome back to Earth" dinner here for moonwalking astronauts in August 1969. Ronald Reagan held his 1980 victory and 1984 reelection parties here. An eight thousand–square-foot Reagan Suite with bulletproof glass, a private elevator, TVs in every room, butler service, free drinks, and forty-seven photographs of Reagan, occupies an entire floor. Its $5,400-per-night price tag hasn't kept away the likes of Elton John, Sylvester Stallone, George Bush, or the kings of Morocco and Sweden. The president of China has stayed in the suite as well; maybe it made him think twice about the glories of peasant life. The property used to be a 20th Century–Fox back lot where Shirley Temple and Marilyn Monroe once worked. It's also where Columbia Pictures prez David Begelman killed himself in 1995.

Dorothy Stratten Murder House
Stiff 80.

10881 Clarkson Road, West L.A., one block from where Westwood Boulevard crosses under the Santa Monica Freeway (Highway 10).

Dorothy Stratten was a naïve small-town Canadian teen working in an ice cream shop when two-bit hustler Paul Snider walked in and changed her life forever. He couldn't help but notice that the leggy, buxom Stratten had the kind of body that drove men mad. So he concocted a plan. He wooed her, seduced her, and eventually sent naked pictures of her to Hugh Hefner. Soon Stratten was in Los Angeles posing for *Playboy* and signing movie contracts. (Her only starring role was in the campy *Galaxina*.) Though Snider was by now Stratten's husband and manager, Hefner regarded him as a meddlesome hanger-on with nothing to offer. When Stratten answered a casting call at the home of director Peter Bogdanovich, one thing led to another and the two began an intense affair. Once Snider found out his meal ticket was leaving him, he went berserk. On August 14, 1980, he brutalized Stratten, raped her, and then blew her head off with a shotgun before turning it on himself. The Playmate of the Year was barely twenty. Several films have since retold the shocking tale, most notably *Star 80,* with Mariel Hemingway as Stratten, and Eric Roberts stealing the show as Snider (many felt he deserved 1983's Best Actor Oscar, yet he was not even nominated). *Death of a Centerfold,* starring Jamie Lee Curtis, flopped. Bogdanovich and Hefner still feud over who was to blame for the tragedy. According to several secondhand sources, the gruesome crime scene was here at 10881 Clarkson Road, just a few miles south of the Playboy Mansion itself. Stratten was buried nearby at Pierce Brothers Westwood Memorial Park; Bogdanovich selected her bizarre, antagonistic epitaph, which reads in part: ". . . you can be sure that it will kill you too but there will be no special hurry."

The Milky Way
Restaurant owned by Steven Spielberg's mom.

> *9108 W. Pico Boulevard, on the south side of the street.*
> *(323) 859-0004.*

The strict rules of *kashrut* apply at this dairy-only eatery where photographs of the owner's son are discreetly positioned here and there. A softly lit dining room is lined with fully stocked yet oddly ornamental bookshelves. Don't touch the books. Choose from cheese chimichangas, pizzas, blintzes, tuna melts, and more. (Like it says in Leviticus, fish doesn't count as meat. How upsetting for the fish.)

The Milky Way

WESTWOOD

Ernie Kovacs Crash Site
At the intersection of Beverly Glen and Santa Monica Boulevards, just west of Century City, lower Westwood.

Beloved TV comedian Ernie Kovacs was more than a little tipsy on the night of January 14, 1962, as he zoomed down Beverly Glen in his car. Legend has it he was trying to light one of his trademark cigars with one hand as he turned east onto Santa Monica. His tires couldn't hold the curve and he skidded into a barrier. The accident crushed his skull, killing him.

Freddie Prinze Death Site
Chico and the gun.

Beverly Hills Plaza Hotel, 10300 Wilshire Boulevard, at Comstock Avenue. (310) 275-5575.

Popular comedian Freddie Prinze seemed on top of the world in 1977. He was starring in his own prime-time TV sitcom (*Chico and the Man*) and had millions of adoring fans. He was credited for breaking the color barrier against Hispanics on white-dominated television. So the public was shocked when Prinze shot himself dead for no apparent reason at the tender age of twenty-two. What seemed at first a tragic accident was later ruled a suicide when the police found a farewell note, though to this day not everyone is convinced he killed himself intentionally. Conventional wisdom holds that the gun went off in room 10C in the west tower of the Wilshire-Comstock Apartments at 865–875 Comstock Avenue in Westwood. But staff at that location, now the Wilshire-Comstock Condominiums, insist that Prinze had never actually moved into his new home there: he was lodging across the street in what was then known as the Beverly-Comstock Hotel while his flat was being refurbished, and it was at the hotel that he committed suicide. Though the hotel has changed owners and names since that time (it's now called the Beverly Hills Plaza), its staff remains tight-lipped about Prinze and any other celebrities who may or may not have ever stayed there: "We're not allowed to talk about that kind of thing." The mystery only deepens.

Pierce Brothers Westwood Memorial Park
Starring Marilyn Monroe.

1218 Glendon Avenue, just south of Wilshire Boulevard. Open daily in summer, 8:00 A.M.–dusk; the rest of the year, 8:00 A.M.–5:00 P.M. (310) 474-1579.

It's cozy but densely packed with stars' graves. Most popular is Marilyn Monroe's flower-bedecked mausoleum crypt in the Corridor of Memories—ex-husband Joe DiMaggio used to send roses regularly, and Hugh Hefner has dibs on the empty crypt next to Marilyn's. Natalie Wood's grave is popular, too. Murdered centerfold Dorothy Stratten has an extremely odd epitaph. Stroll around and pay homage to Jim Backus, Donna Reed, Truman Capote, Carl Wilson, Eve Arden, Burt Lancaster, Mel Tormé, Darryl Zanuck, John Cassavetes, Fanny Brice, Eva Gabor, and Edith Massey, for starters. Frank Zappa has an unmarked grave near a tree a bit to the left of Roy Orbison's. *Family Affair* veterans Sebastian Cabot and Brian Keith are both here. So are Dominique Dunne and Heather O'Rourke, who played sisters in *Poltergeist* and then both died young. Buddy Rich is in the Sanctuary of Tranquility. Dean Martin is in the Sanctuary of Love. Janis Joplin and Elizabeth Montgomery were reportedly cremated on the premises.

University of California, Los Angeles (UCLA)
Where the Nutty Professor taught.

Campus occupies the area between Gayley, Le Conte, and Hilgard Avenues, and Sunset Boulevard. Westwood Boulevard leads directly to a main entrance. (310) 825-4321.

This sprawling, pleasant campus is so conveniently located near the studios that it maintains an ongoing competition with USC as to which appears in more major motion pictures. Eddie Murphy's version of *The Nutty Professor* was filmed here, as were *Higher Learning, The Sure Thing, Scream 2,* and more. Illustrious alumni include Jim Morrison, James Dean, Francis Ford Coppola, Carol Burnett, Rob Reiner, Kareem Abdul-Jabbar, Tim Robbins, and Robert Englund (he's the fella who plays Freddy Krueger).

Dead Man's Curve
Like in the song.

On Sunset Boulevard, just west of Groverton Place, opposite the UCLA football field, between Westwood and Bel Air.

I flew past LaBrea, Schwab's, and Crescent Heights," sang Jan Berry and Dean Torrence in their 1964 hit "Dead Man's Curve." This sad ballad of an impromptu race against a Jag climaxes when its narrator hits a blind curve which "is no place to play . . . you'd best keep away." Berry himself, ironically, later wrecked his car on a *different* stretch of road nearby, sparking confusion ever since over which was the *real* Dead Man's Curve. It was this one, according to the singers themselves. Cartoon voicemeister Mel Blanc nearly died in a crash here, after which road crews were brought in to straighten it out a bit; now it's more of a smooth 120° turn.

Silverlake and Los Feliz

Disney's First L.A. Home and Workshop
4406 Kingswell Avenue, on the south side of the street, just west of Commonwealth Avenue, in the Silverlake district east of Hollywood.

A young Walt Disney first tried his hand at animation in Kansas City. But the two-man cartooning company he founded there quickly went bankrupt for lack of business. So he gave it all up in 1923 and headed west like so many others, drawn by the lights of Hollywood. He mooched off his uncle Robert Disney, who let Walt share this modest Craftsman bungalow in the flatlands of the Silverlake district. Walt wasn't having much luck in the movie world, but he stumbled onto a chance to make cartoon shorts that were to be shown in vaudeville theaters between acts. He set up shop in his uncle's garage, using wooden boxes and borrowed equipment to make a series of crude cartoons, starring stick figures that spoke in word balloons. After landing a few more cartoon jobs, Walt moved out and started his first real professional studio a few blocks away on Hyperion Avenue (see below). For decades the significance of this house and its garage were forgotten. But in the mid-'80s Disney aficionado Arthur

Disney's first L.A. home

"Buddy" Adler bought the garage (but not the land under it), wishing to donate it to the Disney corporation as a historical landmark. Strangely, they weren't interested. So Adler put the garage in storage until he found a willing partner in the Garden Grove Historical Society, which now displays it in a city park not far from Disneyland (see page 18). The garageless 4406 Kingswell, Walt's first L.A. home, sits peacefully in the sun, giving little hint of the career it helped to launch.

Disney's First Studio
Birthplace of Mickey Mouse and feature-length animation.

Original address: Walt Disney Studios, 2719 Hyperion Avenue. Now a Mayfair Food Market, 2725 Hyperion Avenue, at Griffith Park Boulevard, in the Silverlake district. Open daily 7:00 A.M.–midnight. (323) 660-0387. A memorial sign is attached to a light pole in front of the store's parking lot on Hyperion Avenue. The Snow White cottages are around the corner at 2906–12 Griffith Park Boulevard, near St. George Street.

Walt Disney founded his great empire on this unlikely corner lot in 1926. The historians say that Disney's partner and chief animator Ub Iwerks first designed and animated Mickey Mouse in 1928; thus this address must have been Mickey's birthplace, the cartoon world's Bethlehem. For years a sign above the lot proudly declared, "Walt Disney Studios, Mickey Mouse and Silly Symphony Sound Cartoons." And it was here, in the mid-'30s, at his first real L.A. studio (excluding his uncle's garage a few blocks away), that Disney conceived his plan of creating a feature-length cartoon, to be shown in theaters as an

Snow White cottages behind the former Disney Studios

evening's premiere attraction. It was a revolutionary idea. Until then, cartoons had been mere filler between live-action films and newsreels. Disney and the entire company spent years on the project, finally, in 1937, releasing the masterful and immediately successful *Snow White and the Seven Dwarfs*. (A cluster of quaint Tudor cottages just behind the studio served as the architectural inspiration for the dwarfs' home; legend has it the animators lived in these while working on the film. The still-extant cottages are not connected to the Mayfair lot, but can be seen on Griffith Park Boulevard.) Disney took the profits and moved the studio to a much larger lot in Burbank in 1940. The original studio buildings were torn down shortly thereafter. A supermarket now occupies the site. In the center of the store, above the manager's station in front of the check-out counters, an old photo shows how the studio looked in 1929. A sign attached to a light pole on the sidewalk in front of the parking lot indicates the approximate site of the entrance to the studio grounds. Aside from these scant reminders, nothing remains of Mickey's childhood home.

La Bianca House
Manson Family murders, phase two.

3311 Waverly Drive, at St. George Street, just south of Griffith Park's southeastern tip.

Members of the Manson Family killed actress Sharon Tate and her friends one night in the summer of 1969 (see **Sharon Tate House,** page 91). Shortly afterward they made their second strike here, killing grocery store owner Leno La Bianca and his wife Rosemary. The killers stuck a knife and fork in the man's body and wrote messages in blood around the house: "Death to pigs" and the misspelled "Healter Skelter." Someone the Family used to know lived in another house nearby, but the killers didn't know the La Biancas. At the time of the killing, the address was 3301. The address has since been changed to 3311, but the house with its Spanish roof, sundeck, and carport still stands.

Leonardo DiCaprio Computer Center
Log on in the name of Leo.

Los Feliz Branch Library, 1874 Hillhurst Avenue, at Franklin Avenue, just north of Sunset Boulevard. Open Mon.–Tues., 12:30–8:00 P.M.; Wed.–Thurs., 12:30–5:30 P.M.; Fri.–Sat., 10:00 A.M.–5:30 P.M. (323) 913-4710.

As a boy the *Titanic* star lived with his family in a small bungalow on the southeastern corner of Franklin and Hillhurst. By 1999 the building was gone and a new library was being erected in its place. Remembering times past, Leonardo's mother donated funds to establish a public-access computer room at the facility. Though the thirty-some thousand dollars in question were hers, she kindly wanted the computer center to be named after her son. Today *Titanic* posters adorn its walls.

Forrest J. Ackerman Science Fiction Mansion
Open the pod bay door, Hal.

> *2495 Glendower Avenue. (Take Catalina Street uphill to where it forks with Glencairn Road, then bear left; Catalina becomes Glendower.) Open most Saturdays, 11:00 A.M.–noon; call ahead on Friday to make sure: (323) 666-6326 [MOON-FAN].*

F orrest Ackerman has been collecting sci-fi and horror film memorabilia since the 1920s. In fact, he claims to have invented the expression "sci-fi." Today his collection, credited as the world's largest, occupies his expansive home. Visitors line up on Saturdays for a peek at Jane Fonda's *Barbarella* bustier; Bela Lugosi's *Dracula* cape; Tribbles from *Star Trek;* the golden idol from *Raiders of the Lost Ark;* the *Metropolis* robot; and hundreds of thousands of other irreplaceable artifacts. Life masks of Lugosi, Peter Lorre, Vincent Price, Lon Chaney, and Boris Karloff are here, along with monster masks, props, and scads of books and posters. Beam yourself up soon, as Ackerman is searching for a new permanent home for the collection.

Downtown and Nearby

D O W N T O W N

(Entries arranged north to south.)

Union Station
Featured in many movies.

> *800 N. Alameda Street. (213) 683-6875.*

A rt Deco chandeliers as big as dining room tables sparkle above Mission-style accessories in the historic waiting room. For decades moviemakers have been taking advantage of L.A.'s railway hub in all its '30s glory. You can spot it in *The Way We Were, Bugsy, Blade Runner, Ferris Bueller's Day Off,* and many more.

Los Angeles City Hall
> *200 N. Spring Street; the building occupies the block bounded by Spring, Temple, Main, and First Streets. (213) 473-5870.*

L os Angeles City Hall has appeared in more films and TV shows than just about any other single building in the world. Most famous on TV as *Dragnet's* police headquarters and as *Superman's Daily Planet* building, City Hall has also been used in *The Rockford Files; Hill Street Blues; Kojak; L.A. Law; Melrose Place; America's Most Wanted; Unsolved Mysteries; Party of Five; Matlock; Murder, She Wrote;* and so many more that it's impossible to keep count. On the big screen, City Hall was blown to smithereens by Martians in 1953's *War of the Worlds,* earned its film noir credentials in *Mildred Pierce* and *D.O.A.,* and survived the 1990s in Jackie Chan's *Rush Hour* and the remake of *Godzilla.* You're not likely to see it in any films made since 1997, however: the building has been undergoing a restoration project that's scheduled to last at least through 2001. The only way to see the inside nowadays is to impersonate a construction worker.

Los Angeles City Hall

Dorothy Chandler Pavilion
Home of the Oscars.

> 135 N. Grand Avenue, on the crest of the hill between 1st and Temple Streets; most people approach the building from the Hope Street side, through the courtyard it shares with the Mark Taper Forum. (213) 972-7211.

It's the L.A. Philharmonic's home, but more people know it as an Oscars venue. Crowds flock the area on Oscar Day (when the awards ceremony is being held here instead of the Shrine Auditorium), jostling throughout the afternoon and into the evening for glimpses of stars making their way inside. All year round tour buses pull up, disgorging passengers for snapshots. Yet on an ordinary, non-Oscar day, the complex looks stark and spiritless; a hideous sculpture in its courtyard looks remarkably like naked figures hoisting dogs and diapers.

Dorothy Chandler Pavilion

The Bradbury Building
As seen in Blade Runner.

---

304 S. Broadway, at 3rd Street, on the southeast corner.

The Bradbury Building

Inspired in 1893 not only by messages he received via Ouija board from his long-dead brother, but also by a sci-fi novel set in the utopian year 2000, George Wyman designed this office building so that sunshine streaming through its glass roof would fill it with light. Its floors are Mexican tile; its wrought-iron grillwork is French. Its bas-reliefs, ornate wooden doors, and geometrically patterned staircases were featured prominently in *Blade Runner*, which was filmed here. Scenes from *Chinatown*, *Wolf*, and *Lethal Weapon 4* were shot here as well.

Westin Bonaventure Hotel and Suites
Oft-filmed cylindrical towers.

---

404 S. Figueroa Street. (213) 624-1000.

Westin Bonaventure Hotel and Suites

What is it about this hotel, built with great fanfare in the '70s, that inspires the makers of action flicks? Could it be the cylindrical towers shining against the sky like enormous stacks of quarters? Perhaps it's the glassy elevators, which Johnny Depp rode nervously in *Nick of Time*. Also partly filmed here were *True Lies*, *Strange Days*, *Lethal Weapon 2*, *Ruthless People*, *Rain Man*, *In the Line of Fire*, and many more. On level G, below the lobby, is an exhibit of framed posters from movies made here.

Regal Biltmore Hotel
Where the Beatles spent a hard day's night.

---

506 S. Grand Avenue (another entrance is around the corner on Olive Street). (213) 624-1011.

Opened in 1923 with one thousand rooms, this hotel is an island of old-fashioned opulence, complete with frescoes, fountains, massive columns, and cathedralesque ceilings. Past guests have included JFK, Harry Truman, Bill Clinton, Ronald Reagan, and the shah of Iran. In the Crystal Ballroom an original design for what would later become the Oscar statuette was first sketched on a linen napkin.

Several early Academy Awards ceremonies were held here, as well. The Beatles used the Biltmore as a refuge from rampaging fans during their first U.S. tour. JFK set up his headquarters in the Music Room during the 1960 Democratic National Convention. Well over one hundred movies have been filmed here, including *Chinatown, The Buddy Holly Story, The Bad News Bears, Billy Jack Goes to Washington, Splash, Altered States, Pretty in Pink, The Bodyguard, True Lies, Independence Day, The Rock, Fight Club,* and *Rocky and Bullwinkle.* And the hotel's Olive Street entrance is the last place Elizabeth Short, aka the Black Dahlia, was seen alive before her brutal murder.

Los Angeles Conservancy Walking Tours

The Conservancy office is located at 523 W. 6th Street, suite 1216, near Olive Street, downtown, though you need not visit the office in person to make reservations for a tour. Call (213) 623-2489 weekdays, 9:00 A.M.–5:00 P.M., as far in advance as possible, for reservations. The staff will tell you where and when to meet the tour leader. Most tours start at 10:00 A.M., last about two hours, and cost $8 for nonmembers (free for members).

In L.A. when one speaks of "history," one really means "celebrity history." So even though most of the tours offered by the Los Angeles Conservancy focus on historical architecture, you know the stars can't be far away. The "Broadway Theaters" tour (Saturdays at 10:00 A.M.) reveals the secrets behind downtown's glorious old movie houses and even lets you poke around inside buildings otherwise closed to the public while you learn about the glamour days of the film industry. The "Biltmore Hotel" tour touches on scandalous history, while the "Union Station" tour gives a behind-the-scenes look at filming locations for the many classic movies shot there. Call the number above for a complete listing of the many other tours.

Cicada
Where Julia Roberts lost control of her snails.

617 S. Olive Street, between 6th and 7th Streets. Open Mon.–Fri., 11:30 A.M.–2:30 P.M., and 5:30–9:30 P.M.; Sat., 5:30–9:30 P.M. (213) 488-9488.

Julia Roberts struggled with escargot tongs in a famous scene from *Pretty Woman* that was filmed here back when this overwhelmingly Art Deco place was still called Rex II Ristorante. Built in 1928 and resplendent with murals, glass, bronze, massive carved wooden columns, and a dizzying array of zigzags, these premises now house a pricey and popular Italian eatery owned by Stephanie Taupin, ex-wife of Elton John's lyricist, Bernie Taupin.

JJ's Sandwich Shop
Where blood ran in **L.A. Confidential.**

119 E. 6th Street, at Main Street. (213) 625-2363.

Variously called JJ's, J & J, J.J., and JJ, this little slip of a Korean-run restaurant serves "carne spagheti," "camarón teriyaki," and pancakes 'n' shakes. Its retro divey-ness made this the perfect setting for a bloody murder scene in *L.A. Confidential.* In the film it was called the "Night Owl Coffee Shop."

Orpheum Theatre

842 S. Broadway, on the east side of the street, between 8th and 9th Streets. Opening hours vary, but the exterior is always visible. (213) 239-0949.

By the time young Frances Gumm pranced onstage at the Orpheum Theatre in 1936, she was already a hardened vaudeville veteran, a member of the Gumm Sisters—a song-and-dance act—since the age of three. A talent scout in the audience that night got her an audition with Louis B. Mayer. Within a few years, Frances—who became Judy Garland—was the world's most famous actress. This real-life "a star is born" tale is among hundreds of legends spawned at the Orpheum Theatre, which for decades was the premier live venue for the greatest names in show business. The Marx Brothers brought the house down, as did Jack Benny, Bob Hope, and Eddie Cantor. One night, as Gypsy Rose Lee sailed above the audience on a wire during an elaborate striptease, she became entangled in the stage rigging and was saved by several eager male rescuers. Sally Rand took *almost* all of it off, though Duke Ellington preferred to perform fully clothed. Having launched

Orpheum Theatre

many comics' and singers' film careers, the Orpheum is itself a screen star appearing in *The Last Action Hero* (Arnold emerges from the screen), *That Thing You Do, What's Love Got to Do with It?, The Doors, Ed Wood,* and dozens more. As this is still a functioning cinema, you can't just stroll in and inspect the lavish Renaissance-style architecture and decoration. Either take the Los Angeles Conservancy's "Broadway Theaters" walking tour for $8 (see page 124) or come to see a film here.

MacArthur Park
For which the song was named.

> *Alvarado Boulevard at Wilshire Boulevard, just east of downtown.*

Richard Harris had a hit in the summer of 1968 with Jimmy Webb's anguished song "MacArthur Park." Not rock 'n' roll, nor any other discernible genre, it soared up the charts. Listeners puzzled over cryptic lines like the endlessly disturbing *"Someone left the cake out in the rain . . ."* The bifurcated park itself offers few clues. Surrounded with green lawns where local families and trouble-seeking youths lounge, its lake boasts a boathouse. A fountain jets frothily from the middle of the water as white ducks glide past. Roaming Popsicle vendors push their jingly carts. The surrounding streets are thronged with signs in Spanish and doorways pulsing Spanish-language pop—but no trace of Richard Harris.

William Desmond Taylor Murder Site
Hollywood's first murder mystery.

> *Former address: 404B S. Alvarado Street. Current site: a parking lot at the southeast corner of S. Alvarado Street and Maryland Street, next to a Pic 'N' Sav, just north of MacArthur Park, west of downtown.*

On the night of February 1, 1922, in a posh bungalow court near MacArthur Park, silent-screen ingenue Edna Purviance heard desperate yells coming from the nearby home of famed director William Desmond Taylor. Instead of calling the police, she called her friend and colleague Mabel Normand, who she knew was romantically linked with Taylor. Along with companions whose identities remain unknown to this day, Normand rushed to Taylor's bungalow and found he had been shot to death; they spent the rest of the night destroying as much evidence as they could before the police arrived. By the next day the murder was the talk of the nation.

Despite Normand's best efforts, cops found drugs, porn, and incriminating letters stashed all over Taylor's home. Fingers were soon pointing at yet another silent-film actress, the elfin Mary Miles Minter, whose torrid love notes to Taylor became popular reading at the police station. Minter admitted visiting Taylor hours before the murder, but no one could pin the crime on her. Suspicion turned to Minter's mother, who was angry at Taylor for not marrying her daughter. Normand, too, had been at the bungalow just prior to the murder, which is why Purviance had called her. But the public could scarely believe any of these dainty starlets had the capacity to suavely pull off such a brutal crime.

The investigation turned surreal when Taylor's "butler" turned out to be his real-life brother, who was hiding out from the police for unrelated crimes. Behind the scenes, investigators found that Taylor was leading a double life as a bisexual and had male lovers who also came under suspicion. Despite all the leads and all the suspects, the crime was never solved and remains one of Hollywood's great mysteries of the Jazz Age. Taylor was one of his era's top directors; now he is remembered only as a victim. The upscale bungalow court where he fell was demolished long ago to make way for a parking lot, but you can still stand right where it happened (in the approximate center of the lot) and ponder the crime.

Olympic Auditorium
Where Rocky Balboa launched his career.

1801 S. Grand Avenue, south of downtown.

This auditorium was built in the '20s with seats for more than fifteen thousand boxing fans—an early habitué was Al Jolson. Since then the Olympic has inspired viewers worldwide as the place where Sly Stallone won his big match in *Rocky*. Scenes from *Requiem for a Heavyweight*, *The Mike Tyson Story*, and *Baseketball* were shot here as well. And it's where Jim Carrey, as Andy Kaufman, wrestles women in *Man on the Moon*.

Los Angeles River Channel
Hot rods and repo men.

The Sixth Street Viaduct is one block east of the intersection of 6th Street and Santa Fe Avenue, east of downtown Los Angeles.

The Los Angeles River is not much of a river, really. What was once a major waterway—frequently flooding huge areas of the Los Angeles basin—is now little more than a slimy trickle confined to the center of a wide cement channel. This dry strip of traffic-free pavement has been an irresistible lure for hot-rodders and filmmakers since the 1930s. Most famously, John Travolta won Olivia Newton-John's heart during a climactic drag race down the riverbed between the Sixth Street Viaduct and the Fourth Street Viaduct in the 1978 film version of *Grease*. Twenty-four years earlier the giant radioactive ants in *Them!* used the storm-drain entrance at the Sixth Street viaduct as their hideout from the U.S. Army's jeeps and flamethrowers. This section also played a memorable role in Arnold Schwarzenegger's *Terminator 2*. Other films featuring scenes of the river include *Repo Man, To Live and Die in L.A.,* and *Gumball Rally*. Chain-link fences and heavy padlocks discourage drag racers nowadays, but rumor has it that Toyota test-drives its new cars along this stretch of the channel, and that L.A. bus drivers learn how to back up their behemoths here where they can't hurt anyone.

NORTHEAST OF DOWNTOWN

Skeletons in the Closet
The coroner's gift shop.

> Los Angeles County Coroner's Office, 1104 N. Mission Road (room 208), at Marengo. Open Mon.–Fri., 8:00 A.M.–4:30 P.M. (323) 343-0760.

Los Angeles is quite a busy county for a coroner. This is where Marilyn, Janis, and Divine died, just for starters. Riots, earthquakes, celebrity murders—what's a coroner to do? A secretary in this office got the idea of opening a gift shop on the premises. Skeletons in the Closet is a creepy little emporium stocked with T-shirts, coffee mugs, hats, aprons, body bags, and hundreds of other death-themed souvenirs. Many items are proudly emblazoned with the coroner's logo; Mickey Mouse ears just don't hold a candle—and the profits are earmarked for a good cause.

Builders of the Adytum

> 5101 N. Figueroa Street, near Avenue 51 (no, not Area 51), in the Highland Park/Mount Washington area of Los Angeles, northeast of downtown. Services on Sundays at 11:00 A.M. are open to the public. (323) 255-7141.

The Builders of the Adytum are a "mystery religion" in the original sense of the term—they believe spiritual truth can only be understood through ancient texts and rituals in which "ageless wisdom" has been preserved for those clever enough to seek it. The members of BOTA (as they call themselves) know full well that the average Joe could never grasp the esoteric techniques needed to unlock the secrets of the universe. So, unlike some sects we could name, they don't waste their time proselytizing the dregs of society. They leave the door open for people who have half a brain ready to study the Kabbalah and Hermetic philosophy; but the rest of you idiots can go back to the pool hall.

Founded in the 1920s by Jazz Age guru Paul Foster Case, BOTA has survived the last century's upheavals virtually unchanged, a relic of the time when occult spiritualism was trendy. Think tarot cards, alchemy, eyes in the pyramid, and interlocking threads of secret knowledge that descend from the ancient custodians of mystical truth. BOTA symbolism incorporates ideographs and magical tokens from nearly every tradition: lotus blossoms, Stars of David, pentagrams, Maltese crosses, zodiac symbols, the biblical Hebrew name of God, Rosicrucian and Masonic signs . . . the works.

Got the feeling you're one of the Chosen Ones? Drop by and pick up some literature *(Daniel, Master of Magicians and the Name of Names* sounds like a good read) or hang around for one of their services. You never know when some ageless wisdom might come in handy.

Hancock Park/Koreatown Area

Marvin Gaye House
Where his father shot and killed him.

> 2101 S. Gramercy Place, at 21st Street, in the Western Heights district, just south of Washington Boulevard and north of the Santa Monica Freeway.

On April Fools' Day in 1984 Marvin Gaye exited this house mortally wounded and died on its front lawn. After the demise of a career marked by extreme highs and lows—strings of hits, mounting debts, and a drug problem—the man who sang "Let's Get It On" came to live with his parents here, in the home he had bought for them. Half-timbered and impressive, it was built by the same man who designed nearby Venice's canals. On a cocaine–and–porn video jag, the singer was lolling upstairs on the day before his forty-fifth birthday when his father, Marvin Gaye Sr., a former Pentecostal minister, entered the bedroom, searching for a missing document. The men exchanged harsh words before Gaye's father shot him three times point-blank with a .38. The singer staggered outside and fell dead on the lawn, which the current owner keeps well groomed, aware of its significance. At Gaye's funeral, thousands lined up to view the coffin.

Marvin Gaye's home and the lawn where he died

Angelus-Rosedale Cemetery
Here lies Hattie McDaniel.

> 1831 W. Washington Boulevard, between Normandie Avenue and Catalina Street; entrance at Mariposa Avenue. Open generally during daylight hours; call for current times. (213) 730-1219.

Lots of historic graves, juxtaposed with those of fallen gang members, lend spookiness to this inner-city spread. Among the famous spending eternity here are actress Anna May Wong (in grave 5-136-3NE); *Gone with the Wind*'s Hattie McDaniel (near the front gate at D-24-3SW); and L.A. Harbor developer Phineas Banning (J-40-2SE).

Angelus-Rosedale Cemetery

Jazz great Art Tatum lies under a marker that reads, "Though the strings are broken, the melody lingers on" (5-173-2NW). Also here are *Freaks* filmmaker Tod Browning, "Under the Bamboo Tree" lyricist Andy Razaf, and Maria Rasputin, daughter of Russia's notorious "mad monk."

Ambassador Hotel
Where RFK was shot.

3400 Wilshire Boulevard, on the south side of the street.

Looking like part of a glamorous ghost town, the long, low hotel is set way back at the end of a rutted asphalt drive lined with majestic palms. Since 1990 it has been closed to the public and used exclusively for filming—the hundreds of movies shot here include *Forrest Gump, True Lies, Defending Your Life, Barton Fink, Apollo 13, That Thing You Do, Sister Act, Fear and Loathing in Las Vegas,* and *Man on the Moon.* But after it first opened in 1921 the Ambassador and its Cocoanut Grove club enjoyed celebrity hot spot status for many a decade. Exotic actress Pola Negri is said to have once led her pet leopards through its lobby. The first-ever Oscar statuette was handed out during the first of several Academy Awards celebrations held here between 1930 and 1943. For Sammy Davis Jr. this was a home-away-from-home. The Grateful Dead performed here. But the hotel made its biggest headlines when presidential candidate Robert F. Kennedy was assassinated here in 1968. Shortly after delivering his victory speech, having won the state Democratic primary, RFK was in a crowded pantry when Sirhan Sirhan shot him. Theories have since surfaced suggesting that Sirhan did not act alone, that he was brainwashed, that he was not even the actual assassin. A crucial piece of evidence—a door from the Ambassador's pantry that contained more bullet holes than Sirhan had bullets—mysteriously disappeared. More than once, the five hundred–room Ambassador has narrowly escaped demolition. Its future still hangs in the balance.

The Former Brown Derby

Café Namuhana, 3377 Wilshire Boulevard, though technically the restaurant is on the upper level of a strip mall on Alexandria Avenue, 100 yards north of Wilshire Boulevard. Open daily, 5:00 P.M.–2:00 A.M. (213) 480-1223.

For years the elegant restaurant shaped like a hat was an irreplaceable part of L.A.'s skyline. Everyone went there to see and be seen. Today the hacked hat, brimless and painted silver, surveys its surroundings

Café Namuhana, formerly known as the Brown Derby

from the top of a strip mall where it now houses a Korean café-bar. The circular black ceiling sports painted planets, and a toy train zips around and around its perimeter. Thousands mourn the derby's tranformation into a silver yarmulke.

Nat "King" Cole House
401 Muirfield Road, at 4th Street, on the southwestern corner.

Evoking an English manor, this house sports a tall slender chimney and brick walls luxuriant with ivy. Mature trees shade a perfect lawn and steep gabled roof. Bigoted neighbors raised Cain when Cole decided to move here in 1947. At one point, racists even burned the n-word into the grass. But the singer's persistence and friendliness paid off. He lived here until his death in 1965.

Leave It to Beaver House
1727 Buckingham Road, just south of St. Charles Place, on the west side of the street. Enter the neighborhood through St. Charles off Crenshaw Boulevard, as the north and south ends of all other streets are gated to keep automobiles out.

On a quiet street lined with lush foliage and large glamorous homes stands this house. It was used for external shots on TV's *Leave It to Beaver,* whose Cleaver family was said to live on "Pine Avenue" in "Mayfield." The place has been kept up immaculately, and not one detail has been altered in the intervening years. It still seems as if Eddie Haskell is going to cross the expansive lawn any minute now and march up the neat brick walkway on his way to visit Wally.

Leave It to Beaver *house*

Understanding Principles for Better Living
Della Reese's church.

6090 W. Pico Boulevard, at Alvira Street, on the southeastern corner. (323) 655-8617.

After surviving a burst aneurysm, singing legend Della Reese intensified her interest in spiritual matters. Ultimately she founded a church and became ordained. When filming *Touched by an Angel,* she commutes back and forth between

Utah and L.A., where hundreds of the faithful gather on Sunday mornings at 11:00 to hear "the Reverend Della Reese-Lett" in various venues. (Call for current calendar.) The church's offices and meeting room are located in this severe-looking building whose slightly silly sign depicts a hot-air balloon. (The initials UP refer both to "Understanding Principles" and the direction in which balloons rise. Get it?) Tape recording and photography are forbidden during the musical services, which spring from a twelve-steppish ethos. Believers declare their helplessness, surrendering their will to a higher power dubbed "the Master Mind." Churchgoers can even buy souvenir meditation tapes by the angelic Roma Downey.

Understanding Principles for Better Living

West Adams/Olympic Park Area

Black Dahlia Dump Site
Where the cut-up corpse was found.

3925 Norton Avenue, between 39th Street and Martin Luther King Jr. Boulevard, on the west side of the street.

A young mother pushing a stroller near what was then a vacant lot one morning in January 1947 made a shocking discovery. A woman's corpse had been severed at the waist, slit from ear to ear, and mutilated in yet other ways too horrible to describe. The body was later identified as that of Elizabeth Short, a starstruck girl whose time in Hollywood had yielded only frustration and yucky affairs. Nicknamed "Black Dahlia" because of her dark hair, Short had basically lived on handouts from men. An autopsy suggested that, among other indignities visited on Short before her murder, she was forced to eat feces. It was one of L.A.'s most sensational murders ever, yet the killer was never caught. A creepy ex-con came forward with an incriminatingly detailed account of the crime, claiming he had heard it from a friend. Cops suspected the ex-con himself, but before they could nab him, he died in a hotel fire. The vacant

House now on the spot where the Black Dahlia was found

lot where the body was found is now a street lined with stucco homes, built during the early '60s; many sport bonsai trees and immaculate gardens. The body was found on what is now more or less the front lawn of 3925 Norton.

Natural History Museum of Los Angeles County
Hollywood memorabilia.

900 Exposition Boulevard, in Exposition Park, south side of the street; Hollywood section is in Area 11 of the Lower Level, aka the basement. Open Mon.–Fri., 9:30 A.M.–5:00 P.M.; Sat.–Sun., 10:00 A.M.–5:00 P.M. Admission: adults, $8; students, $5; children ages 5–12, $2; under age 5, free. (213) 763-3466.

In the southeastern corner of the California History room, changing displays pay homage to what is, for millions worldwide, the only thing about California that matters. Original props from Charlie Chaplin's *Modern Times* include wrenches, roller skates, and striped overalls, while stills from the film recall Chaplin doing his "dance of the wrenches." Other artifacts on hand might include costumes, makeup, original Disney animation cels, and more.

Chaplin's costume and props from Modern Times

University of Southern California (USC)

The campus is on the block bounded by Exposition Boulevard, Vermont Avenue, Jefferson Boulevard, and Figueroa Street, in the Olympic Park district south of downtown. Call (213) 740-6605 for tour reservations.

More than any other school in the country, USC is an integral part of the film industry. Not only have countless USC graduates (including George Lucas, Ron Howard, Robert Zemeckis, and John Wayne) gone on to fame as actors, directors, and producers, but the campus itself is a star of the big screen. Its picturesque Mudd Hall of Philosophy, on the south side of campus off Exposition Boulevard, was exorcised in *Ghostbusters* and stood in for the New York City Library in *Escape from New York*. Dozens of other films were shot on campus, especially around Doheny Memorial Library, including *Young Frankenstein, Cocoon,* and the graduation

The University of Southern California

scene in *Forrest Gump*. Free campus tours depart Monday through Friday, hourly between 10:00 A.M. and 3:00 P.M., from Trojan Hall 101, though the tours don't focus exclusively on the filmic aspects of campus.

Shrine Auditorium
Where Michael Jackson's hair caught fire.

700 W. Jefferson Boulevard, at Figueroa Street, on the northeastern corner.

Turreted, towered, domed, too white and too big to miss, the Shrine looms above bustling traffic like a hookah-fueled dream. An inscription solemnly identifies this Moorish fantasy as the Al Malaikah Temple and Auditorium. Erected in 1924–25, it is headquarters for the fezzed fraternity chummily known as the Shriners. You know it from scenes in *King Kong,* the first version of *A Star Is Born, Naked Gun 33⅓,* and *The Bodyguard.* The Grammy Awards and, occasionally, the Academy Awards are held inside—amid arches, chandeliers, and scimitar-and-sphinx imagery. Frank Sinatra held his eightieth birthday party here; Dis-

Shrine Auditorium

ney held a huge postproduction party here for *Hercules.* And while Michael Jackson was filming a Pepsi commercial at the Shrine, his hair caught fire, facilitating yet another visit to the plastic surgeon.

Fatty Arbuckle House
649 W. Adams Boulevard, at Figueroa Street, on the north side of the street.

Now it's a residence for mellow Lazarist priests. But comic Fatty Arbuckle was living in this half-timbered house when—on a 1921 trip to San Francisco—he may or may not have killed starlet Virginia Rappe by perforating her organs with a bottle in a botched attempt at hot sex (see **Westin St. Francis Hotel,** pages 198–99). Once nearly as popular as Charlie Chaplin, Arbuckle reportedly owned a car outfitted with its very own toilet. All kinds of antics went on in this then-suburban house, which he dubbed "my jazz pleasure palace." Buster Keaton lived with him here, amid polished

Fatty Arbuckle house

wooden floors, a massive marble fireplace, and other appurtenances. At one point a dogs' wedding was staged in the backyard. After Arbuckle's downfall, the estate became church property.

Doheny Mansion

On Chester Place, midway between Adams Boulevard and 23rd Street, one block west of Figueroa Street, on the campus of Mount St. Mary's College, just south of downtown.

This turn-of-the-twentieth-century French Gothic mansion is a favorite with location scouts, so you've undoubtedly seen its red-roofed spire and stately palms hundreds of times in movies and videos without giving it a second thought. Scenes shot here include some in Mel Gibson's *Payback,* the TV programs *Sliders, Providence,* and *Profiler,* and music videos by Vanessa Williams, Garth Brooks, and nearly every rapper with a recording contract. Some scenes from *The Godfather, Part II* were supposedly filmed here, too. In the '20s the wealthy Dohenys who lived here were horrified by the

Doheny mansion

gin-soaked parties and freewheeling antics of their neighbor Fatty Arbuckle (see above), who lived just across the back fence. Imagine what they'd think of the scantily clad rap-video dancers who get jiggy here so frequently! (One supposes the nuns who now live on the mansion's upper floor concur.)

South and Central Los Angeles

VERNON

Farmer John Pig Murals

Along E. Vernon Avenue, Soto Street, and Bandini Boulevard. (323) 583-4621.

One of L.A.'s best outdoor artworks adorns this wienie facility. To diffuse the meat-packing industry's eyeball-and-spleen reputation, movie-industry artist Leslie Grimes was hired in 1957 to paint whimsical murals on the surrounding walls. But Grimes got drunk and fell to his death from a scaffold while painting clouds shortly before the work was finished. Another artist, Arnold Jordan, took over for the finishing touches. The pastoral array of jolly pigs, farmers, roads, trees, and creeks does its best to make you forget what goes into a hot dog. And the 1964 song "Farmer John," by local boys the Premiers, was about this place.

SOUTH-CENTRAL LOS ANGELES

Reginald Denny Beating Site
The intersection of Florence and Normandie Avenues.

B lack residents of Los Angeles were understandably outraged when the cops accused of beating motorist Rodney King were acquitted of wrongdoing even though the entire assault had been clearly documented on videotape. When the "not guilty" verdicts were announced on April 29, 1992, chaotic violence erupted. Dozens of people were killed in what became known as "the Rodney King riots," and the area suffered over a billion dollars in damage. The horror of that day was epitomized by the fate of Reginald Denny, an unsuspecting white truck driver who naïvely drove into the middle of the wrong neighborhood at the exact wrong moment. Rioters pulled him from the cab of his truck and—as a helicopter film crew broadcast the entire episode live on national TV—beat the innocent Denny, displaying the same racist rage the cops had shown when they beat King. Despite pummelings with fists, feet, and chunks of concrete, Denny managed to survive, though the state of race relations in this country may have suffered even deeper wounds. Years later, the intersection where Denny was beaten looks pretty much like any other in poverty-stricken south-central L.A., though the phrase "Florence and Normandie" still strikes fear in the hearts of many Angelenos.

WATTS

Watts Towers
Big beloved piles of junk.

> *1727 E. 107th Street, at Santa Ana Boulevard. Open Tues.–Sat., 10:00 A.M.–4:00 P.M.; Sun., noon–4:00 P.M. (213) 485-1795.*

I n 1921 Italian-born plasterer Simon Rodia started building these Gaudíesque spires from found materials: steel, wire, bedframes, and broken glass. He kept at it for more than thirty years, then moved away. Having narrowly escaped the wrecking ball not long after their completion, the towers are now a cherished L.A. landmark—yet another testament to the city's eccentric architectural tradition. The tallest of the towers soars nearly one hundred feet over South-Central. Restoration necessitated by the 1994 Northridge earthquake is due to be completed in or around 2000, when the last of the scaffolding and a fence that hides the towers will finally come down. In the interim visitors must peek through the fence.

DOWNEY

World's Oldest Operating McDonald's
10207 Lakewood Boulevard, at Florence Avenue. Open daily 7:00 A.M.–10:00 P.M. (562) 622-9248.

The McDonald brothers built this burger barn in 1953 and ran a thriving business. Later they would sell the company, including their surname, to impresario Ray Kroc. He in turn would launch the rain forest–decimating chain we hear about today. But the brothers' early Downey restaurant—old-time golden arches and all— remains the only one in the world permitted to use the McDonald's name while remaining under private ownership. Though not the first McDonald's ever built (that was in San Bernardino—see page 167), this Downey restaurant wears the crown as the oldest McDonald's still in existence; it alone is not part of the corporation. Sample its noncorporate burgers, nuggets, and fruit pies, then peruse an adjoining museum stocked with vintage McDonald's straws, cups, paper hats, and other artifacts.

INGLEWOOD

Randy's Donuts
Giant rooftop donut.
805 W. Manchester Boulevard, at La Cienega Boulevard. Open daily, 24 hours. (310) 645-4707.

The enormous doughnut perched on the roof is a classic L.A. landmark, making mouths water for miles around. Unsurprisingly, the huge confection has made its way into many movies and TV shows, including *Earth Girls Are Easy, The Golden Child, Mars Attacks!, Volcano, Martial Law,* and *America's Most Wanted.* An animated version has appeared in Fox's *Futurama.*

| HAWTHORNE |

The "Fun, Fun, Fun" Hamburger Stand
It inspired Brian Wilson to write a classic.

> *Foster's Freeze, 11969 S. Hawthorne Boulevard, at 120th Street, across from the Hawthorne Plaza mall. Open daily, 10:00 A.M.–10:00 P.M. (310) 973-9274.*

Brian Wilson and the other Beach Boys used to hang out at this Foster's Freeze, not far from the homes where they grew up. One day as they were goofing off out front, Brian looked up just as a pretty girl he knew whizzed past in a cherry Thunderbird. Inspiration struck, and within a short time he had penned one of his best-loved songs, "Fun, Fun, Fun": "Well, she got her daddy's car and she cruised to the hamburger stand now . . ." Within months it reached the Top Ten, though who knew that the "hamburger stand" in question was a real place? The original Foster's Freeze is still there and going strong. Its '50s-era fast-food architecture makes it a popular filming location for commercials and videos.

Hawthorne Grill Site
As seen in Pulp Fiction.

> *Hawthorne Boulevard at 137th Place, on the southwest corner.*

In *Pulp Fiction,* John Travolta and his colleague Samuel L. Jackson ponder philosophical matters while noshing on coffee shop fare. Suddenly, Amanda Plummer and Tim Roth pull guns and disrupt everything. Those coffee shop scenes were filmed at the Hawthorne Grill, whose brush with glamour sadly failed to keep it afloat. After more than forty years in business, the retro-chic restaurant shut down and was razed in the summer of 1999. Half a block north on Hawthorne Boulevard is Clark Real Estate, whose sign also appears in the movie.

California Uniforms, Inc.
Where Gary Coleman fought with a fan.

> *13248 Hawthorne Boulevard, at 133rd Street, on the east side of the street. (310) 676-9180.*

Habitually down on his luck after his famous days playing Arnold on *Diff'rent Strokes,* Gary Coleman landed a security-guard job at nearby Fox Hills Mall. The diminutive actor was shopping in this store for a new uniform when a woman spotted him and asked for an autograph. A scuffle ensued, and Coleman was charged with assault, though he claimed he was fighting for his own safety since the female fan outsized him. Still, he was fined and given a suspended sentence. By the end of

1999 a bankrupt Coleman was auctioning off his possessions—even a spatula was up for grabs.

CARSON

Carson Bail Bonds
Where Jackie Brown's big deal went down.

> 724 E. Carson Street, on the south side of the street. (310) 549-0033.

This unprepossessing beige stucco storefront appealed to Quentin Tarantino. It features prominently in *Jackie Brown,* his film about an airline hostess who draws a bail bondsman into an alluring but perilous scheme. The office was rearranged in order to create the fictional "Cherry Bail Bonds"— among other things, the filmmakers installed brown paneling. Now the panels are gone and a *Jackie Brown* poster serves as a lone reminder.

Carson Bail Bonds

Pet Haven Cemetery and Crematory
Final home of Bonanza's *leading lady.*

> 18300 S. Figueroa Street, near 190th/Victoria Street, just northeast of where the San Diego Freeway (Highway 405) crosses the Harbor Freeway (Highway 110). Open daily, generally during daylight hours, but the administration office is closed on Sundays. (310) 532-2477.

Somewhere in this modest, avuncular pet cemetery lies the biggest star ever to clipclop across the screen. On *Bonanza,* Michael Landon's character Little Joe Cartwright had a horse named Lady. She died—off camera, thankfully—before the show did and was buried here. Unfortunately, Lady is a popular name for pets. The horse's grave is near the fence on the Figueroa Street side, but you might well become confused by all the other Ladys resting in peace nearby. Ask in the office at the south end of the cemetery, and they'll point you in the right direction.

Beach Towns

MANHATTAN BEACH

McMartin Preschool Site
Where tots said they saw demonic rites.

Strand Cleaners, 927 Manhattan Beach Boulevard, at Walnut Avenue, on the northeast corner.

Kids say the darnedest things! Wee tots attending the preschool that used to occupy this corner made history by insisting that the school's administrators—the McMartin family—had forced them to participate in grisly Satanic rites, including the murder and mutilation of infants. Tales were told of evil doings in secret tunnels under the school. Sparks flew between frenzied parents and the doomed McMartins, whose lawyers sought to prove that the children had more or less been coached by unscrupulous psychologists. This landmark case spawned so many others that "ritual abuse" became a 1980s cliché. The preschool has since been razed and replaced with a dry-cleaning establishment. Most rational observers concluded that either the stories were pure fantasy, or that the McMartins were no more than run-of-the-mill child molesters. But brace yourself: after the trial was over, according to an article in the *Journal of Psychohistory*, little-publicized excavations at the site seemed to show there *had been* tunnels running this way and that, under the school—filled in by persons unknown. Makes your skin crawl.

Manhattan Beach Studios
Where Ally's office really is.

At the western end of 33rd Street, in the northern part of Manhattan Beach—so big you can't miss it.

The Art Deco stylings of this sprawling new complex go on for blocks and blocks in shades of orange, yellow, and green behind a row of massive Canary Island palms. Theses studios are beloved of upstart TV producer David E. Kelley, who tapes *Ally McBeal* here. Steven Spielberg uses the place, too. Throughout the cold war, this region was aerospace industry territory. Ironically, though those days are gone, a paranoid atmosphere remains. A No Trespassing sign marks the private road approaching the studio. Guards at its front gate are anything but friendly, scaring off fans of the skeletal Calista Flockhart.

HERMOSA BEACH

Hermosa Beach Community Center Gymnasium
Where Sissy Spacek's Carrie massacred her classmates.

710 Pier Avenue, at Pacific Coast Highway. Open Mon.–Thurs., 7:00 A.M.–6:00 P.M. (310) 318-0280.

In 1976 Sissy Spacek was nominated for the Best Actress Oscar for her unnerving portrayal of Carrie White, a backward teen with telekinetic powers. Cruel pranksters elect Carrie prom queen, and when Amy Irving and John Travolta dump a bucket of pigs' blood over her head . . . well, things start to go very wrong. The film made household names of Spacek, director Brian DePalma, and author Stephen King, on whose novel it was based. *Carrie's* climactic prom scene was filmed in this gym, which was then part of a junior high school. It looks pretty much unchanged to this day, outfitted with bleachers and banners for the Hermosa Beach Kiwanis Club. Shut your eyes and visualize the screams, the hoses, the locked doors, the flames. The gym in not visible from the street. From the building's main entrance on Pier Avenue, pass the front desk (it might be a good idea to ask directions as you pass), go through the disused men's rest room, and into an interior courtyard. The gym will be the building in front of you; climb the stairs on the left to reach the door. Another entrance to the building is on Pacific Coast Highway through the ARC Adult Development Center. (When the film was shot here, this was Hermosa Valley School, now located a few blocks away—don't go there by mistake.)

The Comedy and Magic Club
Where Jay Leno tests his shticks.

1018 Hermosa Avenue, at 10th Street, just south of Pier Avenue, on the east side of the street. Sunday-night shows start at 7:00 P.M., doors open at 5:00 P.M.; reservations required. (310) 372-1193.

This was the first club where Jerry Seinfeld was a headliner. On Sunday nights Jay Leno works out his *Tonight Show* material here—yes, right here near the beach. Since it opened in 1978 this low-key venue has spawned such illustrious alumni as Tim Allen, Paul Reiser, Jon Lovitz, Dana Carvey, David Spade, and many more. Tuesday through Saturday nights other comics and magicians perform—you never know when Ray Romano, Garry Shandling, or David Brenner will pop by for a guest spot. Even Kato Kaelin took the stage here once, and stories are told of how Leno once drove his Harley into the club during Shandling's act.

TORRANCE

Del Amo Fashion Center
As seen in Jackie Brown.

Hawthorne Boulevard at Carson Street.

Quentin Tarantino, who grew up nearby, chose this shopping mall for key scenes in his film *Jackie Brown*. Pam Grier's character, Jackie, explains and executes part of her plan for a heist at the little blond round tables in the mall's upper-level food court, the International Café, near the entrance to T.J. Maxx. In those scenes a franchise called Teriyaki Donut is featured prominently. In real life it's called Tokyo Grill, and it's right here along with Burger King and Hot Dog on a Stick. Other scenes feature a women's clothing shop, where Pam Grier's character tries on a suit, Bridget Fonda's character goes in search of her, and Robert De Niro's character riffles impatiently through a rack of garments, waiting. That was filmed about a hundred yards from the International Café at Macy's, in the INC section on the second floor. The dressing rooms with their paneled doors and the checkout register are just as you saw them onscreen.

Torrance High School
Where they filmed Beverly Hills 90210.

2200 W. Carson Street, at El Prado Avenue.

An hour as the crow flies south of the real McCoy, this is where outdoor scenes of *Beverly Hills 90210* were shot. The school's Spanish tile roofs, buff stucco structures, and soaring palm trees create an oh-so-Californian effect. So persuasive are its archways and courtyards, in fact, that other TV shows and films have been shot here, including *She's All That, Buffy the Vampire Slayer,* and *Family Law.*

Torrance High School

Peninsula and Harbor Area

| PALOS VERDES PENINSULA |

The Wayfarers Chapel
Where Brian Wilson was wed.

5755 Palos Verdes Drive South, across from Abalone Cove. (310) 377-1650.

Poised breathtakingly on a bluff overlooking the Pacific, this modern and mostly glass Swedenborgian chapel was built in 1951 by Lloyd Wright, son of Frank. It has proved a popular spot for celebrity weddings. Jayne Mansfield married the bodybuilder Mickey Hargitay here in 1958. Dennis Hopper, Gary Burghoff, and Brian Wilson also said "I do" on the premises—though not to each other. Handsome but fictional Dr. Kiley was married here on TV's *Marcus Welby, M.D.* Surrounded by gardens, the chapel lures wealthy young intendeds who fly in all the way from Japan. And they're not Swedenborgians, either.

The Wayfarers Chapel

Chadwick School
Alma mater of the children of the rich and famous.

26800 S. Academy Drive, just northwest of Crenshaw Boulevard, off Palos Verdes Drive North. (310) 377-1543.

Currently it's a posh private day school. But Chadwick, founded in 1935, was for decades a posh private *boarding* school favored by Hollywood types too busy to help Junior with his algebra. Alumni include the offspring of Jack Benny, King Vidor, George Burns and Gracie Allen, Ronald Reagan, Hoagy Carmichael, and Art Linkletter. Like many others on this list, Liza Minnelli and her sister Lorna Luft attended but did not graduate. In her shocking memoir *Mommie Dearest,* Christina Crawford writes fondly of Chadwick, which she loved. While Christina was a student here, adoptive mom Joan Crawford allegedly could only torment her from afar.

Green Hills Memorial Park
Where D. Boon is buried.

    27501 S. Western Avenue, just south of Palos Verdes Drive North, Rancho Palos Verdes. Open daily 6:00 A.M.–6:00 P.M. (310) 831-0311.

After founding his hardcore band the Minutemen with pals Mike Watt and George Hurley, the hefty D. Boon soared to punk fame but stayed true to his roots. The band often sang of their hometown, San Pedro, whose expansive harbor is visible from this cemetery. Killed in a van accident while on tour in 1985, Boon now rests here. His shiny black headstone reads, "Beloved Son and Brother, Dennes Dale Boon, April 1, 1958–Dec. 22, 1985," and bears chiseled images of a Stratocaster guitar and a palette—Boon loved painting as well. (The grave is at Lakeview Lawn 365, Plot B, two-thirds of the way up Lakeview Drive, five rows up from the road: look for the "360" marking on the curb.) Hard-drinking poet and avant-garde icon Charles Bukowski is also interred hereabouts—ask at the office for his location.

SAN PEDRO

Walker's Café
As seen in **Chinatown.**

    700 Paseo del Mar, just east of Gaffey Street, facing Point Fermin Park. Opening hours vary: generally midmorning to early evening. (310) 833-3623.

This folksy and faintly nautical café is quite popular with the biker crowd. Surely they admire the authentic 1940s ambience that has made the place popular with location scouts. TV shows and movies filmed here range from *Walker, Texas Ranger* to *Chinatown* to *Gods and Monsters*. In one crucial scene in *Chinatown*, Jack Nicholson slips a pocketwatch under the tire of a car in front of the café so as to discern the exact time of

Walker's Café

his quarry's departure when the car runs over the watch and breaks it.

Korean Friendship Bell
As seen in The Usual Suspects.

South Gaffey Street, at 37th Street, San Pedro, in Angels Gate Park; across a parking lot from the youth hostel. Open daily, 10:00 A.M.–6:00 P.M.

*T*he Usual Suspects was set largely in San Pedro. One key scene takes place on this lonely bluff which boasts a massive metal bell and a sweeping view of the sea. Wind singing in their ears, the characters make a fateful deal in the shadow of the bell, which in real life was a gift from South Korea to commemorate international friendship. As big as a Volkswagen, it hangs inside a wooden shrine painted with lotuses and dragons. Also filmed here were scenes in *Sergeant Bilko, A Few Good Men,* the *Dragnet* movie, and numerous TV shows, including Sammo Hung's *Martial Law.* The nearby basketball court has appeared in athletic-shoe commercials featuring Michael Jordan and Buddhist monks. And Madonna used the adjoining slope in her "Like a Virgin" video.

Korean Friendship Bell

British European Auto
Served as Primary Colors' *campaign headquarters.*

1525 S. Pacific Avenue, at 16th Street, San Pedro. (310) 833-1525.

A stand-up cardboard John Travolta graces the corner of the showroom, and an autographed portrait of the star remains to remind passersby that *Primary Colors* was filmed here. Stickers, hats, and signs were brought in, and cars moved out, to turn the place into campaign headquarters for the film's presidential hopeful, "Jack Stanton." In other scenes the 600 block of Pacific stood in for a New England street.

Cardboard John Travolta at British European Auto

CATALINA

Natalie Wood Drowning Site
Two Harbors, on the northern part of the island. See below for details.

Just after Thanksgiving in 1981 Natalie Wood set sail from Marina del Rey to Catalina. With her husband Robert Wagner, their friend Christopher Walken, and a skipper, they sailed their yacht, *Splendor*, to the island's main harbor at Avalon. (Wood and Wagner had wed on the island years before.) After spending the night in Avalon, the quartet sailed north to the minuscule seaport of Two Harbors. There they raised a few glasses onshore at Doug's Harbor Reef saloon. Reportedly they downed several bottles of champagne before heading back to the boat. What happened there remains a mystery. According to the skipper, Wagner got angry when Wood flirted with Walken, then she stomped off to bed alone. An hour or so later her companions noticed she was missing. Searchers later found her drowned corpse wearing a nightgown, socks, and a jacket, and floating facedown about a mile northeast of Two Harbors, off Blue Cavern Point. No one knows how or why Wood fell overboard. Some say she was too drunk to remove the wet jacket, whose weight would have dragged her down.

WILMINGTON

Banning Residence Museum
As seen in Primary Colors.

> *401 E. M Street, off Avalon Boulevard, in Banning Park. Tours given Tues.–Thurs., 12:30, 1:30, and 2:30 P.M.; Sat.– Sun., 12:30, 1:30, 2:30, and 3:30 P.M. Admission: $3. (310) 548-7777.*

After the Civil War, state senator Phineas Banning wanted to have a railroad line installed that would connect Los Angeles to the rest of the nation; it happened. The rest is history. Now Banning's twenty-three-room Greek Revival house is open to the public. Furnished with Victoriana, it has portrayed many mansions onscreen. *Primary Colors'* huge Thanksgiving feast took place in front of the Banning House, as did the film's interior kitchen scenes.

Banning Residence Museum

LONG BEACH

Gilligan's Island's "Tropic Port"

At the Alamitos Bay Marina, at the very southeast corner of Long Beach. From Ocean Boule-
vard in Long Beach, follow the flow of traffic up Livingston Drive to 2nd Street and the
Naples district. Turn south on Enna Drive to enter the Marina area, which sprawls across
three small islands bounded by Alamitos Bay, Naples Canal, and Rivo Alto Canal.

I t's one of the great moments in TV history. A boat sails through a sunny harbor
and straight into your subconcious: "Just sit right back and you'll hear a tale, a tale
of a fateful trip, / that started from this tropic
port aboard this tiny ship." The first shot in
the opening sequence of *Gilligan's Island*
shows the SS *Minnow* leaving for a "three-
hour tour." In real life that port was in Long
Beach. Alamitos Bay Marina stood in for
Hawaii in this one quick scene during the
opening credits of every episode. If it doesn't
look as tropical as you remember it, that's because they took away the portable palm trees
when the cameras stopped rolling. The actual *Minnow* is supposedly still docked some-

Alamitos Bay Marina, the Minnow's *home*
port

where in Alamitos Bay. (In an ironic footnote, none of the *Gilligan* cast has ever made
a penny from reruns, which have since generated well over $1 billion in profits.)

Queen Mary

1126 Queens Highway, Long Beach, at the southern terminus of the Long Beach Freeway
(Highway 710). From central L.A., take the San Diego Freeway (Highway 405) southeast;
turn south on Highway 710 and take it all the way to the end. The ship is docked in Long
Beach Harbor, south of the Civic Center. Open daily 10:00 A.M.–6:00 P.M. (later hours in
summer). Admission: adults, $15; seniors over 55, $13; children ages 4–11, $9; children un-
der 4, free. (562) 435-3511.

I n its heyday, this gargantuan pleasure liner hosted nearly every celebrity with sea
legs on both sides of the Atlantic. Mary Pickford, Douglas Fairbanks, William
Randolph Hearst, Alfred Hitchcock, Dorothy Lamour, Joan Crawford, the Duke
and Duchess of Windsor, Bing Crosby, Pearl Bailey, Harpo Marx, Anna May Wong,
Elizabeth Taylor, Winston Churchill, and Alec Guinness, to name but a few, voyaged
aboard the *QM* to England and back. A photo exhibit on the Sun Deck chronicles
the celebrity passenger list. The grand old ship eventually retired to a permanent
berth here in Long Beach and started a new career as a filming location. *The Poseidon*

Adventure, Grumpy Old Men, War and Remembrance, Someone to Watch Over Me, and hundreds of other movies and TV shows have been shot here. A mysterious white dome next to the ship used to house the *Spruce Goose,* Howard Hughes's all-wood seaplane. Now that it's migrated elsewhere, film production crews have seized control of the dome. Some of the most elaborate indoor sets ever built, including those for 1999's *Haunting of Hill House,* various sequels in the *Batman* film series, and Denzel Washington's *Virtuosity* are rumored to have been created inside the dome, which is closed to the public.

San Fernando Valley

GLENDALE

Forest Lawn Glendale
Heaven's casting call.

> 1712 S. Glendale Avenue, at Los Feliz Road, east of Griffith Park. Open daily, 8:00 A.M.–5:00 P.M. (800) 204-3131.

Forest Lawn is a graveyard unlike all others, a showplace where hundreds of grassy acres are dotted with reproductions of major artworks, including Michelangelo's *David* and the *Pieta.* An elephantine painting of the Crucifixion is here, along with an Easter Island head, one hundred thousand shrubs, a big stained-glass *Last Supper,* and replicas of historic chapels. A museum houses replicas of the Crown Jewels. Not only that, but an absolute phalanx of entertainers is buried here. Humphrey Bogart, Sammy Davis Jr., and Mary Pickford are in private, inaccessible areas. Clark Gable, Carole Lombard, Red Skelton, David O. Selznick, and Jean Harlow are in the Great Mausoleum. Nat "King" Cole, Jeanette MacDonald, George Burns, Gracie Allen, Clara Bow, and Alan Ladd are in the Freedom Mausoleum. So are Dorothy Dandridge (in the Columbarium of Victory), Larry Fine (in the Sanctuary of Liberation), Chico Marx (in the Sanctuary of Worship), and Gummo Marx (in the Sanctuary of Brotherhood). Walt Disney is in his own garden nearby, marked with a Little Mermaid statue. Robert Young is in the Graceland section. Ethel Waters is in the Gardens of Ascension. Jimmy Stewart is near the Wee Kirk o' the Heather— where Ronald Reagan married his first wife, Jane Wyman. Also at Forest Lawn are Errol Flynn, Spencer Tracy, Joe E. Brown, Sam Cooke, Norma Shearer, W. C. Fields, Lon Chaney, Theda Bara, Aimee Semple McPherson, L. Frank Baum, Louis L'Amour, and more and more. But this place is so vast that it's not easy to find everything you're looking for in one visit. Bring trail mix.

Hillside Strangler Home and Upholstery Shop

Former name: AB Upholstery, 703 E. Colorado Street. Current name: A&M Auto Repair, 703 E. Colorado Street, just east of Glendale Avenue. (818) 545-3625.

In the space of a few short months from late 1977 to early 1978, the bodies of at least ten women were discovered in the hills around Glendale. All had been tortured, raped, and strangled. The nickname-happy media dubbed their putative serial killer "the Hillside Strangler"; yet the police suspected the crimes were the work of at least two men. Then in 1979 a psychotic security guard in Bellingham, Washington, named Kenneth Bianchi confessed that his misogynistic alter ego had killed women there and in California, including several around Glendale a year earlier. He also fingered his cousin, Angelo Buono, in whose auto-upholstery shop several of the murders had taken place. Within hours the police showed up here at 703 East Colorado and arrested a surprised Buono. A search of the shop and the attached living quarters turned up enough evidence to get both men convicted. Buono's AB Upholstery shop, which was set back a bit from the street, has passed through various owners and now houses A&M Auto Repair. The living quarters seem to have been torn down. Bianchi described horrific torture sessions unfolding here, though Buono himself had little to say on the matter. Though both cousins are in jail for life, some longtime Glendale residents to this day cross the street to avoid passing the building. (See also page 30.)

Margot Kidder Trespass House

407 Ross Street, in the northern part of Glendale.

Having made nearly three dozen movies, Margot Kidder is best known for playing Lois Lane in the *Superman* film series. But the actress was in emotional dire straits by the spring of 1996. After associates reported her missing, an international search for Kidder turned up only rumors. Then, three days into the search, cops were called to this house. Its owner had discovered the actress in her backyard. Wandering along the street, a disoriented Kidder had entered the yard and climbed into a woodpile to sleep. The media descended; Kidder later described her crisis to Barbara Walters on national TV.

| BURBANK |

Warner Bros. Studio
Walk in the Waltons' footsteps.

> *4000 Warner Boulevard. Join tour at Gate 4, off Hollywood Way at Olive Avenue. Tours depart hourly October–May, Mon.–Fri., 9:00 A.M.–3:00 P.M.; half-hourly June–September, Mon.–Fri., 9:00 A.M.–4:00 P.M. Admission: adults, $30; children under age 8 not permitted. (818) 954-1744 or (818) 972-8687.*

Only twelve people at a time are permitted on each "VIP tour" around the Warner Bros. lot. Prowl old sets, soundstages, back lots, wardrobe and prop areas, and more via a cute little electric tram. Also on the two-hour itinerary are an introductory film and a memorabilia museum. Check out the *Casablanca* piano and costumes worn by Ingrid Bergman, Audrey Hepburn, John Wayne, and Joan Crawford. Sets used in *The Waltons, The Dukes of Hazzard, Fantasy Island, Bonnie and Clyde, The Music Man,* and many other classics are scattered around this gigantic property. Allowed to step off the tram now and then, visitors can take close-up looks at a mock Western street, production labs, and other busy parts of the studio.

Dalt's Classic American Grill
Where the mighty eat meat loaf.

> *3500 W. Olive Avenue. Open daily, 11:00 A.M.–midnight. (818) 953-7750.*

In the heart of a district crammed full of big studios, this retro grill serves French dip, cheese steak, chicken pot pie, and patty melts to celebrity carnivores. Patrons spotted here include Quentin Tarantino, Robert De Niro, Kevin Costner, Sinbad, Andy Garcia, and the Olsen twins.

NBC Studio
Behind the scenes at The Tonight Show.

> *3000 W. Alameda Avenue, at Olive Avenue. Meet at guest relations/ticket window on the west side of the studio, off California Street. Tours depart hourly fall–spring, Mon.–Fri., 9:00 A.M.–3:00 P.M.; also, weekends and longer weekday hours in summer. Admission: adults, $7; children ages 5–12, $3.75; under age 5, free. (818) 840-3537.*

Walk through the studio inspecting prop warehouses, ongoing set construction, special-effects machinery, and costumes. Cruise the *Tonight Show* set and even the parking lot where Jay Leno leaves his car. But the tour aims at a rank tourist mentality. Tickets to *Tonight Show* tapings—join the studio audience—are available free at the ticket window. Call in advance for a schedule, then pick up your tix the same day as the taping.

Johnny Carson Park

Riverside Drive at Bob Hope Drive, between NBC Studio and Disney Studios. For more information, call Burbank City Hall at (818) 238-5310.

For years it was called Buena Vista Park. But *The Tonight Show* is created across the street at NBC Studio, and after Johnny Carson filmed numerous segments in the park, the city decided to rename it in his honor. Carson had, after all, welcomed America to "beautiful downtown Burbank." An engraved plaque on the premises features his likeness.

Disney Studios

500 S. Buena Vista Street, Burbank. The studio occupies the block bounded by Alameda Avenue, Keystone Street, Riverside Drive, and Buena Vista Street. (818) 560-1000.

When Walt Disney commissioned the first buildings here at his new studio in the late 1930s, he decreed that the hallways all had to be extra wide. Having sunk every dime he earned from *Snow White* (made at his first studio in Silverlake: see page 119) into this new lot, he needed a contingency plan should his business fail. If the halls were wide enough for gurneys to turn around in, Disney reasoned, he could sell the place as a hospital. But Disney's fortunes soared in Burbank. On this lot he created the films that made Disney what it is today: *Fantasia, Bambi, Cinderella, Peter Pan, Mary Poppins, The Jungle Book, The Little Mermaid,* and virtually every other animated or live-action film with the Disney imprint. Things got so good that Walt drew up plans to turn the Burbank lot into an amusement park he dubbed Disneyland. But eventually he realized it would not fit here, so he bought a huge plot in Anaheim. The studio is a veritable fortress: no tours, no visitors, no kidding. You can stand on the street and peer at some of the buildings, especially the eccentric Animation Department buildings visible from Riverside Drive, and the Team Disney building on the other side of the studio. However, there are two legitimate ways to get on the lot. One day a year, usually on a Saturday in early December or late November, Disney sponsors a Christmas Craft Fair. For $3 a head the public is free to enter, ogle the buildings, visit a unique Disney store that opens its doors to all comers only on this one day, and shop for cutesy Christmas crafts. Costumed Disney characters drop in from Anaheim to entertain the throng. Call the number above in early or mid-November for the date. If you can't wait that long, call Audiences Unlimited for possible tickets to live-action sitcoms that might be currently filming on the lot. You don't get to see much on your way to Stage 6, but at least you can say you've been there.

It's a Wrap! Production Wardrobe Sales
Where you can buy costumes used in movies and TV.

3315 W. Magnolia Boulevard, between Lima and California Streets. Open Mon.–Fri. 11:00 A.M.–8:00 P.M.; Sat.–Sun. 11:00 A.M.–6:00 P.M. (818) 567-7366.

Two stories are crammed with racks of shirts, gowns, leggings, boas, hats, bikinis, and more, with a tag on each identifying the film or TV show in which it was worn: from *General Hospital* to *Spin City* to *Hard Copy* to *Melrose Place,* and beyond. Charts on the walls help you decipher the codes, and the cashier can help with ones that aren't on the charts. Also on the walls, framed museum-style and under glass, are complete movie costumes worn by Dustin Hoffman, Billy Crystal, Sean Penn, and others. Though out on the street your purchase looks like any ordinary tank top, you can gloat, knowing a *Baywatch* babe once soaked it with sweat.

Central Casting
Your shot at being in crowd scenes.

220 S. Flower Street, between Olive and Verdugo Avenues, just south of Burbank's city center, one block west of Highway 5. Sign-ups Mon., Wed., and Fri., 10:30–11:30 A.M. Fee: $20. (818) 562-2700.

When they're looking for extras, the studios search here. To get yourself into the photo files from which they choose, appear at the appointed time bearing your passport, or a combination of driver's license and Social Security card, or driver's license and birth certificate—originals only; photocopies will not do. Bring along a list of your measurements, too. Only those age 18 and over need apply. Twenty dollars covers the pictures they take of you—cash only; no checks or credit cards. Dressing well and/or dressing as the particular "type" you believe you should portray is recommended. Frequent calls to the company will keep you apprised of potential jobs.

UNIVERSAL CITY

Universal Studios Hollywood

100 Universal City Plaza, off the Hollywood Freeway at the Universal Center Drive and Lankershim Boulevard exits. Open in summer, daily, 8:00 A.M.–10:00 P.M.; the rest of the year, daily 9:00 A.M.–7:00 P.M. Admission: adults, $39; children ages 3–11, $29; under age 3, free. (818) 622-3801.

Dating back to Universal's pre–theme park days, its "studio tour" is an old standby. Ride a tram through obsolete back lots to glimpse the Bates Motel from *Psycho* as well as sets used in *The Munsters, McHale's Navy, The Lost World,* and other Universal productions. A fake shark and a fake earthquake "menace" every tram. *Whoops*—we ruined the surprise! This is the world's largest TV and film production studio, and an overpriced theme park is here as well. Its rides and attractions are based on *Back to the Future, E.T., Jaws, Jurassic Park, Backdraft, Terminator,* and more. Stunt shows, live revues, and a wet yet explosive *Waterworld* show compete for your attention, while shops and restaurants crowd faux villages replicating New York, London, Paris, Cape Cod, and the Wild West. Actors impersonating Marilyn, Groucho, and the like unnervingly pop up all over the place.

Hard Rock Café Hollywood

1000 Universal Center Drive, #99, in the Universal CityWalk shopping and entertainment complex. Open Sun.–Thurs., 11:00 A.M.–11:00 P.M.; Fri.–Sat., 11:00 A.M.–11:30 P.M. (818) 622-7625.

The "Hollywood" in its name is merely there to excite out-of-towners. It's in Universal City. Big stars occasionally stop by for a snack when they're working at nearby Universal Studios. Valley girl Jennifer Love Hewitt is a habitué. Rock 'n' roll artifacts on display include Elvis Presley's karate outfit, Ringo Starr's pre-Beatles drum kit, a saxophone played by Bill Clinton, and clothes worn by the Monkees and Elton. And don't miss Bob Dylan's jacket adorned with images of Jesus.

Audiences Unlimited

Where you can get free tickets to television tapings.

100 Universal City Plaza, Building 153, Universal City, near Universal Studios. (818) 753-3470 or (818) 506-0043.

Want to see a star up close and in person? It's easy. Most network television sitcoms are still filmed with a live audience. And anyone can get tickets for free—if you know where to ask. Some studios hand out tickets themselves, but most use the services of Audiences Unlimited, a company that exists for the sole purpose of doling out free tickets. The selection of shows changes with each season's cancellations, but at the time of this writing you could get tickets for *3rd Rock from the Sun, That '70s Show, The Drew Carey Show,* or about fifty others. Popular shows fill up way in advance, so call ahead to reserve a seat. Although its address is here, Audiences Unlimited prefers that you not show up in person. Call the numbers above and they'll mail you the tickets, or order them online at: www.tvtickets.com.

STUDIO CITY

CBS Studio Center
From Gunsmoke *to* Seinfeld *and beyond.*

4024 Radford Avenue, north of Ventura Boulevard, just east of Laurel Canyon Boulevard
(818) 655-5000.

When Mack Sennett ran the place, hundreds of silent films were made here with the biggest stars of the day, including Charlie Chaplin. After Republic Pictures took over in 1935, *The Sands of Iwo Jima* and *The Quiet Man* were filmed on the premises, along with all of Gene Autry's and Roy Rogers's movies. A couple of decades later the studio was used exclusively for TV, and brought you *The Wild Wild West* and *Gilligan's Island*—whose lagoon was, amazingly, still here until 1994. Later offerings from this busy and prolific facility include *The Mary Tyler Moore Show* and its spin-offs, *The Bob Newhart Show, Hill Street Blues, St. Elsewhere, thirtysomething, Falcon Crest, Roseanne, Seinfeld, 3rd Rock from the Sun,* and *Just Shoot Me.* Unfortunately, the studio is off-limits to the public and no tours are given, so you are left to merely stand outside and yelp, "Skipper! Professor!"

Jerry's Famous Deli

12655 Ventura Boulevard, near Coldwater Canyon Avenue. Open daily, 24 hours. (818) 980-4245.

Near the studios and open around the clock, this link in the Jerry's chain attracts lots of industry types. Jason Alexander is—or was, at least—a regular; numerous celebs come here for tostadas, schnitzel, triple-decker sandwiches, and matzah balls.

Sportsmen's Lodge Hotel
Kate Smith's home-away-from-home.

12825 Ventura Boulevard, at Coldwater Canyon Avenue. (818) 769-4700.

In the 1940s and '50s a set of man-made lakes, stocked with trout, dotted this property. And a chef at the Sportsmen's Lodge restaurant would cook your catch and serve it up to you. Clark Gable and his pals avidly indulged in this backwoods pastime. In 1962 a hotel was added, luring entertainers from the nearby studios. Lena Horne, Tallulah Bankhead, and Joan Blondell were steady customers. And Kate Smith reportedly used to zip over here directly from the airport. A rustic setting complete with waterfalls, lagoons, lily ponds, swans, and gazebos still attracts stars who crave country comforts. Pat Boone, Aretha Franklin, and country singers including Garth Brooks and Willie Nelson have been spotted here. Scenes from *Melrose Place* and *Beverly Hills 90210* have been shot here, too.

| NORTH HOLLYWOOD |

Barris Kustom Industries
Where the Batmobile was born.

> *10811 Riverside Drive, just east of Lankershim Boulevard, on the north side of the street. Open Mon.–Fri., 8:00 A.M.–6:00 P.M.; Sat., 8:00 A.M.–2:00 P.M. (818) 509-8454.*

Immortalized in Tom Wolfe's book *The Kandy-Kolored Tangerine-Flake Streamline Baby*, this is the headquarters of kar kustomizer George Barris. It was here that he kreated TV's Batmobile, and klassic vehicles for *Rebel without a Cause, Blade Runner, Jurassic Park, Back to the Future, The Love Bug, The Munsters, The Beverly Hillbillies, The Dukes of Hazzard,* and *My Mother the Car.* (Not only that, but Barris is said to have originated the switching of *k*s and *c*s long ago.) He kustomized vehicles for the likes of Liberace, John Wayne, Frank Sinatra, Zsa Zsa Gabor, and—uh-oh—James Dean, who drove too fast in his and died. Today the showroom has a few of Barris's wares on display, and its walls are plastered with stills from films that have used his kars: *Flubber, Beach Blanket Bingo, Corvette Summer, Revenge of the Pink Panther, Grease, Cannonball Run, Hot Rod Hullabaloo* . . . Hey, who's kounting? The cars on display are changed periodically, so you never know what masterpiece you might find. We were privileged to see the original *Flintstones* car and Batmobile, as well as some souped-up muscle cars.

Academy of Television Arts and Sciences
They love Lucy.

> *5220 Lankershim Boulevard, at Magnolia Boulevard. Plaza visible at all times. (818) 754-2800.*

Decisions are made on these premises that make and break careers—these are the people who hand out the Emmy Awards. Done in soft pastels, the open-air Hall of Fame Plaza outside is peopled with big statues and busts commemorating TV greats. Pay your respects to Mary Tyler Moore, Milton Berle, Bill Cosby, Bob Hope, Jackie Gleason, Red Skelton, Ed Sullivan, Carol Burnett, and others. Topping the plaza's fountain is a shiny, humongous replica of an Emmy statuette.

Western Costume
Rent the real thing.

> *11041 Vanowen Street, at Vineland Avenue. Open Mon.–Fri. 8:00 A.M.–5:30 P.M., but an appointment is required. (818) 760-0900.*

This firm is the world's largest wardrobe maker and provider, supplying Hollywood studios since 1912. Millions of costumes occupy a gigantic warehouse, and while meeting studios' needs is the overwhelming focus, you can rent a sampling from what amounts to miles and miles of gear. Call in advance with a general idea of the costume you want—antebellum, alien, whatever; then a professional costumer will outfit you. Rental prices start high ($100 minimum rental price, with an additional $50 dry-cleaning and labor fee), but these clothes are the real thing. The real *fake* thing.

VAN NUYS

Van Nuys Airport
Where a scene from Casablanca *was filmed—but which one?*

> *The airport occupies the area bounded by Woodley Avenue, Vanowen Street, Hayvenhurst Avenue, and Roscoe Boulevard, in Van Nuys; see below for specific locations. (818) 785-8838.*

A lot of people believe that one of the most famous scenes in movie history was shot here: *Casablanca*'s tearful farewell between Humphrey Bogart and Ingrid Bergman ("We'll always have Paris"). This is stated as fact in brochures and guidebooks, magazines, and Web sites. But records kept at the time, and published interviews with crew members who worked on the set, say that scene was shot in a studio, possibly using a half-size plane and midgets in mechanics' uniforms to give the illusion of distance on a soundstage too small for a life-size runway and plane. The confusion probably arose from the fact that a different scene in *Casablanca was,* in fact, filmed here: a short, early, and mostly unnoticed scene showing a minor character getting off a plane. People jump to conclusions when they see the words *"Casablanca"* and "airport" in the same sentence. (The building supposedly used in the shot has now been converted to a private warehouse at 16217 Lindbergh Street, backing onto Waterman Drive just west of Woodley Avenue, Van Nuys.)

In the years since 1942, camera crews have returned here again and again, either to film airport scenes on location or to use the hangars as soundstages. Flicks filmed in part here range from *Starship Troopers* and *The Last Action Hero,* to *Bordello of*

Blood and *Robosaurus.* Mariah Carey, Ozzy Osbourne, Tina Turner, and KISS have shot rock videos here—not all at the same time, fortunately.

This used to be called Los Angeles Metropolitan Airport and was an important pre-LAX hub. Now it has no passenger or commercial flights and is used only for private planes and cargo. To tour the airport, call for a reservation, then go to Millennium Aviation at 16700 Roscoe Boulevard, Monday through Friday at 9:30 or 11:00 A.M.

Van Nuys High School
Lots of illustrious alumni.

6535 Cedros Avenue, at Hamlin Street, just north of Victory Boulevard. (818) 781-2371.

*F*ast Times at Ridgemont High was filmed on this quintessentially Californian campus. And over the years this school has churned out some dazzling alumni, including Marilyn Monroe (who as Norma Jeane Baker met her first husband here), Jane Russell, Robert Redford, Stacy Keach, Don Drysdale, Vince Van Patten, and Paula Abdul. Celebrity madam Heidi Fleiss's mom and at least three *Playboy* centerfolds are Van Nuys alums as well.

TARZANA

Historic Tarzana
The town that Tarzan built.

Edgar Rice Burroughs's garage, theater, and writing quarters are incorporated into a large Colonial-style home near the southeast corner of Tarzana Drive and Reseda Boulevard. The Edgar Rice Burroughs Inc. offices are on the south side of Ventura Boulevard between Avenida Oriente and Avenida Hacienda. Burroughs's estate occupied all the property between Reseda Boulevard and Avenida Oriente, south of Ventura Boulevard all the way to Mulholland Drive.

*I*n 1919, when the San Fernando Valley was wide-open spaces, *Tarzan* author Edgar Rice Burroughs paid $125,000 for a 550-acre ranch here. He named it Tarzana. The American public adored the apeman, and Burroughs's career was soaring. Ambitiously, he bought a herd of swine and tended his extensive fields. He wrote a song called "My Own Tarzana Ranch." By 1922 he was trying to sell off the pigs and subdivide the property for profit, dreaming of single-handedly starting a new town. Among other promotional schemes, he staged a "jungle barbecue" to lure buyers. In 1928 the area's several hundred residents petitioned the U.S. Postal Service for official recognition. In 1930 Tarzana was granted a postmark. It's a uniquely

Californian tale, this transformation from a backwoods to a suburban sprawl, funded by the profits of a fantasy novel. Although Burroughs himself did not stay—moving all the way to Kauai at one point—his kin recently returned and bought a bit of the old property. Some of Burroughs's original buildings have been incorporated into a home (see location cited above), and the offices of the family business that handle the Tarzan trademark remain in his hometown.

CALABASAS

Los Angeles Pet Memorial Park

5068 N. Old Scandia Lane, north of the Ventura Freeway (Highway 101). From the Ventura Freeway, take the Parkway Calabasas exit north, go back a block east on Ventura Boulevard, and turn north to the park on Old Scandia Lane. Open Mon.–Sat., 8:00 A.M.–5:00 P.M.; Sun., 8:00 A.M–7:00 P.M. (818) 591-7037.

The best-known permanent resident at this quaint graveyard for pets is Hopalong Cassidy's horse, Topper, who starred in many films with his master. Silent-era superstars Gloria Swanson and Rudolph Valentino helped start a celebrity stampede by bringing furry corpses here. The office does not hand out lists of famous people's pets' graves. Humphrey Bogart, Alfred Hitchcock, Diana Ross, Steven Spielberg, Bing Crosby, Betty Grable, Charlie Chaplin, and Aaron Spelling are said to have buried their animals here, but most pets' grave markers don't reveal owners' names—just try finding Mae West's monkey. One mystery is whether the circle-eyed *Our Gang* dog Petey is buried here or in a Maryland cemetery; both claim him. (Over the decades, there probably were several Peteys, so both could be right.) In a well-publicized prank a while back that miffed many, a performance artist held a mock funeral here and then buried a store-bought frozen chicken.

NORTHRIDGE

Northridge Earthquake Epicenter

The intersection of Roscoe Boulevard and Wilbur Avenue, in the southern part of the Northridge district of the San Fernando Valley, near Reseda. The Northridge Meadows apartments were at 9565 Reseda Boulevard, just north of Plummer Street.

One of the most destructive earthquakes in California history struck Los Angeles on January 17, 1994, killing dozens, causing billions of dollars in damage, and destroying thousands of buildings. At 6.7 on the Richter scale, it was severe but nowhere near the magnitude of the 1906 San Francisco quake, the 1989 Loma Prieta quake, or the 1992 Landers quake. The Northridge quake's location is what made it so deadly: its epicenter was in the heart of the highly urbanized San Fernando Valley; epicenters for the other three quakes were in more rural areas. Because they lost so much money in the Northridge disaster, all California insurance companies stopped offering earthquake insurance thereafter, sparking a major real estate crisis.

Geologists pinpoint the epicenter as the intersection of Roscoe Boulevard and Wilbur Avenue, a corner like many others in the Valley. A couple of miles north of here, the bottom floor of a shabbily constructed apartment complex called Northridge Meadows collapsed during the quake, trapping and killing everyone inside. For years the building at 9565 Reseda Boulevard, and the empty lot left after it was razed, was a morbid tourist attraction. Today a new and—we hope—sturdier complex, the Parc Ridge, has risen from the rubble.

MISSION HILLS

Carl "Alfalfa" Switzer Death House
10400 Columbus Avenue, near the corner of Sepulveda Boulevard and Devonshire Street.

Button-cute, freckle-faced Carl "Alfalfa" Switzer charmed millions in the *Our Gang* series between 1935 and 1942. After adolescence, though, life grew tougher. Finding few roles, the short-tempered actor made ends meet as a hunting and fishing guide. In 1959 Switzer borrowed a hunting dog from his pal Moses Stiltz. After the dog ran off, Switzer posted a $35 reward for its return. The dog was returned, but Stiltz and Switzer scuffled over who owed how much cash to whom. When it was all over, Switzer lay dead here in a bedroom of Stiltz's home. Stiltz's shooting of the actor was ruled justifiable homicide and he went free.

San Fernando Mission Cemetery
Fred should have been nicer to Ethel.

11160 Stranwood Avenue, at Sepulveda Boulevard. Open during Daylight Savings Time, daily, 8:00 A.M.–6:00 P.M.; the rest of the year, daily, 8:00 A.M.–5:00 P.M. (818) 361-7387.

This Catholic cemetery's most famous grave belongs to Ritchie Valens, who had a hit with "La Bamba" but died while still a teen in the same plane crash that killed Buddy Holly and the Big Bopper in 1959. The marker on his grave (2-248-C) bears song titles and the singer's actual surname, Valenzuela. Nearby is actor William Frawley (4-66-C), unforgettable as *I Love Lucy*'s Fred Mertz. Chuck Connors is in section C; Walter Brennan, William Bendix, and George Gobel are in section D. Also interred here are June Sprigg and Thomas Noonan of *Our Gang*—not to mention Cecil B. DeMille's son John (12-5-BB), and Clarence Nash, the voice of Donald Duck (25-47-F). Staffers here gladly distribute free maps showing stars' graves. Nearby San Fernando Mission lends a dramatic flair.

Eden Memorial Park
You bet your life he's here.

> *11500 Sepulveda Boulevard, at Rinaldi Street, at the northern edge of Mission Hills. Open Sun.–Fri., 9:00 A.M.–5:00 P.M. (323) 877-5529.*

Both Lenny Bruce and Groucho Marx are interred in this sedate Jewish cemetery. But staffers are loath to point out the exact locations of any famous graves because of a traumatic incident in which Groucho's ashes were stolen from the park— though they were later returned. So, fans trying to pay homage to two of history's greatest comedians face a challenge in finding their final resting places.

LAKEVIEW TERRACE

Rodney King Beating Site
On an open roadside directly across from the Mountainback Apartments, 11777 Foothill Boulevard, near Osborne Street.

After a high-speed chase in November 1993, cops halted motorist Rodney King on this spot; he was drunk and squabbled with the officers. They responded by beating King to within an inch of his life for no apparent reason. When it was over, King had sustained a broken leg, numerous skull fractures, a broken eye socket, and permanent facial nerve damage. A resident at the Mountainback Apartments happened to videotape the entire incident, and the trial that ensued would become one of America's most famous ever. After an all-white jury acquitted the four white cops who had attacked the African American King, rioting erupted across the Southland. King would later win a settlement against the city, but this minor victory did little to assuage the frazzled nerves of the black community. The patch of ground here where it all started remains essentially unchanged from that day.

TUJUNGA

E.T. House
7121 Lonzo Street, at the northern fringe of Tujunga.

Steven Spielberg's 1982 film about a suburban child who befriends an abandoned alien jerked many a heartstring. The San Gabriel Mountains soar behind this astoundingly middle-class home, which served as that of the film's sympathetic young Earthling. The house's appearance was altered only slightly for the film.

CHATSWORTH

Spahn Ranch
Manson Family commune on old western-movie ranch.

Former name: Spahn Ranch. Current name: Country Oaks Estate, 23000 Santa Susana Pass Road, across the street from the Church at Rocky Peak, which is at 22601 Santa Susana Pass Road, Chatsworth. From the San Fernando Valley, take Topanga Canyon Boulevard all the way to the north end of the valley in Chatsworth, turn west on Santa Susana Pass Road, and go about a mile until you see the large Church at Rocky Peak. You can also take the Ronald Reagan Freeway (Highway 118) west from the San Fernando Valley, exit at Rocky Peak Road, and come back to the ranch along Santa Susana Pass Road.

Charles Manson and his followers moved to a ramshackle mountain ranch in the late 1960s to escape the stress of living in L.A. Its owner, George Spahn, for years had rented out the ranch as a western-movie set, but by the time Manson arrived, it was half abandoned. Spahn was old and blind, and kept only a few ranch hands around to maintain the property. So when the Manson Family offered to help out in lieu of rent, Spahn welcomed them. Over twenty of them moved into the old movie-set buildings. Lynette Fromme became Spahn's nursemaid. It is he who reportedly nicknamed her "Squeaky"—based on the sounds she made when he fondled her. The Family had their happiest times here: singing, doing drugs, having sex, listening mesmerized as Charlie ranted. He took smiling pictures of each of them around the property.

But a series of small crises in August 1969 pushed Manson over the edge: it was from here that he sent his minions out to commit the Tate and the La Bianca murders, on August 8 and 9, respectively (see pages 91 and 120). The police raided the ranch immediately after the killings and arrested Manson—for car theft. He was released, and the Family moved out to the desert, supposedly after killing the ranch hand who had snitched on them. There Charlie was finally caught. The ranch burned down in a wildfire not long after and for years was a fenced-off wasteland. Fanatics would scale the fence and trespass on the property to look for remnants of the Family.

New owners have completely rebuilt the property. The multipurpose operation, renamed Country Oaks Estate, has a senior citizens' board-and-care residence, a kennel, stables, and a staging ground for animal shows. Since the area is now populated, you can't just come in and wander around without a reason. (Perhaps you have an aunt or a palomino that needs somewhere to stay?) Do *not* mention the word "Manson," or even "Spahn," to anyone working here—that's the fastest way to get kicked off the property. Some of the outer areas of the former ranch have been incorporated into the new Santa Susana Mountain Park.

Oakwood Memorial Park
Where Fred and Ginger no longer dance.

> 22601 Lassen Street, at Andora Avenue. Open daily 8:30 A.M.–5:00 P.M. (818) 341-0344.

I s this an amazing coincidence or what? Though offscreen they were not a couple, Fred Astaire and Ginger Rogers both happen to be buried here. Fred is just about right smack in the middle of the park: Sequoia section G, lot 82, space 4. Ginger lies southwest of there in the Vale of Memory, section E, lot 303, space 1. And actress Gloria Grahame (aka Hallward, aka Ray) lies near the park's eastern edge in the Pioneer section, lot 242, space 8. Also here is *Hogan's Heroes* star Bob Crane, viciously murdered in an Arizona motel room in 1978. He lies in the Oak Knoll section (lot 34B, space 8) just northeast of Fred Astaire.

San Gabriel Valley

ALTADENA

Mountain View Cemetery
Superman cannot escape from here.

> 2400 N. Fair Oaks Avenue, at Woodbury Road. Open daily 8:00 A.M.–5:00 P.M. (626) 794-6967 or (800) 468-1095.

I n one *Seinfeld* episode George's fiancée Susan dies from licking too many wedding-invitation envelopes. The funeral scene for that episode was filmed here. Then, after *Seinfeld* went off the air, Jerry held a faux funeral for the show here. As comics including Garry Shandling and Paul Reiser "wept" around the "grave," Jerry buried his old material. That's a lotta yuks for hallowed ground. Permanent residents here include George Reeves, who played Superman on TV and died in 1959, an apparent suicide. Zane Grey was cremated on the premises, and Glenn Miller, lost at sea, is remembered here with a cenotaph. Also here are the graves of Richter-scale inventor Charles Richter and California avocado king Rudolph Hass. (Before Mountain View was founded in 1882, locals buried their dead virtually in their own backyards.) This cemetery uses a horse-drawn hearse; but its administrators can also arrange to have your loved ones' ashes scattered in outer space.

> PASADENA

Fenyes Mansion
As seen in Being There.

> 470 W. Walnut Street, at Orange Grove Boulevard. Open Thurs.–Sun. 1:00–4:00 P.M. Admission: adults, $4, children, $3; under age 12, free. (626) 577-1660.

This flamboyant white 1905 Beaux Arts mansion was featured prominently in Peter Sellers's 1979 film *Being There*, in which a simpleminded gardener is thrust into the world of high-stakes politics. The mansion was also a popular backdrop in westerns and other genre films from the early days of moviemaking.

> SAN MARINO

The Huntington Library, Art Collections, and Botanical Gardens

> 1151 Oxford Road, at Allen Road. Open Memorial Day–Labor Day: Tues.–Sun. 10:30 A.M.–4:30 P.M.; the rest of the year: Tues.–Fri., noon–4:30 P.M.; Sat.–Sun. 10:30 A.M.–4:30 P.M. Admission: adults, $8.50; students, $6; children under age 12, free. (626) 405-2100.

Nearly 130 acres of landscaped gardens flank a palatial library and art gallery that houses Thomas Gainsborough's adorable painting *Blue Boy*. Filmmakers cannot resist the Palm Garden, the Desert Garden, the Rose Garden, the Japanese Garden, the Zen Garden, the Shakespeare Garden, the Subtropical Garden, the Australian Garden, or the Jungle Garden. Productions shot here include *The Wedding Singer, A Midsummer Night's Dream, My Best Friend's Wedding, The Nutty Professor, The Great Gatsby, Indecent Proposal, The Little Princess, The Adventures of Rocky and Bullwinkle, Fantasy Island, Matlock, Star Trek, Sliders, Beverly Hills 90210, Beverly Hills Ninja,* and tons more.

| ARCADIA |

The Arboretum of Los Angeles County
301 N. Baldwin Avenue, just south of Highway 210, next to Santa Anita Park Race Track. Open daily 9:00 A.M.–4:30 P.M. Admission: adults, $5; students, $3. (626) 821-3222.

More movies have been filmed "on location" here than perhaps anywhere else in the world. The premiere exotic filmmaking backdrop since the 1930s, the Arboretum has stood in for Hawaii (*Waikiki Wedding*), Thailand (the original *Anna and the King of Siam*), Devil's Island (*Passage to Marseille*), the Mississippi Delta (*Gambler from Natchez*), and every jungle from Brazil to the Congo. Some great movies were partly filmed here: *Notorious, The Best Years of Our Lives, Marathon Man.* And so were some of the worst: *Attack of the Giant Leeches, Bomba and the Golden Idol, Cobra Woman, Pygmy Island.* Many of the Tarzan movies were made here (we're still looking for a copy of *Tarzan and the Slave Girl*), as were scenes from *Wayne's World* and *Terminator 2: Judgment Day.* Several crew members recall filming parts of *The African Queen* here, though officially it was shot entirely in Africa and England. But to many, the Arboretum is most famous as the setting for TV's *Fantasy Island,* including the opening scene where Tattoo rings the bell and shouts, "De plane! De plane!" (It was filmed at the Queen Anne cottage on the lake.) The Arboretum was also the setting for many episodes of *Mission: Impossible, The Love Boat, Lassie,* and *Unsolved Mysteries.*

| SIERRA MADRE |

Invasion of the Body Snatchers Hometown
There goes the neighborhood.

> Sierra Madre town square, at the intersection of Sierra Madre Boulevard and Baldwin Avenue, in the center of Sierra Madre, in the northern part of the San Gabriel Valley, east of Pasadena and north of Arcadia.

Don't trust anyone in Sierra Madre. They're all outer-space aliens, and they've come to Earth to steal our souls! It must be true—*Invasion of the Body Snatchers* was a documentary, wasn't it? Okay, so maybe not. But the 1956 sci-fi classic *was* filmed in Sierra Madre's town square. Scenes in which aliens mimic the behavior of humans they're replaced, unload pods from the trucks, identify the film's lead characters as nonaliens, and chase them into the hills were all filmed in this picturesque square, which will seem eerily familiar if you have seen the movie. Scenes from other

films have been shot here since then, including Hitchcock's *Family Plot,* Adam San-
dler's *Wedding Singer,* and most recently, the Danny DeVito comedy *Drowning
Mona.*

LA PUENTE

The Donut Hole

15300 E. Amar Road, at Hacienda Boulevard, La Puente. Open daily 5:00 A.M.–midnight.
(626) 968-2912.

One of the world's most famous fast-food stands, this looks like two giant
doughnuts half sunk into the ground with a building in between. Customers
drive through the doughnut holes to pick up their orders. A masterpiece of the "pro-
grammatic" architectural style, in which a building's shape reveals its function, the
Donut Hole has survived unchanged for decades. You may have seen it in the background of commercials, music videos, and TV shows set in Los Angeles. Legend has
it that local newlyweds take advantage of the sexual symbolism and drive through
the doughnut tunnel en route to their honeymoons.

CITY OF INDUSTRY

McDonald's Production Studio

17030 E. Green Drive, at Gale Avenue. (626) 965-5920.

It looks like a regular McDonald's. But it's a *mock* McDonald's where the company
tapes its TV ads. This impostor has also appeared on *The Drew Carey Show* and
other productions—whenever they need the look of the real thing without the actual
patrons dribbling Special Sauce. The studio is clearly visible through a chain-link
fence that surrounds it. Signs posted on the fence make it known that you can't come
in, much less eat here—though many a confused, hungry motorist has been lured by
the gleaming sign.

Outer Los Angeles County and Nearby

AGUA DULCE

Vasquez Rocks Natural Area

10700 W. Escondido Canyon Road, Agua Dulce. (Former name: Vasquez Rocks County Park.) From Santa Clarita in northern Los Angeles County, take Highway 14 east for about 18 miles and exit onto Escondido Canyon Road. Go back westward 2 miles to the entrance of the park, which is on the south side of the road. Generally open during daylight hours. (661) 268-0840.

Remember how Captain Kirk always ended up trapped on some desert planet, battling malevolent life forms and seducing alien females? Sorry, but that wasn't really outer space—it was Vasquez Rocks. The geological formations in this back corner of L.A. County are so striking and bizarre that not only were dozens of the original *Star Trek* episodes filmed here, but also several *Star Trek* movies. The film version of *The Wild Wild West* is one of the countless westerns shot amid these crags and pinnacles. Classics like *Lost Planet* and *Charge of the Light Brigade* had scenes that were filmed here, as did *Rambo*. The landscape was a natural for the backdrop of the *Flintstones* movie. And "African" rocks in *The Lion King* were based on sketches made here. Mulder and Scully faced evil here in an *X-Files* episode, and David Carradine kung-fued no-goodniks under its desert sun. The park is named after murderous bandit Tiburcio Vasquez, who terrorized California in the late 1800s. He was a hero to the many Mexicans on whom he lavished his bounty, though not to the gringos he robbed and killed. After a raid he usually retreated to his private hideaway here—the authorities could never find him among these rocks. He was eventually captured elsewhere and hanged.

LA VERNE

United Methodist Church
As seen in The Graduate.

3205 D Street, between Foothill Boulevard and Bonita Avenue, across from Bonita High School, at the eastern edge of Los Angeles County. (909) 593-2013.

In the climactic scene of the 1967 film *The Graduate*, Dustin Hoffman's character has finally decided not to let the love of his life marry another man. He dashes to the church halfway through the wedding. He bangs on a huge window overlooking the congregation and shouts her name ("Elaine!"). Though the scene was supposed to be taking place in Santa Barbara, it was actually shot at this neighborhood church in a remote area of Los Angeles County. Nothing has been altered since the filming, although the film crew installed and removed a set of stairs out front that appears in the movie. The window is still there; enter the church to see it on the second story. The room behind it where Hoffman stood is still called "The Cry Room." Local couples getting married here frequently reenact the banging-on-the-window-and-whisking-away-the-bride scene. Mike Myers and company came here to film a parody sequence of the *Graduate* scene for *Wayne's World 2.*

SAN BERNARDINO

First McDonald's Site and Museum
1398 N. E Street, at 14th Street. Open Mon.–Fri. 10:00 A.M.–5:00 P.M. Admission: free. (909) 885-6324.

In 1940, long before Ray Kroc turned McDonald's into the evil empire it is today, Maurice and Richard McDonald opened a small restaurant on this site, serving barbecued ribs and pork sandwiches. Carhops brought food to sedans' windows. In 1948 they revamped it, jettisoning the carhops and menu, and on December 12, 1948, reopened as McDonald's Hamburgers, with paper-wrapped burgers, disposable utensils, and quick service. The idea immediately took off, and they opened eight more outlets over the next six years. Enter Ray Kroc and . . .

But this is where it all started. Yes, there are other "first" McDonald's—the one in Downey is actually the oldest functioning McDonald's (see page 137); the one in Des Plaines, Illinois, is actually the first Ray Kroc–owned, *corporate* McDonald's; the one in Phoenix, Arizona, is actually the first one to have the golden arches. But *this* was the first one of them *all.* Sadly, the original building was torn down in 1972, replaced with a new one in 1974. It is now the headquarters of the Juan Pollo chicken-restaurant chain, but a McDonald's museum is on the premises. (It's "unofficial"—i.e., not sponsored by the McDonald's Corporation, which never

First McDonald's site and museum

had any connection with this site.) Most of its memorabilia was donated by locals who ate here long ago. Check out old promotional toys, "Happy Meal" boxes, trading cards, McDonald's play-area equipment, Ronald McDonald dolls, and more. The same space also encompasses a small museum devoted to the history of Route 66. A historical marker points the way to the site.

TheCentralCoast

Ventura/Santa Barbara Area

SIMI VALLEY

The Ronald Reagan Presidential Library and Museum
Yo-yos and missiles.

> 40 Presidential Drive, at the western end of town, off Madera/Olsen Road, 2 miles south of Highway 118. Open daily 10:00 A.M.–5:00 P.M. Admission: adults, $5; seniors, $3; children under age 16, free. (800) 410-8354.

Learn in excruciating detail how the star of *Bedtime for Bonzo* and *Girls on Probation* became the Leader of the Free World. Follow Reagan's thrilling life, from an unremarkable Illinois boyhood to naps taken during Cabinet meetings. Stand agog at an actual cruise missile—presumably sans nuclear warhead—in the middle of the museum ("We begin bombing in five minutes"). Exhibits include Reagan's saddles, videos of the 1981 Hinckley shooting, and a rotating selection of off-kilter Christmas gifts that average Americans sent to the White House. Does the museum gloss over embarrassing moments like the invasion of Grenada and the firing of the nation's air-traffic controllers? No! These topics are broached via interactive exhibits that let *you* do the firing. Just don't look for anything here about the Iran-contra scandal. A replica of the Oval Office stands, oddly, next to the toilets. Reagan-themed souvenirs in the gift shop include Reagan yo-yos, erasers, knives (handy for assassination attempts), wine goblets, jelly beans, stuffed elephants, and even Reagan golf balls.

SANTA BARBARA

Juana Maria's Grave
Inspiration for Island of the Blue Dolphins.

In the cemetery of Mission Santa Barbara, at the top of Laguna Street, where it intersects with Los Olivos Street. The cemetery is to the right of the mission building; Juana Maria's plaque is at the back of the cemetery, near the exit gate. Open daily 9:00 A.M.–5:00 P.M. Admission: adults, $3; children under age 12, free. (805) 682-4713.

Island of the Blue Dolphins, the classic children's book and film about a girl who lived completely alone for years on an isolated island, was based on a true story. A small group of Gabrielino Indians had for centuries been living off the California coast on what is now called San Nicolas Island. (It's the most distant member of the Channel Islands archipelago and cannot be visited under any circumstances: it's now part of the Navy's top-secret Pacific Missile Test Center's Sea Test Range, used to monitor Star Wars–era weapons and to service supersonic spy planes.) By the 1830s conflicts with fur trappers and conversion-happy Spanish missionaries had left the Gabrielinos in a sorry state. In 1835 the Catholic padres sent a ship to evacuate the islanders "for their own safety." All the Indians were brought aboard, but at the last minute one of the Indian women, realizing her son had been left ashore, dived into the water and swam back to the island. A storm arose, and the ship was forced back to the mainland. Then it sank. When the woman located her son, he was dead, and all her people were gone. She found herself completely, totally, absolutely alone. For an incredible seventeen years she lived all by herself, scavenging for food, never seeing another soul. She was finally rescued by a hunter searching for sea otters. He brought her back to Santa Barbara, where, ironically, she died within a few weeks. She was baptized "Juana Maria" (her real name is not known) and buried in the Indian cemetery at the Santa Barbara Mission. Her grave plaque is still there, though it may not be over her actual grave, which was left unmarked to discourage nineteenth-century rubberneckers: after death she became a celebrity as "the Lone Woman of San Nicolas Island" and the last surviving member of her tribe.

SANTA YNEZ

The Reagan Ranch
Yet another in a long series of Western White Houses.

> 3333 Refugio Road, in the Santa Ynez Mountains above Refugio State Beach, south of Santa
> Ynez. Reagan Ranch Office (not on the property, but at 812B Anacapa Street, in Santa Bar-
> bara): (805) 957-1980.

Ronald and Nancy Reagan bought this lofty 688-acre spread in 1974 and added their own personal touches. Soon the little nineteenth-century house at Rancho del Cielo had jelly bean dispensers, faux-brick linoleum, and orange Naugahyde chairs. During his presidency Reagan spent about a year here altogether—ridin', canoein', choppin' wood, cuttin' taxes, and hostin' world leaders such as Mikhail Gorbachev and Margaret Thatcher. Supporters say Reagan recharged his batteries here; detractors wonder who was running the country when Reagan was spending nearly 15 percent of his presidency on vacation. After formally announcing that the ex-president was ill with Alzheimer's, Nancy put the ranch up for sale at $5.95 million. The ultra-conservative Young America's Foundation bought it in 1998, planning to use it as part of a training program for collegiate politicos who want to continue where Reagan left off. Viewing the ranch as a national shrine à la Monticello, staffers are preserving it intact: monogrammed cowboy boots, coffee cups, bedside Bibles, windbreakers, taxidermed jackalopes, and all. Due to zoning status and perilous roads, the ranch is not yet open to the public. By prior arrangement, staffers will show the ranch to serious supporters (a Reagan Ranch "Trailblazer" is one who donates $1,000; a "Pioneer" gives $250,000).

LOS OLIVOS

Neverland Ranch
Michael Jackson's private universe.

> About 6 miles north of Los Olivos, between Figueroa Mountain Road and Foxen Canyon
> Road.

Michael Jackson burst onto the world stage in 1969 as an adorable eleven-year-old singing sensation. But by the early 1990s he had metamorphosed into a one-man freak show. Vehemently denying what clearly looked like botched plastic surgeries, Jacko also faced accusations of pedophilia. To escape the nightmare of the real world, he retreated to a vast ranch that he named, with an almost self-deprecating irony, Neverland. Ensconced with a pet chimp, a battalion of yes-men, and more money than anyone could count, he created a childish fantasy world where he could do as he wished without anybody watching. It was from here that he gave a much-anticipated speech in 1993, televised around the world, addressing rumors about his skin-lightening treatments, drug addiction, and unproven child-molestation allegations. He almost wept recalling how the cops had humiliatingly examined "my penis, my buttocks," and other body parts, seeking discolorations his accusers claimed to have seen. As far as anyone knows, Michael still lives here, though the veil of secrecy around Neverland is almost impenetrable. Most locals agree that the main entrance to the ranch is on Figueroa Mountain Road about six miles north of Los Olivos, overlooking the Santa Ynez Valley, but the ranch is so big that it seems to have another entrance on Foxen Canyon Road. Nothing is visible from the road except a gate and a steely-eyed guard who chases away rubberneckers with ruthless efficiency.

Fess Parker Winery and Vineyard
The last outpost for coonskin caps.

> 6200 Foxen Canyon Road, 7 miles north of Highway 154 in Los Olivos. Or, from Highway 101, take Zaca Station Road north for 5 miles to Foxen Canyon Road. Tasting room open daily 10:00 A.M.–5:00 P.M.; tours at 11:00 A.M., 1:00 P.M., and 3:00 P.M. (805) 688-1545.

It all started one evening in 1954, as Walt Disney watched the giant-radioactive-ant extravaganza *Them!* He was struck by the screen presence of an actor named Fess Parker. Disney tapped him for a starring role in a new TV program. Fess Parker immediately became one of the superstars of the midfifties. He didn't merely portray frontiersman Davy Crockett on Disney's early *Disneyland* TV shows: he *was* Davy Crockett, the very essence of the American spirit. Every boy in America threw a tantrum until he got a coonskin cap like Davy's. At Disneyland's grand opening, fans mobbed Fess. In the '60s the towering actor (he's six foot six) went on to further stardom as Daniel Boone. These days Fess has reinvented himself as a master vintner. His classy winery draws oenophiles from far and wide  who sample premium Chardonnays and Syrahs in a friendly tasting room. Fess himself drops by regularly. Best of all, the gift shop still sells Davy Crockett and Daniel Boone souvenirs—knives, videos, frontier cookbooks. This is one of the last places on earth where you can still buy an authentic adult-size Davy Crockett coonskin cap, as even Disneyland only sells them in kiddie sizes.

PHOTO COURTESY OF FESS PARKER WINERY AND VINEYARD, 1999

GUADALUPE

Cecil B. DeMille's *Ten Commandments* Archaeological Site

Under Guadalupe-Nipomo Dunes Preserve, at the western end of Main Street, 5 miles west of Guadalupe. To reach the dunes from San Luis Obispo or Santa Barbara, take Highway 101 to Santa Maria, exit onto Main Street (Highway 166), and take it west all the way past Guadalupe to the beach at the end. The Dunes Center is (for now) at 951 Guadalupe Street, near 10th Street, north of Main in central Guadalupe. (It's scheduled to move a block north to 1055 Guadalupe Street sometime in 2000.) Center open Fri., 2:00–4:00 P.M.; Sat.–Sun., noon–4:00 P.M. (805) 343-2455.

A vast, extravagant, sumptuous Egyptian city lies buried beneath the sand dunes of California's central coast. But it wasn't made by Egyptians: Cecil B. DeMille put it there in 1923. That year he and over four thousand actors and crew members arrived in these trackless dunes to make the era's most lavishly produced epic: *The Ten Commandments*—not to be confused with DeMille's 1956 remake. The astounding set was rivaled in magnificence only by the famed Babylon set built in Los Angeles for *Intolerance*. But Babylon is gone; DeMille's Egypt remains, though cleverly hidden. When the film was done, he ordered the set buried in sand: twenty-one sphinxes, four towering statues of Ramses, city gates as tall as a ten-story building, and over five hundred *tons* of Egyptian-style artwork and statuary. DeMille later wrote that he was half hoping archaeologists would someday be shocked to discover the "ruins."

Ah, but their location was pinpointed in the '80s. Lack of funds keep them from being excavated. The precise spot is kept secret to discourage looters, and even if you visit the dunes and find a bust of Osiris or whatever, you are legally required to hand it over to the rangers who guard the preserve. The Dunes Center focuses on natural history but has an exhibit about the film and ruins, including various bits of Egyptiana that have surfaced over the years. (When they finally excavate the entire set, most of it will be displayed here.) You can also learn about the Dunites, a wacky anarchistic commune that lived near the ruins for decades.

SANTA MARIA

Santa Maria Inn
Valentino slept here.

801 S. Broadway, at Morrison Avenue, Santa Maria. (805) 928-7777.

Built in 1917, this English-style landmark was a favorite hitching post for Hollywood types en route to San Simeon and Hearst Castle. Complete with a taproom, coach room, and wine cellar, it maintains a long tradition of lodging the famous: a sampling includes Charlie Chaplin, Clark Gable, Jean Harlow, Gregory Peck, Shirley Temple, Marlene Dietrich, Marilyn Monroe, Bette Davis, John Wayne, Joan Fontaine, Jack Benny, Basil Rathbone, Oliver Hardy, Eddie Cantor, Ignacy Paderewski, Jackie Coogan, John Candy, and (while filming *G.I. Jane*) Demi Moore. Extensive additions have somewhat deglamorized the exterior. But in the older wing, gold stars on guest-room doors are engraved with the names of those who stayed within: the Rudolph Valentino Suite is said to be haunted.

San Luis Obispo County

SAN LUIS OBISPO

Madonna Inn
Wash like a Neanderthal.

100 Madonna Road, near Highway 101, at the southern end of San Luis Obispo. (805) 543-3000 or (800) 543-9666.

In the mid–twentieth century when theme parties and theme restaurants were at their zenith, Alex and Phyllis Madonna (their actual names!) designed and built this hotel. No 2 of its 109 wacky guest rooms are alike. The popular Caveman Room features walls, ceiling, and floor fashioned of rough natural rock, crags and all—even in the bathroom. Leopard-print bedding completes the picture. Elsewhere you'll encounter cherubs, waterfalls, chandeliers, and heart-shaped furniture. Hilarious surprises lurk everywhere. Past guests include Art Linkletter and Flip Wilson, though staffers keep mum about the current celebs who visit. *Blue Heaven* is among several movies filmed here.

SAN SIMEON

Hearst Castle

750 Hearst Castle Road, San Simeon, 7 miles north of Cambria, off Highway 1. Open for tours (reservations recommended) daily, 8:20 A.M.–3:20 P.M. (later in summer). Tours: adults, $14; children ages 6–12, $8. (800) 444-4445 or (805) 927-2020.

William Randolph Hearst was a towering, flabby, and almost freakishly ugly dork who bore more than a passing resemblance to Boris Karloff playing Frankenstein's monster. His squeaky voice and awkward mannerisms put everyone near him ill at ease. So you'd think he wouldn't be very popular on the Hollywood social circuit. Then again, he *was* the most powerful man on earth, and his villa at San Simeon *was* the most magnificent private home ever built. Throughout the '20s and '30s Hearst Castle saw a veritable parade of world leaders and superstars, from Winston Churchill and J. Paul Getty to Charlie Chaplin, Joan Crawford, and Clark Gable. Watching over all of this was Hearst's mistress, Marion Davies, a once beautiful gold-digging showgirl whose perky hostessing skills were tempered only by ill-concealed alcoholism.

Originally named La Cuesta Encantada, now officially titled Hearst San Simeon State Historical Monument, but known to everyone as Hearst Castle, this place was opulent beyond imagination: Hearst bought European castles and Renaissance buildings, had them disassembled stone by stone, and then reassembled here. Every trinket and end table was a priceless antique. Whispered legends tell of star-studded sex soirees, with Oscar-winning actors hopping from bed to bed. But if it happened, it was not sanctioned by Hearst himself, who—despite abandoning his wife and living openly with Davies—was a party-pooping prude who expelled unmarried visitors whom he suspected of sleeping together. He rigidly enforced dozens of strictures and rituals on his freewheeling guests.

Incredibly, the whole place was built with borrowed money: not only was Hearst not rich, he was millions upon millions of dollars in debt. He just looked and acted wealthy, so everyone thought he was.

By the late '30s the party atmosphere at San Simeon had turned sour. Hearst's ultra-right-wing politics offended liberal Hollywood. Orson Welles's *Citizen Kane,* satirizing Hearst, was the last straw. Hearst moved out in 1947 and his family later donated the property to the state. Now the hoi polloi can tour the splendor on guided walks that gloss over the juicy stuff.

CHOLAME

James Dean Death Site

A few yards east of the Jack Ranch Café, adjacent to the restaurant's parking lot, on the north side of Highway 46 near the intersection of Highway 41, in the town of Cholame, which is 26 miles east of Paso Robles. Memorial always visible. Jack Ranch Café open Mon.–Thurs., 6:00 A.M.–8:00 P.M.; Fri., 6:00 A.M.–9:00 P.M.; Sat., 7:00 A.M.–8:00 P.M. Sun., 8:00 A.M.–9:00 P.M. (805) 238-5652.

On September 30, 1955, James Dean was rocketing down this road in his souped-up new Porsche when a car coming in the other direction slowed down as if to make a turn. "He'll see us," James reportedly remarked to his passenger, a mechanic who had come along to help prepare the car for a hot-rod race in Salinas. They turned out to be the Rebel's final words. The other car, a Ford, turned directly into the Porsche's path, and the rest is bloody history. Fans around the world went into shock, and the now legendary date 9-30-55 became a sort of iconographic shorthand for the broken dreams of the 1950s. In the mid-'80s a Japanese businessman installed a chromium-and-steel memorial to the event (James Dean is practically a deity in Japan) on the approximate site of the crash, in the parking lot of what is now called the Jack Ranch Café.

Monterey Coast

BIG SUR

Henry Miller Library
Remembering the racy writer.

> *Highway 1 in Big Sur, one-quarter mile south of Nepenthe Restaurant, 35 miles south of Carmel. Open April–November, Thurs.–Sun., 11:00 A.M.–6:00 P.M.; winter hours variable. (831) 667-2574.*

In 1944 the controversial author came to Big Sur and resolved to "find peace" and "do the work I was made to do." He spent nearly twenty prolific years here in the damp forest. After Miller's death longtime friend and confidant Emil White converted his own Big Sur home into this library devoted to the writer and stocked it with Miller's books, pictures, and artifacts. Fans come from all over the world to browse the shelves, gaze at Miller memorabilia, and attend concerts, workshops, and other arts events including poetry readings held every Sunday afternoon, in season.

CARMEL AND PEBBLE BEACH

Cypress Inn
Owned by Doris Day.

> *Lincoln Street at Seventh Avenue, on the northeast corner, in Carmel. (831) 624-3871 or (800) 443-7443.*

Doris Day lives in Carmel and owns this 1929 Spanish Colonial hotel. Lavishly tiled, it offers verandas, beamed ceilings, and ocean views. Posters from Day's movies decorate the bar. Yet the inn's popularity has less to do with its owner's film career than the fact that she is an avid animal rights activist. This place is pet-friendly—rare for any hotel, especially one so elegant. Animals are allowed in every one of its guest rooms.

Mission Ranch
Owned by Clint Eastwood.

26270 Dolores Street, Carmel, south of downtown, near the mission. (831) 624-6436.

Carmel is where the *Dirty Harry* star settled down, was elected mayor, and became a local businessman. His Hog's Breath Inn Restaurant, home of the Enforcer Burger, has shut down. But Eastwood bought this hotel a few years ago and filled it with furniture he designed himself. Built in and around an 1850s farmhouse, the place evokes more of a *Paint Your Wagon* ambience than an *Eiger Sanction* one, and is augmented with cozy fireplaces, white fences, and green pastures. You might recognize it as the place where Troy Donahue romped in *A Summer Place,* a sappy drama supposedly set in Maine. The hotel's piano bar is a weekend favorite with locals. T-shirts bearing Clint's picture are for sale in the gift shop.

PACIFIC GROVE

John Denver Crash Site
In the Pacific Ocean, off Ocean View Boulevard, between Asilomar Avenue and Acropolis Street, east of Point Piños at the northern tip of the Monterey Peninsula.

Many mocked the middle-class pop star and his saccharine paeans to country roads and campfires. Yet Denver had legions of loyal fans. When the small plane he was piloting crashed here on October 12, 1997, millions mourned. Denver had moved to the Carmel area not long before. Planning a flight to southern California, he bought a secondhand plane and was giving it a test run the next day when disaster struck. Experts suspect that while checking the gas tank, Denver inadvertently adjusted a rudder and went into a nosedive, an error he was flying too low to correct. (Reports later surfaced that Denver's piloting license was technically invalid because of DUI charges.) Portions of his body were recovered, then cremated and scattered over his beloved Colorado. On the beach nearest the crash site, large groups of fans gather annually on October 12 (and the closest weekend) to mark the anniversary. All-day events include songfests and shore cleanups. Wishing to avoid a Graceland effect, local residents initially shunned the idea of a permanent memorial. However, at last report a plaque was in the works.

MONTEREY

Monterey County Fairgrounds
Where musical history was made.

2004 Fairgrounds Road, off Fremont Street, near Highway 1. (831) 372-5863.

Two years before Woodstock, in June 1967, the Monterey International Pop Festival was held here, inaugurating the era of rock festivals. Later immortalized in D. A. Pennebaker's film *Monterey Pop,* this outdoor Summer of Love extravaganza drew together some of the period's most unforgettable acts: the Who, Jimi Hendrix, Jefferson Airplane, Janis Joplin, the Animals, the Mamas and the Papas, Simon and Garfunkel, Otis Redding, Country Joe and the Fish, Ravi Shankar, and more. The cameras caught Jimi burning his guitar, Pete Townshend smashing his, and Cass Elliott gazing awestruck at Janis. The audience appears amazingly docile, innocent, actually polite. (The Monkees' Mickey Dolenz can be glimpsed in one scene, applauding Shankar's seemingly incessant performance.) Rumor has it that for years afterward an *X* marked the spot onstage where Jimi caressed, then torched, his axe.

Monterey Bay Aquarium
Where Spock saved the world.

886 Cannery Row, on the waterfront. Open Memorial Day–Labor Day, daily 9:30 A.M.–6:00 P.M.; the rest of the year, 10:00 A.M.–6:00 P.M. Admission: adults, $15.95; students, $12.95; children, $7.95. (831) 648-4888.

In *Star Trek IV: The Voyage Home,* the planet's survival depends on whales. Spock engages in a bit of helpful mind-melding at a putative Sausalito Cetacean Institute. Those scenes were filmed here at Monterey Bay Aquarium, mainly in the towering 335,000-gallon Kelp Forest, where today you can watch divers feeding a vast population of sharks and other fish. Scenes were also shot on the outdoor observation deck and in the Marine Mammals Gallery. Not only that, but the aquarium's sea nettles also appeared in *Sphere.*

Salinas/Hollister Area

CASTROVILLE

Marilyn Monroe's "Artichoke Queen" Coronation Site
Where the budding actress had her first taste of fame.

> The former California Artichoke and Vegetable Growers headquarters is at the intersection of Wood Street and Del Monte Avenue, next to the railroad tracks, south of downtown Castroville. The building is now a repair and storage facility for Ocean Mist. (831) 633-3211. Also: Franco's Restaurant in the Franco Hotel, 10639 Merritt Street, Castroville. Open Mon.–Sat., 8:00 A.M.–9:00 P.M.; Sun., 8:00 A.M.–8:00 P.M. Norma Jean's Club in the restaurant is open Sat., 8:00 P.M.–2:00 A.M., with a $5 cover charge. (831) 633-2090.

In February 1948 a starlet who had recently changed her name to Marilyn Monroe arrived in Salinas to do a promotion for a jewelry store. At the time she was an unknown, not yet having appeared in a film or posed nude. A local artichoke grower from nearby Castroville (known as the Artichoke Center of the World) pointed out the ravishing beauty to his colleagues. Why, they wondered, is such a woman wasting her talents on a jewelry store? As a promotional stunt, they convened a meeting of the local artichoke growers' Rotary Club and decided to crown Monroe their "Artichoke Queen." They led her to the headquarters of the California Artichoke and Vegetable Growers and displayed her to the dumbfounded staff. They draped a sash over her shoulder and took photos of Monroe holding an artichoke. Then they all retired to the restaurant in the Franco Hotel for a celebratory luncheon and perhaps more photos. There was no competition for the crown, no artichoke festival: they just handed her the title. The artichoke facility is still at the corner of Wood and Del Monte but is now used as a storage building for Ocean Mist, successors of the California Artichoke and Vegetable Growers. (Ocean Mist recently moved the company offices to the other side of the tracks on Cara Mia Parkway.) The Franco Hotel restaurant (now called Franco's Restaurant) is still there as well, its bar decorated with photos and statuettes of Marilyn. On Saturday nights the bar transforms into Norma Jean's Club, a gay nightspot that hosts an annual Marilyn Monroe look-alike contest on the first Saturday in June to mark the actress's birthday. The winners are usually male. The location of the Rotary Club meeting has been long forgotten. (One eyewitness remembers the luncheon taking place in Salinas, not at the Franco; others disagree. Since all the photos from that day have been lost except a grainy shot that appeared in a newspaper, we may never know.) These days Castroville crowns a new Artichoke Queen every year during its Artichoke Festival.

SALINAS

National Steinbeck Center
Ride the red pony.

> *One Main Street, at Central Avenue and Salinas Street. Open daily 10:00 A.M.–5:00 P.M. Admission: adults, $7; students, $6; children ages 11–17, $4; under age 10, free. (831) 796-3833.*

In his lifetime, native son John Steinbeck was at odds with Salinas, whose residents recoiled at his portrayal of them in his novels. But now, long after his death, the town honors him. (After all, he *did* win the Pulitzer and Nobel Prizes.) Interactive exhibits at this museum include *Cannery Row* sound effects; cool *East of Eden* breezes; *Of Mice and Men* hay bales; migrant cabins; a Mexican-style plaza; and a replica red pony whose mane you can brush. Seven theaters screen films based on Steinbeck's tales, including *East of Eden,* starring James Dean. A vast archive includes original manuscripts. Also here is the green camper in which the author drove cross-country—a trip he described in *Travels with Charley.* Peek inside at his personal artifacts. The author's childhood home is nearby at Central and Stone; the 100 and 200 blocks of Main Street figure prominently in *East of Eden.* And Steinbeck's ashes rest in the Garden of Memories cemetery.

SAN JUAN BAUTISTA

Mission San Juan Bautista
Where Vertigo*'s climactic scene was set.*

> *Mariposa and 2nd Streets, along the northern edge of town. Open daily 9:30 A.M.–4:45 P.M. (831) 623-2127.*

Founded in 1797 by Father Serra's successor, this is the real deal, complete with a refectory, distinctive religious art, and a cemetery packed with dead Native Americans. With its authentic Spanish ambience, the mission appealed to Alfred Hitchcock when he was working on *Vertigo.* After wallowing in a bit of déjà vu amid the livery stables here, the blond heroine (Kim Novak) makes a fateful ascent up a high bell tower. The livery stables, now called the Plaza Stables, await your arrival. Not so that bell tower, which was added to the film via trick photography. Donner Party fans will also want to visit the mission's gift shop, which in 1847 housed a family recently rescued from that frosty, hungry nightmare.

HOLLISTER

The Wild One Motorcycle Gang Riot Site

Johnny's Bar & Grill, 526 San Benito Street (and elsewhere along San Benito Street), in downtown Hollister. Open daily, 8:00 A.M. until things quiet down, usually between 10:00 P.M. and 2:00 A.M. (831) 637-3683.

In the 1953 film *The Wild One*, Marlon Brando and Lee Marvin portrayed the leaders of two rival biker gangs terrorizing a small town. The film caused a nationwide panic as visions of motorcycle-riding hoodlums terrified Middle America. The film was based *very* loosely on an actual event: the 1947 Gypsy Tour in Hollister. The Gypsy Tour was an annual event, a convention where motorcycle enthusiasts showed off their hogs. There had been small gatherings during the 1930s, but World War II had required an interruption, so 1947's tour was the first in a long time. Postwar ennui and wanderlust seized American veterans that year. (Even Jack Kerouac's *On the Road* is based on a 1947 trek.) Thousands of bikers arrived on July 4 weekend, including a large contingent calling themselves the Booze Fighters. Not much happened, really. Some people got drunk, some got in a fight, about fifty were arrested. But sensational media reports culminated in what townies claim was a staged photograph that ran in *Life* magazine: a drunken biker up to his knees in beer bottles. This photo appeared to confirm the so-called Battle of Hollister, and Hollywood took notice. Supposedly shot partly on location in Hollister, *The Wild One* tells a different story, a tale of rival gangs and sadistic cruelty. But it did make Lee Marvin a star. Much of the real-life action centered around Johnny's Bar & Grill, a no-frills roadhouse that serves up steak and beer to this day. Thanks in part to the movie, Hollister is still a mecca for bikers every year on July 4 weekend.

Santa Cruz Area

SANTA CRUZ

Santa Cruz Boardwalk
Dirty Harry had a shootout here.

> Along Beach Street on the waterfront. Open June–mid-September, daily 11:00 A.M.–11:00 P.M.; mid-September–November and January–May, Sat.–Sun., 11:00 A.M.–7:00 P.M.; closed December except the week between Christmas and New Year's, when some, but not all, attractions operate noon–5:00 P.M. (831) 423-5590.

The hero of *Harold and Maude* buys his beloved a souvenir among the arcades here—which she promptly tosses into the waves. In *The Lost Boys,* filmed here, Kiefer Sutherland plays a creepy vampiric teen. And in *Sudden Impact,* Clint Eastwood's "Dirty Harry" Callahan makes the boardwalk echo with gunfire. Vintage attractions along this old-fashioned boardwalk include a 1911 carousel and a 1924 roller coaster whose silhouette is a distinctive landmark poised between mountains and sea.

APTOS

Loma Prieta Earthquake Epicenter

> In the Forest of Nisene Marks State Park, Aptos Creek Road, Aptos. See below for exact directions to the site. (831) 763-7064.

In the old days, when northern Californians said "the earthquake," they meant the 1906 one. But that was before 5:04 P.M. on October 17, 1989. The Loma Prieta earthquake—named for an old logging mill near its epicenter here—registered "only" 7.1 on the Richter scale (not nearly as strong as the 1906 quake), but it felt like the end of the world. From Monterey to Sonoma County, buildings shuddered and collapsed, windows shattered, chimneys disintegrated, telephone poles swayed like rubber. Downtown Watsonville and Santa Cruz were devastated. Structures built on landfill (like San Francisco's Marina District) fared badly, as the ground beneath them liquefied. The quake even interrupted a World Series baseball game, seen live on TV nationwide. Before that day no one outside of Aptos had ever heard of Loma Prieta, and even now few people know how the earthquake got its name.

Here's how to reach the epicenter: From Santa Cruz, take Soquel Drive (or Highway 1, and then exit onto Soquel Drive) east to Aptos and turn north on Aptos

Creek Road. Park at the end of the road and continue on foot up Aptos Creek Road, which becomes a dirt road. After about a mile and a half, look for a sign mentioning the epicenter. Continue past the sign onto a side path called Aptos Creek Trail. Follow it uphill until you reach another sign indicating the real epicenter. (Not recommended in muddy conditions.)

TheCentralValley

Stockton

Cleveland Elementary
Scene of a massacre.

20 E. Fulton Street, between El Dorado Street and Pacific Avenue. (209) 953-4245.

At this ordinary public school hundreds of youngsters were capering on January 17, 1989, when a young man wearing an army-surplus outfit walked up and started shooting. Having brought no less than three guns, including an assault rifle, he killed five kids and wounded dozens more, then shot himself. The dead marauder was Patrick Purdy, a former Cleveland student obsessed with war—the Vietnam conflict in particular—though he was far too young to have served. (He singled out Asian kids as his victims.) His lodgings were later found to be full of toy soldiers. Little did anyone know at the time that Purdy's evil spree was to be the first in a spate of 1990s shootings by students or former students killing their classmates.

Sacramento

Squeaky Fromme/Gerald Ford Attempted Assassination Site

On a curving pathway in Capitol Park that runs diagonally from the intersection of 12th and L Streets to the State Capitol Building; the incident happened about 10 yards from the sidewalk, near a magnolia tree.

Manson follower Lynette "Squeaky" Fromme devised an elaborate, if unlikely, plan to free Charlie from jail. If she were to get involved in a high-profile criminal trial, she reasoned, he would be called as a witness. Once on the stand, Manson would explain his philosophy to the world, and he would be immediately set free and hailed as a savior. All he needed was a platform. All she needed was a high-profile crime. When Gerald Ford visited Sacramento on September 5, 1975, she saw her chance. Just after 10:00 A.M. Ford exited the Senator Hotel at the corner of Twelfth and L Streets, crossed into the broad park that surrounds the Capitol, and began shaking hands with a small crowd that had gathered to greet him. Wearing a long red robe and standing among the crowd, Squeaky pulled out a Colt .45, aimed it at Ford, and pulled the trigger. Had there been a bullet in the chamber, it would have killed him. But the gun was not loaded properly, and emitted only an impotent *click*. Squeaky was immediately tackled, and Ford stoically kept his scheduled appointment with Governor Jerry Brown in the Capitol Building. Squeaky's plan backfired. Manson was never called to testify at her trial, and though she probably had never actually intended to kill Ford, she received a life sentence. (Two decades later she escaped after hearing that Manson was sick, but she was recaptured before she could reach him.) The Senator Hotel has been converted into an office building, but otherwise the pathway and the Capitol look much the same as they did on that day. (See also **Westin St. Francis Hotel, San Francisco,** pages 185–186.)

Dorothea Puente House
Where the landlady buried her tenants.

> 1426 F Street, between 14th and 15th Streets, on the northern edge of downtown, south of the American River.

The crafty Dorothea Puente may have been as young as thirteen the first time she was married. By the 1980s she was an ex-con on parole, having been jailed for stealing and forging checks. Yet the ladylike, grandmotherly Puente was a darling of local social-service officials and was allowed to care for the elderly and operate a boardinghouse. In November 1988 seven of her former tenants' corpses were unearthed in the yard and garden surrounding this graceful Victorian. Two more corpses would be found near the river. Puente had poisoned each with drugs and continued to cash their Social Security checks. She had fled Sacramento and was a fugitive in L.A. when an elderly man saw her picture on TV and turned her in—she'd flirted with him in a bar and asked whether he was on Social Security.

Oroville

Ishi Discovery Site

A memorial plaque marks the site, at 2547 Oroville-Quincy Highway, at the intersection of Oak Avenue, 2 miles east of downtown Oroville.

It was August 29, 1911. A team of Oroville butchers heard dogs barking in the corral next to their slaughterhouse. They went outside and discovered a nearly naked man crouching terrified in the mud, surrounded by snarling hounds. His skin was a deep bronze, and his hair was burnt almost to the scalp. He was severely emaciated and seemed near death. But who was he? They brought him inside and tried talking to him in English, Spanish, and even some Native American languages. But the mysterious man didn't understand any of them. UC Berkeley anthropologist Alfred Kroeber read the ensuing sensationalistic newspaper accounts of "the wild man of Oroville" and rushed north to rescue him. Kroeber slowly uncovered the truth: the man was the last surviving member of the Yahi, a Native American tribe that had never been driven onto a reservation and was long thought to be extinct. As far as anyone knew, the Yahi had never had any contact with Western culture aside from a few bloody battles with white settlers. Because this starving Yahi refused to reveal his name, Kroeber simply called him "Ishi," the Yahi word for *man*. Within months Ishi was world-famous as "the last wild Indian in America." Indeed, Ishi was a Stone Age man forced by fate into the twentieth century. Kroeber brought him to the Bay Area, where Ishi spent years teaching anthropologists about his life in the northern California wilderness. Before dying of tuberculosis in 1916, Ishi did a bit of reverse anthropology of his own, incisively assessing American society thus: "[White men] are smart but not wise, knowing many things including much that is false." Many historians think Ishi's discovery that August day was a pivotal event in New World history, the final act of a terrible tragedy that started when Columbus set sail in 1492. By now the slaughterhouse is long gone, and all that remains to mark the site are a small plaque and a picnic table.

Chico

Bidwell Park

As seen in Gone with the Wind.

> Just northeast of the center of town, between Vallombrosa and Woodland Avenues. Highway 99 bisects the park.

The scene in *Gone with the Wind* where Gerald O'Hara has his first horseback ride was filmed here—a far cry from the Old South. Punctuated with a winding creek, the long narrow park has appeared in other classic films as well, including *The Adventures of Robin Hood, Waterloo Bridge,* and *Friendly Persuasion.*

The Gold Country

COLOMA

Marshall Gold Discovery State Historic Park
Where a shiny pebble changed the course of history.

> On Main Street (Highway 49) just north of Mt. Murphy Road, in Coloma, which is 7 miles north of Placerville. The exact site of the gold discovery is on the east side of Main Street, north of the sawmill, right on the banks of the American River; a walking trail and signs clearly point the way from the road. The museum and visitors center are across the road at 310 Back Street. Open daily, 10:00 A.M.–5:00 P.M. (530) 622-3470.

"Monday 24th. This day some kind of mettle was found in the tail race that looks like goald, first discovered by James Martial, the Boss of the Mill."

With these fatefully misspelled words in the diary of millworker Henry Bigler, California's destiny changed forever. In January 1848 frontier businessman John Sutter had paid an employee of his named James Marshall to build a sawmill on the American River to cut wood for Sutter's various construction projects. The mill was powered by water that ran through an artificial channel Marshall had dug from the river. But the lower end of the channel that drained off the water and guided it back to the river (called a tailrace) was clogged with rocks and mud, so workmen were struggling to clear it. On January 24 Marshall was inspecting the tailrace when he noticed a few shiny flecks in the water. Rudimentary tests convinced him it was gold. Word got out. By 1849 an avalanche of humanity descended on California (and hence the name of the San Francisco football team, the '49ers). By 1850 the craze was worldwide, and California went from being an unknown backwater to the focal point of history's largest gold rush.

Much has been written about the significance of Marshall's discovery and the $50 billion worth of gold later found in the Sierra foothills. It is thought that the Union would have lost the Civil War if the federal government had not had the California gold reserves to pay for military mobilization. The U.S. certainly would have developed much more slowly, and California would not be the economic power-

house it is today. At the park you can visit the approximate discovery site, a recon-
structed sawmill (the original was washed away years ago), and more. (The nugget
Marshall found is now displayed in UC Berkeley's **Bancroft Library,** see page 251.)
You can even try your hand at gold panning on the river's opposite bank.

COLUMBIA

High Noon Filming Location
Along Main Street. Columbia is just off Highway 49, north of Sonora. (209) 536-1672.

Considered by some to be the best western ever made, 1952's *High Noon* tells the
story of a stoic sheriff facing off against vengeful killers. The townspeople of
Hadleyville turn their backs on him and force him to face his destiny alone. Gary
Cooper won a Best Actor Oscar; the film won three more as well. But the film's real
star was the town of Columbia, its real-life setting. *High Noon*'s plot was based in
part on an actual incident in Columbia's past. The scriptwriter, who was soon scheduled to appear in front of the House Committee on Un-American Activities
(HUAC), reportedly put in the part about the cowardly townspeople as a jab at his
turncoat Hollywood friends who refused to help him fight the witch hunt. As the
state's best-preserved gold rush town, Columbia has been the setting for over two
hundred other films, among them Clint Eastwood's *Pale Rider.*

JAMESTOWN

Petticoat Junction Filming Location
*Railtown 1897 State Historic Park, 5th and Reservoir Streets, just east of the center of
Jamestown, which is south of Sonora on Highway 49. Open daily 9:30 A.M.–4:30 P.M. Ad-
mission: adults, $2; children, $1. Trains run April–October, Sat.–Sun., 11:00 A.M.–3:00 P.M.;
November, Sat. only, 11:00 A.M.–3:00 P.M. Train rides: adults, $6; children, $3. (209) 984-3953.*

Though it was set in the 1960s, *Petticoat Junction* evoked the Wild West. Its
Shady Rest Hotel—isolated on a spur line of a semi-abandoned railroad—was
caught in a time warp. Viewers loved the adventures of its staff, especially the beautiful sisters Billie Jo, Bobbie Jo, and Betty Jo. The show had a successful seven-year
run and even inspired a popular spinoff, *Green Acres.* Most of *Petticoat Junction*'s
outdoor scenes were filmed at Railtown, a collection of antique trains and railroad
paraphernalia. The famous opening scene where the sisters undress in a water tank
and flip their petticoats over the rim was filmed here as well—the water tower is
about a quarter-mile up the track from the depot at the entrance. Nearly a thousand

movies, TV shows, and ads have been shot at Railtown, including *The Wild Wild West*, *Little House on the Prairie*, *The Unforgiven*, and scenes in *High Noon* and even *Back to the Future, Part III*. Anytime you see an antique steam locomotive onscreen, chances are this is the place. Fatty Arbuckle and Mary Pickford made movies here in the 1920s. *Petticoat's* famous Engine No. 3 is still gleaming in the roundhouse.

The Sierras

TRUCKEE

Donner Memorial State Park
Where pioneers became cannibals.

12593 Donner Pass Road (old Highway 40), just west of Truckee. The Emigrant Trail Museum is open daily 9:00 A.M.–4:00 P.M. Admission: adults, $2; children ages 6–12, $1; under age 6, free. (530) 582-7892.

Trying to take a shortcut on their westward trek, the Donner Party—a group of pioneer families emigrating to California—was trapped in this remote pass during the terrible winter of 1846. As one after another in the party died of cold and hunger, survivors resorted to eating the corpses. By the spring of 1847, after several rescue teams had reached the encampment, about half of the original party had died. The site of their cannibalistic nightmare is now a state park. The museum recalls life on the Emigrant Trail, with a film that recounts the Donner fiasco. Plaques mark the sites of cabins where desperate emigrants struggled to survive.

SOUTH LAKE TAHOE

Sonny Bono's Death Slope
Watch out for that tree!

Heavenly Ski Resort, just west of the Nevada border, south of Stateline and South Lake Tahoe. From Highway 50, take Ski Run Boulevard and follow the signs to Keller Road. See below for exact location. (775) 586-7000 or (800) 243-2836.

On January 5, 1998, sixty-two-year-old Sonny Bono was vacationing here with his wife and kids. After riding a gondola together, the four set off to enjoy themselves on the easy-to-intermediate Upper Orion ski run. But when one child took a minor tumble, the pop star–turned–congressman went on ahead while the others aided her. When he failed to join them at the bottom of the slope, they grew very worried. That evening Bono's body was discovered about 150 feet off the trail, near the top of the slope. He had skied headfirst into a 40-foot pine. Like many skilled skiers, he had intentionally veered off the clear snow into the more challenging wooded area.

EL PORTAL

Cedar Lodge
Scene of "the Tourist Murders."

> *9966 Highway 140, just west of Yosemite National Park. (209) 379-2612 or (800) 321-5261.*

Snuggled tight against a forested slope, this unassuming inn with its plushly furnished $100 rooms and $300 suites looks very safe indeed. In room 509, out-of-towners Carole Sund, her teenage daughter Juli, and their young Argentinian friend Silvina Pelosso were enjoying the last night of a vacation in February 1999 when hotel handyman Cary Stayner appeared at their door. Saying he needed to fix a leak, Stayner ended up killing all three—then covered his tracks, disposed of his victims, and evaded capture for months. Only after beheading a Yosemite naturalist was Stayner caught, at which point he confessed to the earlier killings, telling a horrifying tale of rape, strangulation, and throat-slitting.

LONE PINE

Alabama Hills

> *From Lone Pine, take Whitney Portal Road 2½ miles west; Movie Road (also known as Movie Flat Road) will be on your right (north), and a short distance beyond that, Horseshoe Meadow Road will be on your left (south). The hills and rock formations will be clearly visible, though identifying which is which can be difficult. Always open. Lone Pine Chamber of Commerce: (760) 876-4444.*

These bulbous rocks and barren hills have been an extension of the studios' back lots since the movie industry's earliest days—it was Fatty Arbuckle who first "discovered" the Alabama Hills and used them as a filming location. Since then hundreds of westerns, ranging from *Across the Plains* to *Yellow Sky,* have included this picturesque landscape as a backdrop. (Actual cowboy-and-Indian massacres here stained the soil red in the 1860s.) The bizarre formations also make the area an ideal setting for sci-fi adventures—*Star Trek: Generations* and *Star Trek V: The Final Fron-*

Financial District/Embarcadero

"Preparedness Day" Bombing Location

At the intersection of Market and Steuart Streets, near the Embarcadero and Justin Herman Plaza, on the sidewalk on the west side of Steuart.

By the summer of 1916 World War I (known at the time as "the Great War") had been raging for nearly two years. But the United States was not yet involved. Tensions were running high, and many Americans were ready to go to war at a moment's notice. July 22, 1916, was unofficially declared "Preparedness Day," and militaristic parades were staged nationwide. San Francisco's was one of the largest: up to fifty thousand people marched down Market Street past tens of thousands of spectators. At precisely 2:06 P.M., as the Spanish-American War veterans were rounding the corner from Steuart Street onto Market Street, a suitcase sitting on the sidewalk on the west side of Steuart exploded with a deafening boom. One bystander was decapitated instantly, nine others were killed, and at least forty sustained serious injuries. Windows were shattered, buildings damaged. A hat with a piece of skull lodged inside landed on a rooftop over one hundred feet away. Bloodied bodies were strewn on Market.

In the ensuing panic, people found a scapegoat in union agitator Tom Mooney, who was popular with socialists but hated by big business. Mooney and a cohort were quickly arrested, tried, and convicted of the bombing, and Mooney was sentenced to death. But he was innocent. Not only did witnesses place him nowhere near Steuart Street on the day of the bombing, but also a photograph (suppressed at the trial) showed him watching the parade from a roof over a mile away, with a clock in the background showing the time near 2:06. Later investigations proved that right-wing business interests had coerced witnesses and manufactured evidence, in a successful attempt to frame Mooney. His case sparked an international furor; workers in Russia rioted on his behalf. Foreign journalists condemned the U.S. as corrupt. Mooney became a martyr to the cause of workers' rights. After his sentence was commuted to life, he languished in San Quentin for two decades before being pardoned in 1939. A jubilant throng accompanied Mooney down Market. By now the corner has been repaved and rebuilt, leaving not the slightest hint of what had occurred

tier were both filmed here, as were episodes of *The Twilight Zone,* and others. The 1939 classic *Gunga Din,* in which California doubled for India, put this place on the map. A *Gunga Din* marker on the east side of Horseshoe Meadow Road shows where the film's now vanished temple was. Areas around Movie Road (mostly accessible along rough tracks or on foot) have been named for movies shot there and their stars: Lone Ranger Canyon, Gary Cooper Rock, Gunga Din Bridge, and more. Ask for a map of movie locations at the tourist office in Lone Pine (call number above for location), or join a tour during the Lone Pine Film Festival in October. Though faves such as *High Sierra* and *The Long, Long Trailer* were partly filmed here, so were bombs like *Bamboo Saucer, Monolith Monsters,* and *Tarzan's Desert Mystery.*

Manzanar Internment Camp

On Highway 395, 5 miles south of Independence and 12 miles north of Lone Pine, on the west side of the highway just north of Manzanar Reward Road. Open daily during daylight hours. Admission: free. (760) 878-2949 or (760) 878-2932.

Less than three months after Pearl Harbor was bombed, FDR signed Executive Order 9066, authorizing the imprisonment of Japanese Americans in detention centers. Its racist justification was that these citizens might in fact be loyal to Japan, working as spies or saboteurs. (So why didn't they lock up Americans of German ancestry?) Not wanting to hinder the war effort, a patriotic Japanese community submitted. After short stays in various transit camps, nearly all southern Californian Japanese Americans were imprisoned here at Manzanar for over three years. (In Europe the Nazis had a similar plan for their own internal "enemies.") By comparison, despite the humiliating conditions, Manzanar's internees received adequate food, clothing, and shelter. Families were usually allowed to stay together, and camp guards were generally decent. But while they were away, many internees lost their homes and businesses to unscrupulous whites. Some ten thousand people were interned here at Manzanar, which had its own temples, hospital, schools, and gardens. Now it's a National Historic Site. But of this shameful chapter in American history, all that remains are two sentry posts, an auditorium, and a cemetery. Elsewhere around the huge site, all you'll find are foundations. Try to join one of the frequent walking tours. (See also **Tanforan Park Shopping Center, San Bruno,** page 246, and **Tule Lake Internment Camp, Newell,** page 269.)

here. The Preparedness Day bombing remains unsolved and still stands as the worst mass killing in San Francisco history.

101 California Shooting Spree Site
101 California Street, at Market Street.

This is the quintessential modern steel-and-glass sky-scraper. Exotic trees fill the atrium, and plaques identify the varieties of marble with which the elevators are paneled. On July 1, 1993, mortgage broker Gian Luigi Ferri entered the building with a bag containing guns and ammo. Blaming his current financial woes on advice he had taken from attorneys at the Pettit and Martin law firm, Ferri rode the elevator to their thirty-fourth-floor offices. In a hail of bullets he killed three and seriously wounded another, then went down to the thirty-third floor. There he killed two more. On the thirty-second floor he killed another three and wounded several more before committing suicide as police converged. In a note found later, Ferri raged against the law firm and also about food additives. In San Francisco parlance the phrase "101 California" has since become synonymous with this type of crime. The law firm is gone, and interiors have been rearranged.

101 California shooting spree site

Palace Hotel
Hosting high society since 1875.

2 New Montgomery Street, at Market Street. (415) 512-1111.

Oscar Wilde stayed here, as did Thomas Edison, Mark Twain, Woodrow Wilson, Theodore Roosevelt, Amelia Earhart, Sarah Bernhardt, Charlie Chaplin, Guglielmo Marconi, Andrew Carnegie, Winston Churchill, D. H. Lawrence, Madame Chiang Kai-shek, Bill Gates, and the crowned heads of England, Belgium, Yugoslavia, Norway, the Netherlands, and Brazil—not to mention Kevin Bacon. When the Palace opened in 1875 it was the world's largest luxury hotel, with over seven hundred rooms. Newspapers reported that it was a

Palace Hotel

quarter of a mile across, its walls two feet thick. Its builder bought a furniture factory to fill the place. Among many celebrity guests was Hawaii's King Kalakaua, who died here. The 1906 earthquake vaulted a stunned Enrico Caruso out of bed; the following fire burned the hotel, and it had to be rebuilt. A chef here invented Green Goddess salad dressing. Victorian splendor prevails via fat marble columns, gold leaf, potted palms, chandeliers, and dramatic glass ceilings. Memorabilia is on display amid overstuffed furniture and an original Maxfield Parrish mural.

Museum of the Money of the American West
Home of the Broderick-Terry dueling pistols.

> Basement, Union Bank of California, 400 California Street, at Sansome Street. Open Mon.– Fri., 9:00 A.M.–5:00 P.M. (415) 705-7000.

On display here are two souvenirs from what was then San Francisco's most sensational killing. David C. Broderick was a popular San Francisco abolitionist and senator. He had swiftly made a fortune by clandestinely minting $5 and $10 gold pieces. And David S. Terry was the state's chief justice, a pro-slavery Southerner. In 1859, after a spate of slander, the two Davids scheduled a duel near Lake Merced, with eighty witnesses. Of the two pistols on offer, one had a defective trigger. Broderick got that one, and Terry took advantage. When Broderick misfired, Terry shot him in the chest. Thousands mourned. In their day

Broderick-Terry dueling pistols

these two guns had all the makings of a major tourist attraction. They languished in a remote British museum for decades. Finally they were sold at auction and returned 112 years after the duel to San Francisco, where they are now displayed alongside gold rush nuggets and coins, and an ultra-rare $3 bill personally signed by Mormon prophet Joseph Smith. (See also **Broderick-Terry Duel Site,** pages 240–41.)

Bank of America Building
Where a sniper set off Dirty Harry *and flames ignited* The Towering Inferno.

> 555 California Street, between Kearny and Montgomery Streets; Carnelian Room is on the 52nd floor. There are several entrances to the building, but the main entrance is at California and Kearny. Carnelian Room open Mon.–Fri., 3:00–11:30 P.M.; Sat., 4:00–11:30 P.M.; Sun., 10:00 A.M.–2:30 P.M. and 6:00–11:30 P.M. (415) 433-7500.

Dirty Harry's opening sequence shows a psychopathic sniper picking off victims at random from his perch atop the city's tallest building. The scene was filmed from the Carnelian Room, a swanky cocktail lounge on the top floor of Bank of America's headquarters. Look out the restaurant area's north-facing windows to see a bright blue swimming pool some distance below, where the sniper spotted one of his unwitting victims. That pool is on the roof of the Holiday Inn at 750 Kearny Street. (Ride the hotel's elevator up to the pool and see the sniper's perch from the victim's point of view.) The Bank of America building was also the setting for 1974's camp epic *The Towering Inferno,* featuring *Bullitt's* Steve McQueen and native San Franciscan O. J. Simpson. However, fifty-two stories was not "towering" enough for director Irwin Allen: special effects added eighty-six more stories to make that fictional building the world's tallest.

View of sniper's perch from Holiday Inn pool

Montgomery Block Site
Where Mark Twain met the real Tom Sawyer.

600 Montgomery Street, at Washington Street; now it is the Transamerica Pyramid, on the block bounded by Montgomery, Washington, Sansome, and Clay Streets.

The towering Transamerica Pyramid, San Francisco's most distinctive skyscraper, occupies a site steeped in literary history. A massive four-story commercial and residential building dubbed the Montgomery Block— its address was 628 Montgomery—was home to Ambrose Bierce, Frank Norris, and Joaquin Miller. Sun Yat-sen, while working to finance a Chinese revolution, wrote the English version of a new constitution in his office here. And at a Turkish bath in the building's basement, Mark Twain is said to have met a onetime firefighter named Tom Sawyer. Sawyer told fascinating stories that Twain transformed into America's favorite novel. The Montgomery Block had been built in 1853 at great expense out of redwood logs and ships' planking. Bohemians of all kinds loved the place, which was a hotbed of art and ideas. It survived the great earthquake and fire but was torn down in 1959. In 1978 a madman climbed into the ventilation shaft of the newly built pyramid and fell twenty-nine stories to the solid cement ground floor. To everyone's amazement, he survived.

Transamerica Pyramid, on the site of the Mongomery Block

Union Square Area

Westin St. Francis Hotel
Where Fatty ruined his career, Ford dodged a bullet, and Jolson keeled over.

Originally named the St. Francis Hotel; now called the Westin St. Francis, 335 Powell Street,
between Post and Geary Streets, facing Union Square. (415) 397-7000.

Roscoe "Fatty" Arbuckle was once America's best-known and best-loved comedian. From 1913 to 1921 he starred in scores of popular slapstick comedies whose titles in retrospect seemed to foreshadow the disaster awaiting him: *Fatty's Wine Party, A Reckless Romeo, Fatty's Magic Pants, The Village Scandal, Fickle Fatty's Fall.* On Labor Day weekend 1921 Roscoe and some Hollywood buddies drove up to San Francisco for a few days of fun. They rented a three-room suite on the twelfth floor of the St. Francis Hotel: rooms 1219, 1220, and 1221. Room 1219 was Fatty's bedroom, 1220 was converted into the party lounge, and 1221 was apparently reserved for making whoopee. The party rolled on for days. On September 5 a drunken Fatty escorted an even drunker starlet named Virginia Rappe into room 1221 and shut the door. What happened then is the stuff of legend. Either he raped her with a champagne bottle (or a Coke bottle, or a sharp piece of ice, or all three), or he compressed her delicate frame with his huge body (estimates of his weight range from 266 to 340 pounds), or they engaged in sloppy consensual sex. Rappe's alcohol-filled bladder burst inside her. Screaming, she was taken to a hospital. Yet the party continued as if nothing had happened.

When Rappe died of peritonitis days later, Fatty's nightmare began. Arrested at his Los Angeles home (see page 134), he was charged with manslaughter. The ensuing scandal was O. J.–esque. Though Fatty was acquitted of wrongdoing after three agonizing trials, the bad publicity ruined his career. And it almost ruined the movie industry, which the public now viewed as one vast den of iniquity. Fatty never again acted onscreen, though he later directed a few films, using a pseudonym. He died young, his spirit crushed. To see the suite, wander the twelfth-floor hallway until you see a short cul-de-sac branching off, with four doors. Room 1221 is in this cul-de-sac, its door dark with gold trim like all the rest.

Strangely, the suite saw another celebrity death in 1950. Al Jolson—star of 1927's *Jazz Singer,* the first-ever feature film with dialogue—had just returned from entertaining troops in Korea. He rented rooms 1220 and 1221 and was settling down to a game of gin rummy with his manager when he felt his pulse stop. Jolson fell to the floor and was soon declared dead of a massive heart attack.

A quarter century later the hotel again made headlines. On September 22, 1975, Gerald Ford ate lunch here and was heading for the Post Street exit. The crowd awaiting him on Post included a disturbed woman named Sara Jane Moore.

SAN FRANCISCO / **UNION SQUARE AREA** **199**

An ex-housewife who later got into radical politics, Moore had at one point foolishly agreed to spy on her friends for the FBI. Even more stupidly, she told her friends she was doing it. So the radicals kicked her out and the FBI dumped her. Desperate and lonely, Moore wanted to prove what a true revolutionary she was. So she stationed herself across the street from the entrance, on the north side of Post, approximately where the Disney Store is today. As Ford walked through the Post Street doors, Moore raised a gun and fired. Although she missed, Ford grabbed his chest as if in pain (see also **Squeaky Fromme–Gerald Ford Attempted Assassination Site, Sacramento,** page 185). As guards whisked him away in the presidential limousine, Moore was apprehended, her plan foiled. She was later sentenced to life in prison. Visiting dignitaries still use the Post Street exit rather than face huge hordes at the front door.

Union Square
Where **The Conversation**'s *conversation took place.*

> The square bounded by Stockton, Geary, Powell, and Post Streets, across from the Westin St. Francis Hotel.

In Francis Ford Coppola's classic 1974 film *The Conversation,* Gene Hackman plays a San Francisco surveillance maestro. In a crucial scene a young couple strolls around and around Union Square while our hero uses a parabolic receiver to tap their conversation. (*Laverne and Shirley* fans will recognize the female half of the couple as Cindy Williams.) The pair has deliberately chosen to circumambulate the square, believing that in this way they cannot possibly be overheard. They are wrong—and what our hero hears will change his life forever.

Hotel Diva
Celebrity signatures in cement.

> 440 Geary Street. (415) 885-0200.

The owner of this purple-accented postmodern hotel has been soliciting celebrity autographs for the sidewalk out front since the place opened in 1985. Signators range from Mary Martin to Stevie Wonder, with Anjelica Huston, Leontyne Price, Lily Tomlin, and Tommy Tune in between. Tune left his footprints, too, and Tomlin left a Milk Bone–shaped impression that she labeled as her funny bone.

Former Location of the Pinkerton Detective Agency

The James Flood Building, 870 Market Street at Powell Street; another entrance is at 71 Ellis Street next door to John's Grill.

This imposing twelve-story structure, with its marble walls, marble floors, and carved wooden banisters, survived the 1906 earthquake. Decades later the Pinkerton Detective Agency had its offices here, in suite 314. One of the firm's detectives was Dashiell Hammett, who drew on his experiences as a gumshoe when writing the novels that made him world-famous.

John's Grill
Described in The Maltese Falcon.

63 Ellis Street, between Powell and Stockton Streets. Open Mon.–Sat., 11:00 A.M.–10:00 P.M.; Sun., 5:00–10:00 P.M. (415) 986-0069.

Dark wood and period furnishings adorn this 1908-era restaurant that Dashiell Hammett, a frequent patron himself, used as a setting in *The Maltese Falcon.* Now the place is a favorite with Hammett's fans: the Dashiell Hammett Society is headquartered here. On the walls are pictures of satisfied customers, including George Lucas, Hillary Clinton, Jerry Lewis, Lauren Bacall, and Matt Dillon. Hammett and *Falcon* memorabilia decorate both the upper and lower levels.

The *Maltese Falcon* Murder Site

Burritt Alley, which branches south off Bush Street just west of Stockton Street.

The street sign marking this alley is swiped regularly, but a brass plaque marks this as the spot where Brigid O'Shaughnessy killed Sam Spade's partner Miles Archer, thus launching *The Maltese Falcon*'s rapid-fire plot. Another tiny street, across Bush, has had its name officially changed from Monroe to Dashiell Hammett.

Robert Louis Stevenson House

608 Bush Street, above the Stockton Tunnel, across from Burritt Alley.

The roaming Scot would later say he spent some of the poorest, sickest, and most miserable days of his life at this address. Before moving out of the rooming house in early 1880, he is said to have ridden ferry-

Plaque marking the site of the Robert Louis Stevenson house

boats for inspiration and eaten cheap meals at nearby cafés all winter. Today a plaque outside the San Miguel barbershop explains that the down-and-out yet prolific RLS wrote essays, poems, autobiographical works, and fiction during his winter here.

Civic Center and the Tenderloin

CIVIC CENTER

San Francisco City Hall
Site of the Moscone/Milk assassination, and Marilyn's wedding.

> City Hall occupies the block bounded by McAllister, Polk, and Grove Streets and Van Ness Avenue. The main entrance faces the Civic Center park on the Polk Street side; the Dan White window (see below) is at the center of the bottom level of the McAllister Street side. Open for business Mon.–Fri., 9:00 A.M.–5:00 P.M., though free tours are given daily; call (415) 554-6023 or (415) 554-5780 for details. General information: (415) 554-4000.

George Moscone was a popular, progressive mayor, a breath of fresh air after a century of mayor's-office deals and backroom graft. Harvey Milk was the most liberal member of the city's Board of Supervisors and the nation's first openly gay politician to successfully run for office, elected in 1977. Dan White was everything Moscone and Milk were not, a reactionary conservative supervisor (and former cop) who was heavily influenced behind the scenes by big business. After serving a year on the board, Dan White resigned his elected position in November 1978 (see also **Dan White's Hot Potato Stand,** page 223), unable to support his family on the minuscule salary and frustrated by incessant political battles with liberals like Milk. But within days White's financial backers convinced him to change his mind, so he asked Moscone for his job back. Moscone refused, setting the stage for the most famous crime in San Francisco history.

White was humiliated, confused, enraged; he paced around all weekend, eating Twinkies and other junk food. On Monday morning, November 27, 1978, White packed his old police revolver and went to City Hall. Fearful that his gun would set off the metal detectors at the front door, he crawled through a basement window on the McAllister Street side of the building, muttering excuses to the dumbfounded city engineer into whose office he had climbed. White went upstairs to Moscone's office, was let in by the helpful secretary, and again demanded his job back. Again, Moscone refused. White pulled out his gun and shot Moscone four times, killing him instantly. Then he reloaded and scampered across the building to Milk's office. After a short verbal confrontation White shot Milk five times, finishing him off execution-style, as he had Moscone. Then-supervisor (later mayor and senator) Dianne Feinstein heard the shots and rushed into Milk's office seconds after White had fled. When she announced the killings a short time later, Milk's blood still damp on her clothing, the city went into shock. White turned himself in a few hours after the shooting.

At his trial, lawyers broke new legal ground by using what infamously became known as the "Twinkie defense": White was not responsible for his actions because eating too much junk food had clouded his judgment. The jury actually bought it, handing out the lightest possible sentence. The shocking verdict sparked a night of violence later dubbed "White Night," as outraged gays and other Milk supporters rioted and burned police cars in front of City Hall.

White served his short sentence at Soledad, befriending Sirhan Sirhan, of all people. After his release, the self-loathing White committed suicide in 1985 rather than live an as outcast. You can still see the window through which White entered the building; now covered with bars, it's on the ground level, in the middle of the McAllister Street side of City Hall. The room he broke into is no longer an office: it was converted into a day care center in 1999. The actual rooms where the killings took place are still used as offices and are not open to the public.

On a cheerier note, Marilyn Monroe and Joe DiMaggio were married in City Hall on January 15, 1954, though it was not under the central dome, as is traditional for marriages performed here. The pair apparently tied the knot in a third-floor room, but no one knows exactly which one.

Former Location of the Fillmore West
San Francisco Honda, 10 South Van Ness Avenue, at Market Street. (415) 441-2000 or (415) 913-5160.

In 1968, when this was still called the Carousel Ballroom, it hosted concerts by Jefferson Airplane, the Grateful Dead, Chuck Berry, Moby Grape, and other greats. That year rock impresario Bill Graham left the original Fillmore and took over the Carousel, renaming it Fillmore West. Performers at its grand opening included Big Brother and the Holding Company, and Sly and the Family Stone. Cream, the Who, and more of the era's best played here before the club closed in 1971. Now it is the second floor of a large Honda dealership. Its walls and ceiling sport fancy Moorish openwork. Evocative graffiti in a rear stairwell are rumored to be a genuine souvenir of the Fillmore West.

THE TENDERLOIN

Phoenix Hotel
Where the rock stars stay.

601 Eddy Street, at Larkin Street. (415) 776-1380 or (800) 248-9466.

This '50s motor lodge–turned–retro paradise attracts the ultracool likes of Keanu Reeves, the Beastie Boys, Everlast, Everclear, Third Eye Blind, Sonic Youth, Sinéad O'Connor, Joey Ramone, R.E.M., the Cardigans, the Red Hot Chili Peppers, 10,000 Maniacs, the B-52's, k.d. lang, Linda Ronstadt, Woody Harrelson, Smashmouth, Ziggy Marley, Vanilla Ice, No Doubt, Jane's Addiction, and dozens more hip types. When it was new this was a hangout for visiting Hollywood personages; then the place grew more and more decrepit. In 1987 it underwent a costly renovation. Now it has wacky original artworks and tropique furnishings. A "rock 'n' roll hairstylist" is at your service, and you never know who will pop up in the sculpture garden, or at the Backflip, a "see and be seen" lounge. A swirly mural decorates the floor of the pool.

Phoenix Hotel

Dashiell Hammett Apartment

891 Post Street, just east of Hyde Street.

Circa 1927 and 1928 Hammett lived in apartment 401 of this ho-hum brick house above a laundry while working on several of his most important novels, including *The Maltese Falcon, Red Harvest,* and *The Dain Curse.* His private dick protagonist Sam Spade lives at this address as well, the very place where Hammett is said to have first conceived his alter ego.

Billie Holiday Arrest Site

Formerly the Mark Twain Hotel; now the Ramada Inn at Union Square, 345 Taylor Street near Ellis Street. (415) 673-2332.

This was still the Mark Twain Hotel when jazz diva Billie Holiday came for a visit in early 1949. On January 22 cops arrived and—the story goes—broke down her door. She flushed a little parcel down the toilet but did not escape being hauled away, along with her manager, on drug charges. On one of the second floor's cheery yellow walls a plaque somberly marks Lady Day's suite, number 203.

Nob Hill

Crocker Mansion "Spite Wall" Location

Former address: 1150 California Street (mansion); and the southwest corner of Sacramento and Taylor Streets (wall). Current address: Grace Cathedral, 1100 California Street, between Jones and Taylor Streets, on Nob Hill. Plaque is just to the right of the California Street entrance. Cathedral open Sun.–Fri., 7:00 A.M.–6:00 P.M., Sat., 8:00 A.M.–6:00 P.M. (415) 749-6300 or (415) 749-6304.

Charles Crocker was one of the "Big Four," the California robber barons who made uncountable millions off the flood of hopefuls who came west during the gold rush. He was also one of the worst neighbors in history. In 1877 Crocker bought almost the entire block where Grace Cathedral now stands, tore down the houses thereon, and built a grotesquely gaudy mansion. Only one homeowner, Nicholas Yung, refused to sell. Crocker's grand estate was ruined by a single interloper: Yung's house jutted into the middle of Crocker's property. No matter how much money Crocker offered, nor how extreme his threats, Yung wouldn't budge. Vowing revenge, the millionaire built a thirty-foot-high "spite wall" around three sides of Yung's house. This effectively plunged the Yung home into perpetual darkness, since the only exposed side of the house faced north. Yung retaliated by putting a ten-foot-long coffin adorned with skull and crossbones on his roof in full view of the Crocker bedrooms. This bizarre standoff became a tourist attraction in Victorian San Francisco. After both men died, their heirs patched things up. The 1906 earthquake and fire leveled the whole block anyway, and the Crocker family donated the land to the Episcopal Church, which built this cathedral. Crocker's mansion was on the California Street side (marked today by a plaque at the church's entrance), and the spite wall was on the other side of the block on the south side of Sacramento Street, just west of Taylor Street.

Brocklebank Apartments
As seen in Vertigo.

   1000 Mason Street, at Sacramento Street.

In *Vertigo* this luxurious 1926 apartment building was the home of Kim Novak's blond character, Madeleine. She is shown repeatedly walking in and out of its grand façade. Other movies and TV shows filmed here include *The Lady in Red, The Streets of San Francisco,* and *Hart to Hart.* Columnist Herb Caen lived here for years.

York Hotel
Vertigo's *"Empire Hotel."*

   940 Sutter Street, at Leavenworth Street. (415) 885-6800.

York Hotel

I n *Vertigo* this was the home of Kim Novak's *non-*blond character, Judy. Shots of the exterior and an upstairs room were used in the film, though today no trace can be seen of the green neon sign that glowed outside Judy's window. While the film's "Empire Hotel" was a bit of a fleabag, the real thing has attractive stained glass, a piano bar, and a stylish European flair.

Another Dashiell Hammett Apartment
   1155 Leavenworth Street, at Sacramento Street.

H ammett fans making a pilgrimage must pay a visit to this address, where the author lived in number 4 (according to current residents) and finished writing *The Maltese Falcon.*

Sally Stanford's Bordello
Where the elite used to come.

   1144 Pine Street, between Jones and Leavenworth Streets, on the north side of the street.

S ally Stanford was the Heidi Fleiss of her day, procuring for high rollers. Later the popular madam entered the political ring herself and was elected mayor of Sausalito. During the '40s a large Victorian home on this property was Stanford's main place of business. Regular clients included heirs and stars and other discerning types. But by the late 1960s the high-class whores were gone, the once lush house decrepit. It was razed, and the garden apartments that replaced it, considered avant-garde for their time, found their way into *Sunset* magazine.

Hard Rock Café

1699 Van Ness Avenue, at Sacramento Street, on the west side of the street. Open Sun.–Thurs. 11:30 A.M.–11:00 P.M.; Fri.–Sat. 11:30 A.M.–midnight. (415) 885-1699.

A gratifying array of guitars on display here includes souvenirs from Nirvana, Pearl Jam, George Harrison, Frank Zappa, Roger McGuinn, and oodles more. Also on the restaurant's walls are Björk's coat, Mick's blouse, Elton's platforms, Clapton's jacket, and Dennis Wilson's aloha shirt. An entire wall dedicated to John Lennon offers his own drawings, historic photos, and a hat. Autographed items, vintage concert posters, and gold records are everywhere. Examine an elaborate hash pipe made from a hand-painted tambourine: poster artist Rick Griffin gave it to Jimi Hendrix in 1969.

Björk's coat, Hard Rock Café

Trailside Killer Apartment

1140 Sutter Street, between Polk and Larkin Streets, in the "Nobberloin" area at the base of Nob Hill.

Though he was charged in his youth with numerous sex crimes, San Francisco's David Carpenter grew up to be an apparently ordinary husband and father. But soon after the birth of his third child, Carpenter beat a woman nearly to death with a hammer in the Presidio. He went to prison and his wife divorced him. Upon his release Carpenter married a second time. The newlyweds are said to have been living in this apartment house when the ex-con committed a string of violent rapes in 1970; Carpenter was caught and jailed. Not for long enough, though, because when next released he swung into action again, as the Trailside Killer, murdering hikers all over northern California. (See also **Trailside Killer** entries, pages 239–40.)

Trailside Killer apartment

Avalon Ballroom Site

Regency II Theater, 1268 Sutter Street, at Van Ness Avenue.
(415) 776-8054.

In the '60s this address belonged to one of San Francisco's greatest rock venues, the Avalon Ballroom. (Reportedly its motto was "May the good Lord shut your mouth and open your mind.") With the help of hippie concert promoters the Family Dog, every band that mattered was booked here. Fans grooved on the Doors, Canned Heat, Blue Cheer, the Grateful Dead, and Jefferson Airplane while swirly colored lights made it all *so* trippy. Janis Joplin debuted here with Big Brother and the Holding Company. Today what used to be the ballroom is an upper story above the cinema, inaccessible to the public.

Regency II Theater, once the Avalon Ballroom

Chinatown

Golden Dragon Massacre Site

Golden Dragon restaurant, 822 Washington Street (another entrance is at 816 Washington), between Grant Avenue and Stockton Street, on the north side of the street. Open daily 8:00 A.M.–11:30 P.M. (415) 398-3920.

Throughout the summer of 1977 tensions had been rising between two Chinatown street gangs. An argument over turf (including protection rackets and even illegal firecracker sales) sparked sporadic violence. At 2:40 A.M. on September 4 three masked gunmen burst into this all-night restaurant and sprayed the place with bullets. Five died, eleven were seriously injured. The intended targets—rival gang members—managed to dodge the gunfire, and survived. Though the gunmen were later caught, Chinatown's image as a friendly tourist haven was tarnished forever, business sagged—and diners shunned the Golden Dragon. But tourists soon had other things on their minds with the Dan White assassinations and the Jonestown disaster a year later. A refurbished Golden Dragon is again open for business.

Bruce Lee's Birthplace
Enter the Dragon.

> Chinese Hospital, 845 Jackson Street, between Stockton and Powell Streets. (415) 982-2400.

The kung fu king's shocking death in 1973 sparked endless speculation. Was it murder, or merely an allergic reaction? At least we can be sure about his birth: on November 27, 1940—the year of the dragon—a baby boy named Lee Jun Fan was born at what was then known as Jackson Street Hospital. His father was far away, reportedly performing with a Chinese opera troupe in New York. As the new mother had not yet thought up an American name for her infant, a hospital staffer came up with Bruce. Soon after, parents and baby went home to Hong Kong. A plaque in the hospital's lobby, donated by his family, denotes this as his birthplace.

Duncombe Alley Opium Den Sites
> Duncombe Alley branches north off Jackson Street, midway between Grant Avenue and Stockton Street, opposite Ross Alley.

This short alleyway was once crowded with opium dens, especially along the west side (on your left as you look into the alley from Jackson Street). Despite sensationalistic stories in the newspapers of the day, most opium dens in the 1800s were not pestilential hellholes of vice where white girls were led astray by the evil poppy. Rather the typical den served the same purpose as a neighborhood bar ("where everybody *forgets* your name"). It was a place for Chinese laborers to spend a relaxing evening. (The British once went to war with China to ensure that English merchants could sell opium to the Asian populace, a practice the Chinese national government was trying to eradicate.) Though it sounds exotic and dangerous today, opium was legal in the nineteenth century. It was a common ingredient in patent medicines sold in corner stores all over the country. Public opium smoking was frowned upon, however, so many Chinatown shops had a cozy spot in the back where customers who brought their own could light up without

Duncombe Alley

offending any passing missionaries. If you didn't have any of your own, or wanted to really make a night of it—or a weekend, or a lifetime—you came here to the "opium resorts," as they were sometimes called, and dreamed away your troubles. A fence now blocks the alley's entrance, though it always seems to be unlocked. And the buildings

here were completely redone after the 1906 earthquake, so little evidence remains of
the past.

Jackson Street Opium Den Sites
*The dens were at 720–730 Jackson Street, between Grant Avenue and Stockton Street, on
the north side of the street.*

An informal 1885 census counted no less than twenty-six opium dens in Chinatown. Most catered to Chinese, but some had white patrons as well. A veritable
opium emporium flourished here on Jackson. It became quite well known for its
mixed clientele, and because so many of its patrons became desperate addicts. (Doctors came up with a solution, developing a substitute that could be ingested without
smoking. It was called heroin.) The original buildings are long gone; 730 Jackson is
an apartment house, and 728 Jackson is home to Wing On Trading Inc., which sells
exotic herbs. The Wo Chong produce store at 720 Jackson has behind its cash register what looks like a mysterious small doorway leading down into a dark basement,
where one of the most infamous dens was reported to be.

Jackson Street Prostitute "Cribs" Site
The cribs were along Jackson Street on either side of Grant Avenue.

The world of prostitution in old San Francisco had a clearly delineated hierarchy.
On top were the parlor houses and brothels with their fancy whores; next,
dance halls and saloons with their hard-drinking party girls; then the streetwalkers,
who couldn't find work anywhere else. At the very bottom were "cribs," grungy little
pens where the scum of San Francisco sought relief. The cribs were often in converted cellars partitioned into four-foot-by-six-foot cubicles, each furnished with a
cot. Only the unluckiest, most desperate girls wound up here, confined like beasts in
stalls. Mainly they were diseased, aging, or homely ex-streetwalkers; mentally ill or
drug-addicted prostitutes; or Chinese slave girls who had no way to escape. The girls
would expose themselves through gates near ground level, enticing down-and-outers
with promises of cheap sex. And cheap it was. The only English many crib girls knew
was the then-familiar chant, "Ten-cent lookee, twenty-five cent feelie, fifty-cent
doee." Some were forced to take in forty or fifty men a night. Many crib girls died of
VD or hunger before their twentieth birthdays—sometimes long before. Many were
kicked out to make room for newcomers, who usually started at age twelve or thirteen. To numb the psychic and physical pain, many became addicted to opium,
worsening their plight. This system was tolerated by law enforcement until around
1917, when a coalition of temperance groups, suffragists, missionaries, and those
urging civic "purification" thankfully brought an end to the cribs. Jackson Street was

famous as the center of the red-light district and is said to have been lined with cribs, which were sometimes in the basements of legitimate businesses. Today it's a bustling commercial district lined with groceries and restaurants.

Teenage Prostitute Slave Market Location
At the back of St. Louis Place; the entrance to the alley is on the south side of Jackson Street, about a hundred feet west of Grant Avenue.

This obscure dead-end alleyway was once the setting for California's only slave market. The sort of slave market where captured Africans were sold to work on plantations was always illegal in California; what went on here was *sexual* slavery. Prepubescent and young teenage girls in China were lured to California with promises of jobs; some were bought from starving parents; many were simply kidnapped. After a miserable voyage the duped girls were brought to this alley, stripped, and sold to pimps and madams. The girls were led to believe that by law they had to pay off the cost of the voyage though many had sailed against their will. Purchasers received contracts, such as this one: "An agreement to assist a young girl named Loi Yau. Because she became indebted to her mistress for passage, food, etc., and has nothing to pay, she makes her body over to this woman Sep Sam to serve as a prostitute. . . ."

The contracts often specified an amount to be repaid through "labor," or a specific period of servitude (which could be extended if the girl "misbehaved"). In practice many died before becoming free. This system was illegal, but the white police rarely intervened. Between 1850 and 1906 thousands of Chinese girls lived short, agonizing lives as enslaved prostitutes in San Francisco. Before it was rebuilt after the 1906 earthquake, St. Louis Alley (as it was then called) had two branches, one of which (no longer extant) exited onto Grant Avenue. Where these two halves of St. Louis intersected—now the alley's southern end—was a small vacant lot in the center of the block, not visible from either Grant or Jackson. It's reasonable to surmise that the slave market was on this hidden corner, which is now the site of the building just to the right of the sign that says "DW Family Assn" at the back end of the alley.

Sullivan's Alley Whorehouse Locations
Sullivan's Alley is now named Jason Court, which branches off northward from Jackson, half a block west of Grant Avenue.

In days of yore Sullivan's Alley—like Bartlett Alley (see below)—was densely lined with whorehouses of every description. By day it looked much like any other Chinatown street, but at night it was thronged with pleasure seekers. Most gold rush–era Chinese immigrants were men. A few managed to bring their families, but racist anti-immigration measures soon shut the door. Antimiscegenation laws banned sex between partners of different races. So with so few marriageable Chinese women in town, many men visited Sullivan's Alley. It was dense with slave prostitutes smuggled here solely to service Chinatown's male population. The old Sullivan's Alley was once much, much longer than Jason Court is now, with several side alleys and cul-de-sacs branching off in every direction.

Bartlett Alley Whorehouse Locations

Bartlett Alley is now named Beckett Alley, which is just a few yards east of Grant Avenue between Jackson and Pacific Streets.

Now almost deserted, Beckett Alley gives no clue to its sordid past; before 1906 both sides of the street were wall-to-wall whorehouses. Almost all the girls who worked here were Chinese, though their clients came from all over the world. Some of the houses on Bartlett were high-class, but not all: Bartlett had more slave-girl prostitutes than any other street in San Francisco—a virtual sex factory with no escape for the young unfortunates imprisoned here. The buildings on the street now are of fairly recent vintage, but the ghosts are very, very old.

Ross Alley Gambling Parlor Locations

Ross Alley is located a half block west of Grant Avenue, running from Washington Street to Jackson Street.

So notorious were the rough-and-tumble underground casinos that occupied nearly every building on either side of this famous alley that Ross was for decades called "the street of the gamblers." Although some of the illegal gambling halls offered Western-style dice and card games, most featured Asian games. (Fantan, which involved guessing the number of buttons remaining after multiples of four were removed from a large pile, never caught on with Anglo gamblers, but a lottery game that evolved into the modern keno and a dominoes variant called pai gow are popular to this day in the high-tech casinos of Reno and Las Vegas.) Ever fearful of police raids, each gambling parlor had a thick metal sliding door that would slam shut when spotters stationed in the street gave the danger signal. By day the alleyway was sedate, but at night gamblers crowded Ross cheek by jowl, desperate to squander their wages. The parlors are now but a dim memory along the blocklong alley, but today's smells, graffiti, and shadowy doorways are probably not much different than they were back then.

Jun Yu Barbershop
Snipping the stars.

> 32 Ross Alley, at Jackson Street, on the east side of the street. Open daily 9:00 A.M.–6:00 P.M. (415) 362-7776.

I t's not Vidal Sassoon, but this tiny slip of an old-fashioned barbershop has earned quite a reputation among visiting movie stars and film crews. Snapshots filling the window in its pink façade reveal satisfied customers, including Clint Eastwood, Michael Douglas, Matt Dillon, Russell Wong, Carl Reiner, Eric Roberts, the late River Phoenix, and many more.

Pictures in window of Jun Yu Barbershop

Sun Yat-sen's Office
Where a popular hero organized the overthrow of the Chinese government.

> Ghee Kung Tong headquarters, 36 Spofford Alley, on the east side of the street, between Washington and Clay Streets.

S un Yat-sen was a revolutionary, but not the wild-eyed kind. He was a *nice* revolutionary who simply wanted to throw off the yoke of centuries of oppression and set his people free. A wanted man in China, Sun came to San Francisco in 1904 and settled in the office of a Chinese secret society called the Ghee Kung Tong (sometimes also transliterated as Chee Kung Tong). Sun had free rein to use the tong's newspaper, the *Chinese Free Press,* to rally support for his cause. For six years Sun's articles and editorials were devoured by Chinese all around the world. He whipped up support for his government-in-waiting and generated international pressure against the old regime. When the Manchu Dynasty— Mongolian conquerors who had ruled China since the 1600s—finally fell on October 10, 1911, jubilation filled the streets of Chinatown. Men were finally allowed to cut

Ghee Kung Tong headquarters, Spofford Alley

off their queues, the long ponytails that the Manchus made every Chinese male wear as a sign of subjugation. Sun was elected president of his country's first democratic government, and for a while this building at 36 Spofford Alley functioned essentially as a branch office of the new administration, selling bonds to eager buyers.

The rest of the story is not so pretty. Sun's government only lasted a short time before squabbles between the army and a large band of peasant Communists led to a messy civil war that was complicated by a full-scale Japanese invasion. The squabbling groups cooperated to boot out the Japanese, but the civil war rages to this day. The Chinese Republicans—Sun Yat-sen's political descendants—retreated to Taiwan in 1949, while the Communists gained control of the mainland. Each side still claims to be China's only legitimate government. Whatever the eventual result, this major chapter in world history started right here in this Chinatown alley. The Ghee Kung Tong occupies the building to this day: beneath its name the door reads "Chinese Free Mason of the World," revealing the group's Masonic origins. Along the alley, birdsong competes with the clack of mah-jongg tiles as laundry flutters in the breeze and shoppers walk past with bags of bok choy. Revolution or no revolution, life goes on.

Waverly Place Tong Wars Location

Waverly Place is a half block west of Grant Avenue, running from Sacramento Street to Washington Street.

You can't tell by looking at it, but little Waverly Place has seen more violence and bloodshed than almost any street in America. From the 1870s until the turn of the century, this narrow alley was a major battleground for rival Chinese tongs settling their differences the hard way. Tongs were mutual-protection societies for immigrants from the same province in China or with the same profession. Not unlike the Teamsters or the Calabrian Mafia, tongs did not shy away from violence when it was needed to protect their status or economic position. While respectable elders ran the business side, street toughs trying to prove themselves did the dirty work. Since the Chinese did not have much access to guns in those days, the battles were often fought with razor-sharp hatchets, meat cleavers, or martial-arts weapons. In a scene reminiscent of a grainy old kung fu movie, one famous battle in 1879 saw fifty men fighting hand to hand over the right to exploit a beautiful teenage prostitute. At least four men were hacked to death that day. (Ironically, in the late 1800s the southern block of Waverly, between Clay and Sacramento, had a dozen brothels staffed exclusively by white prostitutes.) Similar "wars" raged periodically until the 1906 earthquake put a damper on things by leveling the neighborhood. Prohibition brought a new round of gang violence to Waverly Place in the '20s, but its repeal in 1933 brought an end to the tong-war era, making way for today's comparatively benign tong presence. Dashiell Hammett mentioned these latter-day tong wars in some of his stories, and the goofy action-comedy *Big Trouble in Little China* depicted a supernatural version of a San Francisco tong war in which some of the fighters had magical powers. A scene in *The Joy Luck Club* (one of whose characters is named Waverly, after the street) was filmed on location here as well. It's now the prototypical

Chinatown alley, with flower shops, rusty fire escapes, and—still—offices for many of the community's leading tongs.

North Beach

hungry i Location
Where Lenny Bruce was arrested.

Former address: 599 Jackson Street, at Kearny Street.

Later it moved to another address and became a sleazy nightspot, but during the '50s and '60s the hungry i was right here. A folk-music and comedy club, it regularly featured Lenny Bruce, Bob Newhart, Bill Cosby, Jonathan Winters, Shelley Berman, Mort Sahl, the Limelighters, the Kingston Trio, and others. Hepness abounded. Bruce was arrested here, an incident that failed to silence him. In the late '50s Winters reportedly gave bizarre stand-up performances in which he mumbled and wept and disparaged Harry Truman. (Another story is told from that time, in which cops found Winters clinging to a ship's rigging in San Francisco harbor, claiming to be from outer space. He was taken to San Francisco General Hospital for observation.) There is now no trace of the old hungry i at its original location.

The Purple Onion
Where Phyllis Diller cracked them up.

140 Columbus Avenue, at Jackson Street, on the east side of the street. (415) 389-8415.

In the '50s and early '60s the Purple Onion was a rich spawning ground for comedians and singers who later became legendary. The Kingston Trio and the Smothers Brothers were regulars on its stage. So were Phyllis Diller, Lenny Bruce, Red Buttons, the Mamas and the Papas, Mort Sahl, Pat Paulsen, the New Christy Minstrels, Robert Goulet, and Bill Dana—better known as his character "Jose Jimenez." Barbra Streisand and Woody Allen are said to have done a few early stints as well. That incarnation of the Purple Onion closed in the mid-1960s; its current one opened circa 1993. Now the purple-awninged club hosts up-and-coming punk, retro, and garage bands.

Vesuvio
Bohemian watering hole.

255 Columbus Avenue, near Broadway. Open daily 6:00 A.M.–2:00 A.M. (415) 362-3370.

L egend has it that the night Jack Kerouac was supposed to meet Henry Miller in
Big Sur he spent here instead, drinking himself silly. Ever since it opened in
1949, this bar has attracted bohos of every stripe; it was a beat hub. Murals out front
depict peace signs, psychedelia and poetry. Inside are collaged tables and walls
crowded with photos, newspaper clippings, and altered-consciousness-inspired artworks. Prominently displayed are framed photos of former habitués including Kerouac, Allen Ginsberg, and Lawrence Ferlinghetti (whose City Lights bookshop is
across the alley). Vesuvio is a must on any beat pilgrimage; Kerouac aficionado
Johnny Depp stops by whenever he's in town. And the alley running alongside this
bar is now named Jack Kerouac Place.

City Lights Bookstore

261 Columbus Avenue, at Broadway. Open daily 10:00 A.M.–midnight. (415) 362-1901.

M ixing business with pleasure, beat poet Lawrence Ferlinghetti cofounded this
rambling two-story shop circa 1953. Right in the heart of Beatsville, it became a hangout for writers and their acolytes. Deciding to publish books, too, Ferlinghetti released a City Lights edition of his pal Allen Ginsberg's epic *Howl,* later to
successfully ride out an obscenity charge. In his book *Big Sur,* Jack Kerouac writes
fondly of the store and its owner. Beat books are still a specialty here, and a gruff but
tolerant ambience persists.

The Condor
Where topless dancing was born.

300 Columbus Avenue, at Broadway. Open daily 11:00 A.M.–2:00 A.M. (415) 781-8222.

T hese days it's a sports bar whose patrons enjoy televised football and boxing. But
this is where, in 1964, topless dancing got its start. A male worker got the idea
to (un)dress busty dancer Carol Doda in a topless bikini, a style popularized by
avant-garde couturier Rudi Gernreich. Doda's act was the first of its kind, and the
club became wildly famous. For years San Francisco was the only city in America
where performers could legally bare their breasts during shows. In a bizarre 1983
mishap, two workers were making whoopee after hours atop a trick piano when the
instrument (rigged on cables to move up and down from ceiling to stage) ascended
unexpectedly and crushed the man to death, pinning his terrified girlfriend between
his corpse and the piano till morning.

Tosca Café
As seen in **Basic Instinct.**

242 Columbus Avenue. Open daily, 5:00 A.M.–2:00 A.M. (415) 391-1244.

In *Basic Instinct,* Michael Douglas's troubled character loiters here with colleagues. The movie makes lesbians look bad, and during the filming at Tosca, savvy gay activists protested out front. The Italianate nightspot was temporarily transformed into a fighter-pilot bar for *The Right Stuff,* whose cast made themselves at home while the movie was being filmed here. Pictures and memorabilia on display recall those days, when Chuck Yeager himself played pool here with the actors. Latter-day habitués include Jack Nicholson, Robin Williams, Francis Ford Coppola, and Tom Waits.

Caffé Trieste

601 Vallejo Street, at Grant Avenue. Open Sun.–Thurs. 6:30 A.M.–11:00 P.M.; Fri.–Sat. 6:30 A.M.–midnight. (415) 392-6739.

Jutting out like a hitchhiker's thumb, this corner café was a fave among beat writers and their finger-snapping, espresso-sipping, black-stockinged imitators. Its rich heritage has lured literati and poseurs ever since, and the place is usually packed—particularly on Saturdays, when the proprietors do impromptu operatic concerts. Rumor has it that Francis Ford Coppola worked on his script for *The Godfather* here.

Co-Existence Bagel Shop Site
Where the Beats ate borscht.

Now North Beach Video, 1398 Grant Avenue, at Green Street. Open daily noon–10:00 P.M. (415) 398-7773.

When North Beach was Beatsville, this café stayed open well into the wee hours—till 4:00 A.M. on weekends. Its wall-size bulletin board overflowed with blurbs announcing poetry readings and jazz gigs. The era's most happening writers and artists hung out here before the place shut down circa 1960. Now it's a video store; filmmakers remodeled it when they were shooting 1999's *EdTV* here.

"The Place" Site
Where Kerouac courted disaster.

1546 Grant Avenue, between Union and Filbert Streets.

A tavern called the Place once occupied this address. And in the first part of Jack Kerouac's novel *Big Sur,* that tavern is allegedly where the dissolute protagonist (hmm, who might that be?) gets really drunk. The bar boasted avant-garde art and popular "Chatterbox Nights," aka "Blabbermouth Nights," which had in turn evolved from "Dada Nights." For three minutes any patron could stand and say anything from the bar's built-in pulpit. The storefront structure is still here but new occupants, unaware of its history, removed the historic pulpit.

Mabuhay Gardens Site
Punk rock mecca.

> 443 Broadway, on the south side of the street, between Kearny and Montgomery Streets. The site is now occupied by the Velvet Lounge.

This story's unlikely hero is a cranky and completely unhip producer named Dirk Dirksen. In the mid-1970s he approached a struggling Filipino supper club ("mabuhay" is a multipurpose Tagalog word similar to the Hawaiian "aloha") and wangled the job of booking offbeat acts for late-night shows on its stage. When punk rock hit San Francisco in late '76, Dirksen made "the Mab" into a West Coast CBGB. No punk himself, Dirksen became the patron saint of the punk community, emceeing the shows like an ill-tempered baby-sitter with a Hitlerian mustache. Local faves like the Mutants, the Dead Kennedys, and the Avengers dueled for the ever-swelling audience's attention with visiting stars like Devo, the Ramones, and Blondie. But times changed, and the Mabuhay closed sometime in the mid-'90s. Now the site is occupied by the Velvet Lounge, a dance bar that features unironic '70s and '80s revival nights.

Allen Ginsberg Apartment
Where he wrote Howl.

> 1010 Montgomery Street, at Broadway.

These days a Chinese child care service operates on the ground floor, with apartments above. In 1955 one furnished unit in this sun-washed gray edifice was home to Allen Ginsberg. Many agree that this is where, inspired by jazz phrasings and the idea of making poems with looong lines, he wrote a major part of *Howl*.

Allen Ginsberg apartment house

Dark Passage House

1360 Montgomery Street, north of Union Street, on the east side of the street, near the top of Telegraph Hill.

Adorned with silvery bas-reliefs depicting boats, heroic figures, and the Bay Bridge, this three-story Moderne apartment house is a glass-brick-studded work of art. An etched-glass nautical motif decorates its entryway. An apartment here featured prominently in *Dark Passage,* where Lauren Bacall's character hides an escaped prisoner played by Humphrey Bogart. Both exterior and interior scenes were shot at the house, which has been dubbed by some "the Bogey building." The current resident of Bacall's apartment has been known to place a life-size cardboard Bogart in the window, to the astonishment of passersby.

Dark Passage *house*

Philo T. Farnsworth Laboratory Site
Where TV was born.

200 Green Street, at Sansome Street.

Today several different companies occupy the complex at what used to be 202 and is now 200. In the Aspen Graphics print shop downstairs a small display area on one wall tells the tale of how, on this spot on September 7, 1927, humble Mormon farm boy Philo T. Farnsworth invented the world's first all-electronic television system when he was only twenty-one. Three years later, he made the first-ever long-distance TV broadcast from here as well. Arguably a genius, Farnsworth beat RCA to the punch and later won a legal case against them, but he never received much in the way of royalties. He died broke in 1971. Upstairs in the building a TV production company—having fondly named itself "Philo" and named its editing suites after members of the Farnsworth family—makes infomercials. Outside, a metal plaque on the corner commemorates the "U.S. pioneer in electronics" who made history pretty much all by himself "in a simple laboratory on this site."

Philo T. Farnsworth laboratory site

Russian Hill

Neal Cassady–Jack Kerouac House
29 Russell Street, between Hyde and Eastman Streets, on the south side of the street.

Wedged tightly between two neighboring houses along a teensy-weensy street, this brown-shingled A-frame is where Neal and Carolyn Cassady lived in 1951. Their pal Jack Kerouac came for a visit and settled into the attic the following year, while creating great literature and banging both husband and wife. Today the chimes of passing cable cars echo up and down the lane.

Neal Cassady–Jack Kerouac house

Jimmy Stewart's *Vertigo* Apartment
900 Lombard Street, at Jones Street, on the northwest corner.

In *Vertigo*, Jimmy Stewart's neurotic cop lives in a streamlined bachelor apartment. After saving the life of the cryptic blond object of his desire, he brings her here. The pair warm up in front of a cheery fireplace. Later we see him outside the building, where a metal grille at the entryway has a Chinese motif. Today that grille is gone, but this cream-colored stucco two-story still stands at the foot of Lombard Street's famous zigzags. Hitchcock filmed all exterior and front door scenes here, but—as always—he recreated the interior scenes in a studio, using footage filmed out the door here as a backdrop.

Jimmy Stewart's Vertigo *apartment*

VERTIGO FILMING LOCATION TOUR

In Alfred Hitchcock's 1958 thriller *Vertigo*, retired cop Jimmy Stewart is hired to spy on the wife of an old acquaintance. The striking blonde, played by Kim Novak, leads him on a bizarre chase; Stewart is soon convinced she's either crazy or the reincarnation of a long-dead relative, or both. His obsession takes him through an astounding series of plot twists that still leave audiences astonished after nearly half a century. Many consider *Vertigo* the quintessential San Francisco film: while Hitchcock shot almost all of *Vertigo*'s interior scenes in a studio, its unforgettable exteriors were filmed all over the City by the Bay. Here's a self-guided tour to *Vertigo* filming locations; some have their own complete listings elsewhere in the book, as noted.

- **Brocklebank Apartments.** *1000 Mason Street, at Sacramento Street.* This real-life apartment building was Kim Novak's fictional home in the first half of the film (see page 204).
- **Jimmy Stewart's Apartment.** *900 Lombard Street, at Jones Street.* Jimmy Stewart brings Kim Novak here after saving her life (see page 219).
- **Ernie's.** *847 Montgomery Street.* Though two scenes were set in this venerable (now closed) North Beach restaurant, neither was filmed on location: Hitchcock re-created Ernie's on a soundstage.
- **Podesta Baldocchi.** *224 Grant Avenue (old location).* Kim Novak buys flowers at this florist, but it has since moved to a different location and there is no trace of the shop depicted in the film.
- **Mission Dolores Cemetery.** *Enter through the church gift shop on the west side of Dolores Street, between 16th Street and Chula Lane.* Kim Novak visits a mysterious grave at this old cemetery (see page 235).
- **Palace of the Legion of Honor.** *Entrance at Thirty-fourth Avenue and Clement Street, in Lincoln Park.* Jimmy Stewart follows Kim Novak here as she views a mysterious portrait.
- **"McKittrick Hotel."** *1007 Gough Street, at Eddy Street.* This imaginary Victorian hotel where Kim Novak becomes Carlotta Valdes was in fact a private home that was torn down a short time after filming. Modern apartments now occupy the site.
- **Fort Point.** *At the end of Marine Drive, directly under the Golden Gate Bridge, at the northernmost tip of the Presidio and San Francisco.* One of *Vertigo*'s most famous scenes takes place here under the Golden Gate Bridge (see page 238).

- **Big Basin Redwoods State Park.** *On Big Basin Way (Highway 236), northwest of Boulder Creek in Santa Cruz County.* A short scene in a redwood forest was supposedly set in Marin County's Muir Woods, but *Vertigo*logists say it was actually filmed here in the Santa Cruz Mountains where the redwoods are a bit grander.
- **York ("Empire") Hotel.** *940 Sutter Street, at Leavenworth Street.* Kim Novak's second cinematic home was here at the "Empire Hotel" (see page 205).
- **Mission San Juan Bautista.** *Mariposa and Second Streets along the northern edge of San Juan Bautista, near Monterey. Vertigo's* dizzying climax takes place here, though the famous bell tower was merely an optical effect added later (see page 181).

Bullitt Chase Scene

The streets around Russian Hill, including Chestnut Street and the intersection of Taylor and Vallejo Streets. See below for more details.

Many consider *Bullitt*'s rip-roaring high-speed pursuit through the streets of San Francisco the greatest car chase ever recorded on film. Other cinematic chases may be flashier or have more explosions, but none match *Bullitt*'s gritty authenticity. It was all filmed in real time, with Steve McQueen and two stunt drivers piloting real cars down real streets at up to 110 miles an hour—almost no other car chases have been filmed "at speed" like this. McQueen (and the other drivers) practically destroyed his Mustang's inner workings as he leaped over hills, careened down dizzyingly steep slopes, and turned impossible corners. Every shudder and jerk, every smoking wheel, every crunching landing was recorded by cameras mounted in the cars without shock absorbers. Ever since the film's 1968 big-screen release, countless viewers have asked: can *I* follow the route of the chase? Well, not really. It is a pastiche of scenes filmed all over the hills of San Francisco. From all accounts, many of the scenes were shot on Russian Hill's clifflike thoroughfares: McQueen's car goes airborne at the intersection of Taylor and Vallejo. Later both cars plunge down Chestnut Street. Other segments are up for debate. Fillmore Street between Broadway and Green is especially *Bullitt*esque, and Army Street (now Cesar Chavez Street) is often cited as a filming location as well. The chase seems to be heading for the Golden Gate Bridge, but city officials nixed permission to film there, so the drivers unexpectedly pop up on the Peninsula, south of the city—defying geographical logic.

The Marina and Pacific Heights

THE MARINA

Alcatraz

In San Francisco Bay, north of San Francisco. To reach the island, take a Blue & Gold Fleet ferry from Pier 41, on the Embarcadero near the intersection of Powell and Jefferson Streets, between Fisherman's Wharf and Pier 39. Ferries leave at 9:30 A.M., 10:15 A.M., and then every half-hour until 4:15 P.M. (2:15 P.M. in winter). Return ferries also depart every half-hour until 6:30 P.M. (4:30 P.M. in winter). Visitors can stay as long as they wish (though not overnight). The tour is popular, and the lines to buy a ticket for same-day travel are very long; it is easier (though more expensive) to order tickets in advance by phone. Prices by phone: $14.50 with audio tour (children, $9.25); $11 without audio tour (children, $7.75). Prices in person: $12.25 with audio tour (children, $7); $8.75 without audio tour (children, $5.50). Call (415) 705-5555 for tickets, or (415) 556-0560 for information.

After a seventy-year stint as a grim military prison, Alcatraz started a new career in 1934 as a federal penitentiary specifically designed to hold escape artists, incorrigibles, and celebrity criminals who posed a security risk. The worst of the worst from federal prisons nationwide were transferred here, including Al Capone, George "Machine Gun" Kelly, Alvin "Creepy" Karpis, and Robert Stroud, the "Birdman of Alcatraz." Within a year it was the world's most famous prison and remained so until 1963, when Attorney General Robert F. Kennedy closed it—the place just cost too much to run. Many of its official records were subsequently lost or thrown away; some were loaned to a researcher who never returned them. Thus crucial details about Alcatraz's history are unknown. Modern visitors, for example, always want to see Al Capone's cell, and although one in B Block is identified as his, no one knows for sure. (He *did* prefer to play a banjo in the shower room rather than risk violence in the exercise yard.) "Machine Gun" Kelly stayed somewhere in C Block, but again the exact location is a mystery. But both gangsters were saintly compared to Robert "Birdman" Stroud. Forget about Burt Lancaster's nicey-nice portrayal: Stroud was a psychopath. An Alaskan pimp, he went to Leavenworth for murdering a bartender. It was there he studied birds (not on Alcatraz, despite the movie) when not snitching on fellow inmates, raping new arrivals, and killing guards. All of this earned him a one-way ticket to Alcatraz. After six years in solitary confinement in D Block, cell 42, he was transferred to the hospital ward, where his obsessive, constant masturbation so revolted the staff that they installed a wooden door to block their view of him. (This still-extant "masturbation door" is *not* discussed on the audio tour.)

Some prisoners couldn't stand prisondom's deepest dungeon. A squad of desperate inmates staged a bloody but futile takeover on May 2, 1946. The only ones to make it off the island did so in coffins—the rest were subdued and tossed into solitary confinement. (Bullet holes from this disastrous "Battle of Alcatraz" can still be seen in D Block.) For the story behind a more successful escape attempt, head down to cells 138, 140, and 144 in B Block. It was from here in 1962 that Frank Morris and the Anglin brothers escaped, becoming the only three prisoners ever to make it off Alcatraz without an escort. Officially, they were presumed dead, washed out to sea by the strong currents, but it is likely that they actually made it ashore. Either way, cops never found them. The incident was glamorized in the Clint Eastwood vehicle *Escape from Alcatraz*, which was filmed on location in C Block (*The Rock* was shot here as well).

After the prison closed, government officials in the '60s and '70s entertained bizarre and far-fetched plans for the island: covering it with a Plexiglas dome; using it as an anchorage for a new bridge to Marin County; installing a wax museum; even erecting a gigantic West Coast counterpart to the Statue of Liberty, to be called the Statue of Justice. Instead, the island lay dormant, abandoned. So on November 20, 1969, a band of Native Americans seized it, citing a century-old treaty allowing Indians to occupy unused government land. Their claim was completely legitimate, and public opinion was heavily in their favor. So they stayed. After a year and a half the government displaced them by finding a "use" for the land—as a tourist attraction.

Dan White's Hot Potato Stand

The Hot Potato was at the entrance to Pier 39, directly in front of where Burger Café and Burrito Wraps now stand, on your left as you first enter the pier. Pier 39 is next to the intersection of the Embarcadero and Beach Street, at the northeast tip of San Francisco.

Dan White was having trouble making ends meet on his modest supervisor's salary. So in October 1978 White's political supporters arranged for him to get the franchise to run a baked-potato stand at the new Pier 39, at that time also known as North Point Pier. He donned a chef's apron and gave it a go. The stall, called the Hot Potato, was not a full-fledged restaurant, but a small cart. (Perhaps *this* Republican Dan knew how to spell "potatoe.") It didn't last long. Driven to a murderous frenzy by Twinkies and hate, White assassinated Mayor George Moscone and Supervisor Harvey Milk just two months into his potato career (see page 201). (Perhaps he should have eaten more potatoes and less junk food.) The cart is now long gone as well, replaced by the traditional Burger Café and the more avant-garde Burrito Wraps.

Longshoremen's Hall
Musical spawning ground.

400 North Point Street, at Mason Street. (415) 776-8100.

Jefferson Airplane and the Charlatans entertained at a dance held here on October 16, 1965. That show is now considered the first hippie concert ever. Ahead-of-their-time rock promoters the Family Dog put it on, and the rest is history, man. Later concerts here debuted other future greats, including the Lovin' Spoonful. One show in January 1966 featured not only the Grateful Dead, Big Brother and the Holding Company, and Ken Kesey with his Merry Pranksters, but also a Chinese lion-dancing troupe.

6 Gallery Site
Where Ginsberg howled.

Now the location of Silk Route International, 3119 Fillmore Street, between Lombard and Union Streets. (415) 563-4936.

Now it's a carpet and antiques outlet on a trendissimo shopping street. But it was a gallery on October 13, 1955, when a now legendary reading was held here. The reading, *6 Poets at 6 Gallery,* included Allen Ginsberg, Gary Snyder, Phil Whalen, and Michael McClure. Philip Lamantia, the fifth, would read the work of the late John Hoffman. As emcee, Kenneth Rexroth was dismayed at the behavior of Jack Kerouac, who had elected not to read his own work but to sit drunkenly onstage shouting praise. (Kerouac later wrote of passing a jug of wine around the audience.) It was here that Ginsberg debuted *Howl.* From the moment he began—"I've seen the best minds of my generation destroyed by madness . . ."—the crowd was mesmerized.

PACIFIC HEIGHTS

Mrs. Doubtfire House
2640 Steiner Street, at Broadway.

With a widow's walk and round tower, this Victorian was used as the home where a divorced dad (portrayed by Robin Williams) uses a clever drag ruse to rejoin his kids. The home next door, to the south, portrayed the none-too-nice neighbor's house in the film.

Mrs. Doubtfire *house*

Zodiac Killer Murder and Escape Site

At the northeast corner of the intersection of Cherry and Washington Streets, at the curb in front of 3898 Washington Street, in the Presidio Heights neighborhood, just below the Presidio.

With his cryptographic notes to the cops and an airtight MO, the serial killer known as Zodiac still strikes fear in the hearts of northern Californians, even thirty years after his crime spree apparently ended. Zodiac was never caught, though cops came very close after witnesses in this exclusive neighborhood spotted him in the act. Sometime during the evening of October 11, 1969, Zodiac climbed into a taxi and asked to be driven to the corner of Washington and Maple Streets. Just before 10:00 P.M. two children looking out of the middle upstairs window of their home a block away, at 3899 Washington, spotted a man stealing the wallet of someone slumped in the front seat of a car. They called the police, who showed up almost immediately to discover cabbie Paul Stine shot to death in his taxi, parked in front of 3898 Washington, across the street from the witnesses. The police dispatcher mistakenly (and racistly) broadcast a description of the suspect as a black man. So when, moments later, police stopped a chunky white man walking north on Cherry Street just one block away from the crime, they believed his tale of having spotted a black man fleeing in a different direction. After they zoomed off, the real killer turned west from Cherry Street onto Jackson Street, then north through the Julius Kahn Playground into the impenetrable undergrowth of the Presidio. It was only when police received a corrected description of the suspect as a white man that they realized the man they had stopped was the killer. Too late. A frantic manhunt turned up nothing.

Days later Zodiac mailed a coded letter describing the incident in full: the killing, the police blunders, his escape route. He included in the envelope a piece of Stine's bloody shirt as proof. It was never explained why the cab was parked a block away from its intended destination, nor why Zodiac cut off a piece of the shirt, as if he knew ahead of time that he was going to elude capture and wanted evidence to prove he had been there. At no other time did the cops even come close to capturing Zodiac, though plenty of true-crime writers think they know who the killer is. The case has spawned dozens of books and was the inspiration for Clint Eastwood's *Dirty Harry* (in which the killer is called "Scorpio"). The corner where the crime happened looks very much the same today as it did then; but the million-dollar homes at Washington and Cherry are mute regarding the horror they witnessed. (See also **Zodiac Killer Tour, Vallejo,** pages 262–63.)

Western Addition and Nearby

People's Temple Site
1859 Geary Boulevard, near Fillmore Street.

A new four-story post office looms on the spot where megalomaniac Jim Jones charmed hundreds of admirers. Operating along vaguely Christian principles, his temple attracted down-and-outers, ex-cons, and ordinary folks, mostly African American, who gave up all they had to join him. Tales of torture and sexual misdeeds later surfaced, and in 1978 Jones led more than nine hundred cultists in a mass suicide in Guyana. Yet in 1977 Jones was a darling of political bigwigs who admired his ability to turn wasted lives around: Jimmy Carter, Jerry Brown, Jane Fonda, and doomed San Francisco mayor George Moscone were among Jones's ardent supporters. He received a plum humanitarian award. Before moving to Guyana he allegedly held a practice mass suicide here at his San Francisco temple, distributing a drink which he told his followers (untruthfully) was poisoned.

Fillmore Auditorium
1805 Geary Boulevard, at Fillmore Street, on the southwestern corner, upstairs. (415) 346-6000.

This theater was built in 1910, and what a long, strange trip it's been. Taking over around 1965, rock promoter Bill Graham booked bands that would soon become legendary. Jefferson Airplane was among the first to play at Graham's Fillmore. Jimi, Janis, the Yardbirds, Country Joe, the Four Tops, the Turtles, the Velvet Underground, the Mothers of Invention, Love, the Association, the Temptations, Sam the Sham and the Pharaohs, and the Dead trod its stage as well. Psychedelic fashion shows, tarot readings, and other events heightened the hippie factor. Live shows are still staged here sporadically.

Fillmore Auditorium

Winterland Site
2000 Post Street, at Steiner Street.

Nothing remains today of the historic concert hall where Janis and the Dead made a name for themselves, and where the Sex Pistols gave their last-ever concert in 1978, right before breaking up at the nearby Miyako Hotel. In 1986 an enormous apartment complex was built on the property where Winterland had recently been torn down. In the lobby at its Post Street entrance a photo exhibit shows the entertainment palace when it was still called Dreamland, circa 1928, then through the ensuing decades when Winterland was enjoyed by ice skaters, tennis players, and dancing fools. One of rock's most famous lines—"Ever get the feeling you've been cheated?"—was snarled by Johnny Rotten to the audience here as the Sex Pistols left the stage, ending their final concert.

Sex Pistols' Breakup Site
Anarchy in the U.S.A.

Now the Radisson Miyako Hotel, 1625 Post Street, at Laguna Street. (415) 922-3200.

On tour in mid-January 1978, the Sex Pistols were scheduled to appear at Winterland, San Francisco's venerable rock venue. The band's manager, Malcolm McLaren, booked himself, Steve Jones, and Paul Cook into the plush, Japanese-themed Miyako Hotel. But he booked band members Sid Vicious and Johnny Rotten into the run-down Cavalier Motel miles away, near the airport. During a spit-soaked and cynical show that allegedly netted the band $66, Rotten insulted the audience while his bandmates staggered through a ridiculously short set. Afterward the band gathered in McLaren's room at the Miyako and fought over a proposed trip to Brazil to visit exiled train robber Ronnie Biggs. Rotten had learned of the trip by chance from an outsider and suspected McLaren was trying to ditch him. Drugged and uncomprehending, Vicious smashed the room's mirror. Bitter arguing ensued— over motels, South America, and mistrust. Rotten quit—and found himself alone in San Francisco with twenty dollars to his name. The band promptly disintegrated, ending an era.

The hotel consistently attracts a rock 'n' roll crowd. John and Yoko used to stay here. Photos adorning a wall in the mezzanine-level bistro depict former guests including Steve Miller, Johnny Winter, Journey, Kitaro, and Roberta Flack. The Sex Pistols' picture has been removed.

Mary Ellen Pleasant Memorial
Remembering a voodoo queen.

Octavia Street at Bush Street, on the southwestern corner.

Some say she was a practitioner of magic and a procuress who found attractive young partners for the city's wealthiest men. Some say she was a skilled black-mailer. Some say she pushed one of those men, her boss, off a third-floor balcony. Yet to many she was a hero. Born a slave, the mysterious woman known in her day as Mammy Pleasant fought for abolition and helped finance the Underground Railroad. Her mansion at 1695 Octavia is long gone, but a porcelain plaque set into the sidewalk declares this as "Mammy Pleasant Memorial Park," honoring the "legendary pioneer" who "lived on this site and planted six trees." Her eucalyptus trees soar overhead, gigantic and gnarled.

Patty Hearst Captivity Apartment
1827 Golden Gate Avenue, #6, just west of Broderick Street.

Members of a self-styled revolutionary band calling themselves the Symbionese Liberation Army kidnapped heiress Patricia Hearst from her Berkeley home in 1974. They subsequently brought her to this unremarkable apartment house, indistinguishable from dozens surrounding it. And here, in an upstairs unit, they imprisoned Hearst for three months in a small hall closet, subjecting her to physical and mental abuse, repeated rape, starvation, and brainwashing. Eventually she snapped, joined her tormentors, and helped them rob a San Francisco bank.

Patty Hearst captivity apartment house

Westerfield House
Former home of Anton LaVey and Kenneth Anger (and possibly Ken Kesey).

1198 Fulton Street, at the northeast corner of Scott Street, on Alamo Square.

Who knows what secrets this five-story 1882 Italianate mansion harbors? Anton LaVey once lived here but was evicted for keeping a lion cub as a pet, giving it free run of the house. LaVey decamped to California Street, where he presided over his Church of Satan. Another satanic celebrity, Kenneth Anger, lived here and reportedly made some of his underground films, including *Scorpio Rising,* in its upstairs rooms. In *The Electric Kool-Aid Acid Test,* Tom Wolfe referred to this as one place where Ken Kesey dropped acid, but there is no evidence that Kesey actually lived here. For nearly a decade Westerfield was a crash pad where freaks, dropouts, and social revolutionaries passed through for a night—or a year. New owners have painted the house el-

Westerfield House

egant shades of olive and purple, and beautifully restored its Victorian detailing. The interior retains original gaslight fixtures from the era when radio pioneer Guglielmo

Marconi is rumored to have conducted early wireless broadcasting experiments on the top floor.

Interview with the Vampire House
503 Divisadero Street, at Fell Street.

Offices now occupy yet another lavish purple-and-green Victorian replete with stained glass, whimsical gingerbread, and ornate columns. When Anne Rice wrote *Interview with the Vampire,* she was living here, in an upstairs flat. The novel's first paragraph evokes the house: "He stood there against the dim light from Divisadero Street . . . a wash basin hung on one wall." The fictional interview happened here, too.

Interview with the Vampire *house*

Jefferson Airplane House
The Airplane's hangar.

2400 Fulton Street at Willard Street North, facing the northern side of Golden Gate Park.

Their star was on the rise, so Jefferson Airplane were hardly keeping a low profile when they moved into this mansion. Enormous Corinthian columns make it feel like a grand old library or a city hall. The band held legendary parties here, attended by the top rock celebrities of the '60s and '70s. These days security is high, and surveillance cameras scan the porch.

Jefferson Airplane house

Haight-Ashbury

Kenneth Rexroth Flat
Where writers dished dirt.

250 Scott Street, at Page Street, on the east side of the street.

Poet and powerful literary critic Kenneth Rexroth lived for years in a flat occupying the uppermost floor of this red-and-yellow Victorian apartment house. The building is now teetering on the verge of decrepitude, but in Rexroth's day, circa 1957, it was *the* literary hot spot. Literati were drawn to Rexroth's salons like moths to a flame. While the poet-critic was famous in his own right, many now remember him best for his dislike of Jack Kerouac, whom he blamed for facilitating an affair between another writer and Rexroth's wife. Decades after his departure, mail addressed to Rexroth is still delivered now and then to the record shop downstairs.

Big Brother and the Holding Company House
1090 Page Street near Broderick Street.

Rather slapdash and noodling musically, Big Brother and the Holding Company might not be remembered today if a certain young Texan vocalist hadn't joined them. Janis Joplin herself lodged for a while at their house here, which has since been torn down. Condos were erected on the spot in the mid-'70s. But way back when, one of the group's albums was recorded on the premises.

Condos on the site of the Big Brother house

Janis Joplin House

124 Lyon Street, at Oak Street (another entrance is at 1387 Oak). See below for details.

With then-boyfriend "Country Joe" McDonald, Janis lived—and lived it up— in this four-story Victorian. Its living room was painted black. The pair met after she moved into the house in 1967, soon to make waves at the Monterey Pop Festival. An argument with the landlord over Janis's dog ended with her eviction in 1968. In June 1999 the place was transformed into a rehab center for homeless drug-addicted mothers and their babies. (The 1968 phone book lists her official address as 122 Lyon—presumably upstairs in the same building. But other sources place her at 112 Lyon, a few doors up the street.)

The Herb'n Inn and Flower Power Walking Tours

525 Ashbury Street, just north of Haight Street. Tours depart 9:30 A.M. on Tuesdays and Saturdays. Tickets: $15. (415) 553-8542.

This bed-and-breakfast is a museum of psychedelic history, stocked with original concert posters, paraphernalia, photos, hemp products, and scrapbooks full of clippings tracking Haight-Ashbury's glory days. Proprietor Bruce Brennan, who runs the place with his sister Pam and readily spouts "I was there" reminiscences, leads twice-weekly walking tours through the district. The 2½-hour tours (open to all, not just the inn's guests) busily probe the ghosts of Jimi Hendrix, Jerry Garcia, the Diggers, the Human Be-In, and the Summer of Love.

Jimi Hendrix's "Red House"

Ashbury Tobacco Center, 1524 Haight Street, near Ashbury Street. (415) 552-5556.

On the second and third floors of the old Victorian at 1524 Haight Street, upstairs from what is now a head shop, Jimi Hendrix reportedly kept two girl-friends—one on each floor. Though he never actually lived here, he did spend many a night here in one bed or another. In his song "Red House," Jimi supposedly refers to this building (no longer red).

The Ashbury Tobacco Center below the former "Red House"

Grateful Dead House

710 Ashbury Street, between Waller and Frederick Streets.

Generations of Deadheads make the pilgrimage to this big purple Victorian with its gold trim and stained glass. In 1966–67, when they were the toast of the neighborhood, Jerry and the band lived here and just kept truckin' on. Today a securely locked front gate prevents bouquet-bearing pilgrims from blubbering all over the current occupants.

Grateful Dead house

Rudolf Nureyev–Margot Fonteyn Bust House

42 Belvedere Street, between Haight and Waller Streets.

After a performance one night in 1967 famed ballet dancers Rudolf Nureyev and Margot Fonteyn attended a party at this house in the heart of hippieland. The cops arrived sometime after 3:00 A.M. and found joints, suspicious pills, and a few rolls of film suspected of being pornographic. And they found Dame Fonteyn cowering on the roof in a fur coat. She and Nureyev were among the eighteen partiers arrested. After spending a few hours in jail all were released, and the charges were dropped the following day. Incised long ago in the once-wet cement out front, graffiti still adorn the triplex: flowers, a peace sign, and "Love Is Where It's At."

Manson Family House

636 Cole Street, between Haight and Waller Streets.

In 1967, surrounded by his hippie harem, Charles Manson lived in this stucco duplex with its charming marble entryway. Later they would move to southern California and murder people.

Manson Family house

Suzan and Michael Carson Murder House
Where the killer couple struck first.

825 Schrader Street, near Frederick Street.

Self-professed Moslem assassins Suzan and Michael Carson mooched off mellow hippies while dealing dope in the Haight, circa 1980. Many disliked their self-righteous religious mumbo jumbo—they were fond of deeming people "evil witches." Young Keryn Barnes became the couple's acolyte, following them everywhere and adopting their twisted form of Islam. Using her SSI payments, Barnes secured a basement apartment in this building for all three of them to share. It may have been sexual jealousy that made Suzan goad Michael into murdering the girl with a frying pan. The Carsons fled town and killed two more before being caught nearly two years later.

Suzan and Michael Carson murder house

Hippie Hill
In Golden Gate Park, just south of John F. Kennedy Drive, north of the children's playground, about 200 yards west of Kezar Drive, at the eastern end of the park.

At the height of the hippie era, this grassy slope in Golden Gate Park was an irresistible mecca. Crowds gathered here to make the scene, being sure to wear flowers in their hair. Because it was so close to Haight Street, and because the south-facing slope caught the sunshine, hippies and dropouts flocked to this lush lawn for years, earning it a nationwide reputation as hangout central.

South of Market and Potrero Hill

"Make My Day" Diner
Where Dirty Harry acquired his catchphrase.

Burger Island: original location, 701 Third Street; current location, 695 Third Street, at Townsend Street, south of Market near China Basin. Open Mon.–Fri. 11:00 A.M.–8:00 P.M.; Sat. 11:00 A.M.–6:00 P.M. and Sun., 11:00 A.M.–5:00 P.M. (415) 541-9166.

Clint Eastwood's character "Dirty Harry" Callahan doesn't suffer fools gladly. The obsessive San Francisco cop metes out vigilante justice whenever and wherever he likes. In the fourth film about him, *Sudden Impact,* Harry confronts a villain who is holding a hostage at this diner. When the villain threatens to kill his hostage, Harry sneers, "Go ahead. Make my day"—i.e., sans hostage, you're dead meat. For some reason this simple phrase immediately entered the popular lexicon. And though he has made fifty films and delivered thousands of memorable lines, this is the one that seems to sum up Eastwood's career. And this run-down hamburger stand in a run-down neighborhood is where it happened. The venerable burger joint stood for years at 695 Third, which is where Harry did his thing. In the mid-1990s it moved across the street to 701 Third, while the building that appeared in the movie was torn down. A McDonald's now stands on the original site—and it's not making anyone's day.

Pacific Heights filming location
1243 19th Street, at the southeast corner of 19th and Texas Streets, on top of Potrero Hill.

In 1990's psycho-thriller *Pacific Heights,* maniacal tenant Michael Keaton torments naïve landlords Melanie Griffith and Matthew Modine. The film takes place in this turreted yellow Victorian with panoramic views. All the exteriors were shot here, and residents say some interior scenes were filmed here, too, though some sources claim all interiors were filmed on a soundstage. The delicious irony is that the house is nowhere near Pacific Heights, despite the movie's title, resting instead at the crest of Potrero Hill, miles to the south. That's show business.

O. J. Simpson's Childhood Gym
Potrero Hill Recreation Center, at the intersection of Arkansas and Madera Streets, just north of 23rd Street, on Potrero Hill.

O. J. Simpson may be an outcast everywhere else in the country, but at the Potrero Hill Recreation Center he's still a hometown hero. Young Orenthal James spent his boyhood afternoons here, playing and running and strengthening those big muscles that he would use to such great effect later in life. A large 1977 mural on the front of the gym still shows O. J. as a USC football hero, dashing downfield in his trademark number 32 uniform. Inside the gym, along the back wall at the east end of the basketball court, a photo gallery of Potrero Hill alumni includes one exhibit entitled "O. J. Simpson returns to make a commercial," showing our hero filming a TreeSweet Orange Juice ad. In the snapshots he's playing Ping-Pong with awestruck fans. The hall leading to the gym's offices has framed newspaper

O. J. mural, Potrero Hill Recreation Center

clippings on the wall, including some about O. J.'s early days here. For a while the gym was nicknamed "the O. J. Simpson Gym," but in light of recent events, the name has fallen into disuse.

The Mission and the Castro

Mission Dolores Cemetery
Where Kim Novak visits her own grave in Hitchcock's **Vertigo.**

Enter through the church gift shop on the west side of Dolores Street, between 16th Street and Chula Lane (though the official address of the mission is 3321 16th Street). Open May–October, daily 9:00 A.M.–4:30 P.M.; November–April, daily 9:00 A.M.–4:00 P.M. Admission: $2 donation. (415) 621-8203.

A curious Jimmy Stewart follows the entranced Kim Novak to this graveyard in an early pivotal scene in *Vertigo*. She wanders among the headstones in a daze until she stops in front of one inscribed "Carlotta Valdes." To say any more would give away the plot. The old cemetery, partly overgrown with roses and ivy, looks much the same today as it did during the filming in 1957, with rustic nineteenth-century headstones tilting to and fro.

Mission Dolores Cemetery

Don't bother looking for the grave of Carlotta Valdes, though—the headstone was a prop, taken away as soon as the cameras stopped rolling. However, real graves here include those of Arguello (first governor of California), de Haro (first mayor of San Francisco), and three victims of gold rush–era vigilante justice.

Miraculous Hydrant
It single-handedly saved the Mission District.

Church Street at 20th Street, on the southeast corner; between the street and the tram tracks.

N ow painted bronze, this ordinary fire hydrant performed an apparent miracle during the devastating fire—still known as "the Great Fire"—that followed

Miraculous hydrant

the big 1906 quake. An accompanying plaque explains how, "though the water mains were broken" by the quake, this lone hydrant gave forth "a stream of water allowing the firemen to save the Mission District." Meanwhile the rest of the city burned to ash. To this day no one knows how this hydrant alone managed to keep the water flowing, when every other hydrant in the city was bone dry.

Janis Joplin Apartment
892 Noe Street, at 22nd Street, on the northwest corner.

This 1911 apartment house has bay windows, rounded towers at either end, and a cunningly sculpted cornucopia design over its main doorway. The doomed songbird lived here in 1969—in apartment D, where she loved to drink Chianti.

Harvey Milk's Camera Shop Site
Now Skin Zone Retail Skin and Hair Care, 575 Castro Street, between 18th and 19th Streets. Open Mon.–Sat. 10:00 A.M.–9:00 P.M.; Sun., 10:00 A.M.–7:00 P.M. (415) 626-7933.

Janis Joplin apartment

Harvey Milk was the first openly gay person elected to political office in California. He was wildly popular in his home district, where he was dubbed "the Mayor of Castro Street." His career started in the mid-1970s when his modest camera shop (named, creatively, the Camera Shop) little by little became a gay social center where locals would come to talk politics. When Milk ran for supervisor, the shop became his campaign headquarters, the nexus of gay activism. Years after his assassination by fellow supervisor Dan White, mourners painted a mural of Milk on the wall above his former shop and installed a memorial plaque on the sidewalk out front, both of which are still visible. The building's interior has since been remodeled, leaving no trace of the original shop.

Skin Zone, once Harvey Milk's Camera Shop

Richmond District and the Presidio

Church of Satan Site

6114 California Street, between Twenty-third and Twenty-fourth Avenues.

Church of Satan site

In 1966 a circus-animal trainer, actor, and organist named Anton LaVey founded the Church of Satan, espousing nonconformity, individualism, and a troth with you-know-who. Rumors ran wild about what went on here at its headquarters: black masses, cannibalism, naked girls' bodies used as altars. . . . And those stories include a Hollywood celebrity or two. (Hints: One of the rumored habitués had a glass eye. The other had a pink house.) LaVey's book, *The Satanic Bible,* sold well over a million copies. At the time of this writing the late LaVey's former home (and pilgrimage spot for Satanists worldwide) was boarded up, fenced off, and abandoned, while the once-lustrous black paint slowly peels in the fog.

Sutro Baths Ruins
As seen in **Harold and Maude.**

Just north of Cliff House and Sutro Heights Park, near the end of Point Lobos Avenue, at the far western edge of San Francisco. A pathway leads to the ruins from next to Louis' Restaurant, 902 Point Lobos Avenue.

One of *Harold and Maude*'s most memorable scenes happens here at Sutro Baths, where a confrontation between the unlikely duo and a bilious soldier ends with Maude falling through the floor. The shot did not take palace in the flooded remnants of the pools themselves but on the circular cement overlook just a few steps north of the baths. Aficionados claim to have identified the patched-up hole, but there are so many patched-up-seeming spots that it's hard to tell which is which. Crashing surf and crumbling ruins lend an otherworldly air to the setting. Sutro Baths was once one of the world's largest swimming complexes, a pleasure palace with seven huge pools, trapezes, Egyptian and Chinese antiquities, three restaurants, and more. Changing tastes and a disastrous 1966 fire put an end to the fantasy.

Human Be-In Site

Polo Fields, Golden Gate Park, between John F. Kennedy Drive and Middle Drive West, just south of Spreckels Lake, in the western part of the park.

On the afternoon of January 14, 1967, an acid-fueled "Gathering of the Tribes," organized in part by Allen Ginsberg, attracted thousands to Golden Gate Park. Flowers, beads, and bell-bottoms were everywhere. A stoned and ecstatic crowd grooved on Jefferson Airplane and other local talent. Speakers included Ginsberg, along with Lawrence Ferlinghetti, Timothy Leary, and Jerry Rubin. Having circumambulated the territory to sanctify it, Ginsberg and fellow poet Gary Snyder led a chant and blew a conch shell at dusk to signal the festival's end. The Summer of Love was on its way. Pop-culture historians now consider this original "Be-In" to be a turning point of the '60s, the culmination of the hippie movement and the beginning of the "New Age."

Fort Point
As seen in **Vertigo.**

At the end of Marine Drive, directly under the Golden Gate Bridge, at the northernmost tip of the Presidio and San Francisco. From Lincoln Boulevard, take Long Avenue, which becomes Marine Drive.

It was here at Fort Point that Kim Novak's character in *Vertigo* attempts suicide by jumping into the bay, only to be rescued by Jimmy Stewart's character. The exact spot is easily recognizable: it's a few feet east of the fort's tip, where the brick wall comes almost up to the water's edge. Of course, when you peer over the chain rail, you will *not* see the steps and landing that Jimmy runs down—they never existed. Kim's dive in the first half of the scene was filmed on location here, but the rescue attempt was filmed in an L.A. studio. The giveaway is the calm, murky water from which Jimmy pulls her in the film. In reality the swells and waves smashing ashore here would have finished them both off in no time flat. *Fort Point*

Golden Gate Bridge

On San Francisco's far northern tip, linking the city to Marin County.

It's one of the world's most romantic spans, the subject of countless postcards and dreams. Thus it is the world's most popular suicide spot. (Not only that, but *Star Trek IV* and *A View to a Kill* were filmed here.) The first jumper, a World War I vet, did it just a few months after the bridge was erected in 1937. These days two or so jump every month, most choosing the east side, facing the city. Some years back word got out that the toll was nearing five hundred. Fifteen jumpers reportedly vied to become the five hundredth. This taught officials to zip their lips regarding exact tallies, though by all estimates the total has now passed one thousand. The drop is about 220 feet and lasts just a few seconds. But at speeds reaching eighty miles per hour, the impact is enough to jam femurs into chests. Some survive. Most don't. In August 1993 Victoria's Secret founder Roy Raymond committed suicide here, devastated by recent bad investments.

Sunset District and the Southwest

Patty Hearst Bank Robbery Site

Now Hollywood Video, 1450 Noriega Street, at Twenty-second Avenue. (415) 681-3265.

In April 1974, when this was a Hibernia Bank, four fully armed robbers entered wearing combat gear. They stole around $10,000, and two passersby were wounded in the fracas. Surveillance cameras identified one of the robbers as kidnapped heiress Patty Hearst. Days earlier she had announced via an audiotape that she wished to "stay and fight" under the name "Tania" with her Symbionese Liberation Army captors. Those video images of a machine gun–toting Patty are among the most famous of the entire decade. The bank later closed, and a video store has taken its place. Culture vultures love to come here and rent copies of John Waters's *Serial Mom*, featuring none other than Patty herself.

Trailside Killer Childhood Home

152 Sussex Street, opposite Van Buren Street, on the north side of the street, in the Glen Park neighborhood.

In 1981 he would be dubbed the Trailside Killer, convicted of raping and murdering hikers in lovely northern California forests. But as a child David Carpenter lived in this unprepossessing stucco house, where his parents terrorized him emotionally and physically. A chronic stutterer, he had few friends. Ironically, at the time of his arrest for murder Carpenter was living with his parents on this very street, in another house (see below, and page 206).

Trailside Killer Arrest Site
38 Sussex Street, near the east end of the street where Sussex becomes Bemis Street, in the Glen Park neighborhood.

F ear gripped residents from Santa Cruz to Point Reyes when a string of female hikers turned up murdered, clearly the work of a crazed serial killer. More than half a dozen died before a surviving witness whose girlfriend had been killed helped cops finger fifty-year-old David Carpenter. A repeat sex offender who worked at an Oakland print shop, Carpenter lived with his aged parents at 38 Sussex, having grown up in another house down the street. During his crime spree he had called the cops anonymously, taunting them. Early one morning in the spring of 1981 they arrested him here on the sidewalk in front of the house. Today the gray house looms forbiddingly behind a gate, up a high cement staircase.

Trailside Killer arrest site

Broderick-Terry Duel Site
San Francisco's first political assassination.

> *Near 1100 Lake Merced Boulevard, south of Lake Merced Hill and north of John Muir Drive, in the far southwest corner of the city. Enter the tennis court parking lot on the east side of Lake Merced Boulevard about 200 yards north of John Muir Drive and the city limits; at the far end of the parking lot, go past the plaque describing the duel, through the opening in the fence, and bear left along the lawn to the granite memorial shaft that supposedly (but erroneously) indicates the site of the duel. Following the arrow on its base, continue past this shaft straight ahead about 100 yards to the two stone markers in the grove of eucalyptus and pine trees, near the chain-link gate. The markers indicate the exact spots where each of the duelists stood.*

D an White's 1978 killing of two city officials was not the first time in San Francisco history that a right-wing activist got off nearly scot-free after murdering a political opponent. David Broderick was a California senator, the state's voice in Washington D.C. An abolitionist, he despised the crooked tactics of the pro-slavery "Chivalrists." David Terry was the chief justice of the California State Supreme Court, a pro-slavery Southerner whose rulings allowed slaves to be held in the state under certain circumstances, though slavery was illegal here. Terry and his Chivalrist cohorts tried to force Broderick to vote their way when questions of slavery arose in the U.S. Senate. Broderick insisted on his independence, maintaining his anti-slavery stance. Terry insulted Broderick in a speech. Broderick openly declared his low opinion of Terry. Further slurs were exchanged, and Terry challenged Broderick to a duel. Fearful of being branded a coward, Broderick accepted.

Stone markers show where the duellists stood

The two met at dawn on September 13, 1859, on the very site indicated by the two duel markers that still stand today. Terry supplied the two suspicious-looking antique pistols (see **Home of the Broderick-Terry Dueling Pistols,** page 196). When the time came to fire, Broderick's gun discharged prematurely, before he could even raise it. Under dueling rules Broderick was then forced to stand there, unarmed, as Terry took aim and shot him in cold blood. It was later discovered that Terry had tampered with Broderick's pistol, filing down its trigger until it would not fire properly. When local papers began referring to the incident as an "assassination" instead of a duel, Terry skipped town. He was never prosecuted for the crime. The incident caused such an uproar that dueling was thenceforth rigorously banned in California. Broderick's bravery is not forgotten. Visit the site on the day after the duel's anniversary and you are likely to see a makeshift shrine on Broderick's marker, complete with flowers and a memorial candle.

Excelsior and Hunter's Point

Patty Hearst Capture House

625 Morse Street, between Guttenberg and Lowell Streets, in the Crocker-Amazon district.

After kidnapping the nineteen-year-old heiress Patricia Hearst from her Berkeley apartment in February 1974 (see page 288), the self-styled revolutionaries calling themselves the Symbionese Liberation Army confined her in a closet. After undergoing physical and emotional torment there, she donned combat gear and the name "Tania" and helped them rob a bank and spat-

Patty Hearst capture house

ter a sporting-goods store with gunfire. It all fueled one of the century's biggest media blitzes. Cops caught up with Hearst and some SLA cohorts here a year and a half after she was kidnapped. When SLA hanger-on Wendy Yoshimura answered a knock on the door here and found herself face to face with FBI agents, she reportedly wet her pants. During her trial Hearst maintained she had been brainwashed. The jury convicted her of bank robbery and Jimmy Carter later commuted her seven-year sentence.

Candlestick Park
Where the Beatles gave their last concert.

> Off Highway 101, in the southeastern corner of the city, on Candlestick Point, surrounded by Gilman Avenue, Jamestown Avenue, Hunter's Point Expressway, and Giants Drive, just north of the San Mateo County line.

On August 29, 1966, thousands of fans filled San Francisco's venerable baseball stadium to worship at the feet of John, Paul, George, and Ringo. A stage was erected at second base, with the best seats in the house going for $6.50. Garage rockers the Remains, "Red Rubber Ball"ers the Cyrkle, and the way-past-their-prime Ronettes opened the show. Though the Fab Four were enjoying unprecedented success, and though they continued to make dazzlingly popular records, this was their last public concert together. At present the blustery stadium is being phased out as the city's official major-league sports venue, and its fate is uncertain.

The Peninsula and Silicon Valley

SAN JOSE

The Rosicrucian Egyptian Museum and Planetarium

1342 Naglee Avenue, at Park Avenue (the property occupies an entire block; the museum entrance is on the Park Avenue side). Museum is open daily, 10:00 A.M.–4:30 P.M. Admission: adults, $7; students, $5; children ages 7–15, $3.50; under age 6, free. (408) 947-3636.

In this museum built to resemble an ancient Egyptian structure, prowl a reconstructed rock tomb. Inspect mummies, gleaming sarcophagi, and other ancient artifacts. Then wander the landscaped grounds admiring papyrus, Egyptian statuary, and remarkable structures. (For $1 the gift shop sells a walking-tour map.) Since 1927 this has been home base for the Rosicrucian Order, a mystery tradition whose adherents claim roots dating back before the birth of Christ. A key figure is the monotheistic, sun god–worshiping Pharaoh Akhnaten. Modern practitioners claim to be the direct descendants of an ancient secret society that clandestinely practiced spiritual healing and other occult skills during the spiritually stressful Middle Ages. Serious seekers can join its intricate training program to this day.

Winchester Mystery House
Proof that guns drive people crazy.

525 S. Winchester Boulevard, near Stevens Creek Boulevard. Open January–February and November–December, daily 9:30 A.M.–4:00 P.M.; March–April, daily 9:00 A.M.–5:00 P.M.; May and September–October, Sun.–Thurs., 9:00 A.M.–5:00 P.M., Fri.–Sat., 9:00 A.M.–7:00 P.M.; June–August, daily 9:00 A.M.–7:00 P.M. Admission: adults, $13.95; children, $7.95; under age 5, free. (408) 247-2000.

The widow Sarah Winchester inherited a gun fortune. She visited psychic mediums, who told her that only by continuing

Winchester Mystery House

construction on her house for the rest of her life could she placate the spirits of all those ever killed by Winchester rifles. Begun in 1884 and under construction twenty-four hours a day for the next thirty-eight years, this sprawling crazy quilt of a home now has 160 rooms, dozens of fireplaces, and weird "mystery" details scattered throughout, such as stairways going nowhere and doors opening onto blank walls.

LOS ALTOS

Apple Garage
Where the Macintosh seed was planted.

2066 Crist Drive, off Grant Road, at the southern end of Los Altos, next to Cupertino and Sunnyvale.

In the garage adjoining his boyhood home, young Steve Jobs and his pal Steve Wozniak are rumored to have manufactured the first Apple computers. Both Steves had been tinkering with techno-gizmos since junior high; then in 1975 Wozniak developed a primitive personal computer. As the legend goes, neither Hewlett-Packard nor Atari wanted his new creation, so the pair set up shop in this garage. The rest is history.

PALO ALTO

Hewlett-Packard Garage
Where Silicon Valley was born.

367 Addison Avenue, just north of the Stanford campus.

In this beige wooden garage behind a house on a sedate suburban street, Stanford University alumni William Hewlett and David Packard developed an audio oscillator in 1938. Disney would later buy eight of their oscillators and use them to make *Fantasia,* and an industry was born. Today a metal plaque mounted in stone out front hails the humble garage as "the birthplace of the world's first high-tech region, 'Silicon Valley.'"

Hewlett-Packard garage

Filoli

The Dynasty *mansion.*

Cañada Road (no number), just north of Edgwood Road, just off Highway 280. Open mid-February–early November, Tues.–Sat., 10:00 A.M.–2:00 P.M. Admission: adults, $10; children under age 12, $1. (650) 364-8300.

This redbrick Georgian Revival house portrayed the fictional Carringtons' home on *Dynasty.* (A soundstage was eventually created to precisely replicate some of its interiors.) The opulent spread also appeared in *Heaven Can Wait* and doubled as both California and Shanghai in *The Joy Luck Club.* Sixteen acres of formal gardens surround the mansion, which was built circa 1915 for a gold-mine owner who created its name by truncating his motto, "Fight–Love–Live." Parquet floors, seventeen-foot ceilings, period furnishings, and artworks complete the picture.

Rose Court Mansion

As seen in Harold and Maude.

On the south side of the cul-de-sac called Stacey Court, which branches off Redington Road.

In this 1971 cult film a wealthy but suicide-obsessed youth (portrayed by Bud Cort) rejects the debs his mother tries to set him up with. Then he meets his soulmate, Maude (portrayed by Ruth Gordon). Sixty years his senior, she changes his passion for death to a passion for life. A wide cobblestoned courtyard behind a screen of trees fronts this Italian-style villa whose doorway sports a green awning. Ivy-covered stonework further enhances the mansion's glamour. Once owned by the famous DeYoung family, it was used in *Harold and Maude*'s interior and exterior scenes as the home of wealthy but unhappy young Harold.

SAN BRUNO

Tanforan Park Shopping Center
Formerly a World War II internment camp.

   El Camino Real at I-380 and Sneath Lane. (650) 873-2000.

M any of the shoppers browsing for bath beads and woofers at JCPenney and
Radio Shack have no idea that this mall was first a racetrack and then, to its
eternal shame, a wartime internment camp. When anti-Japanese paranoia was at its
peak in 1942, all foreign- and American-born Japanese in California were ordered by
law to evacuate their homes. Forced to uproot abruptly, many lost everything. Several sites around the state, such as this one, were designated assembly points: temporary camps where evacuees were lodged before being transported to the long-term
detention centers where they lived as prisoners, their heritage their only "crime." At
one point nearly eight thousand people were confined at Tanforan—housed in horse
stables. (See also **Manzanar Internment Camp, Lone Pine,** page 193, and **Tule
Lake Internment Camp, Newell,** page 269.)

COLMA

Cypress Lawn Memorial Park
William Randolph Hearst's final resting place.

   *1370 El Camino Real, south of Serramonte Boulevard. Open daily 8:00 A.M.–dusk. (650)
   755-0580.*

O ne of California's last Victorian-style cemeteries, Cypress Lawn is heavy on the
stained glass and somberly beautiful statuary. One prominent occupant is
newspaper czar and Hearst Castle king William Randolph Hearst, the inspiration for
Citizen Kane. (He rests with his kin in the eponymous William Randolph Hearst
Mausoleum.) Also here are sugar tycoon Rudolph Spreckels, baseball champ "Lefty"
O'Doul, martyred politician David Broderick, and actress Laura Hope Crews, who
played Aunt Pitty Pat in *Gone with the Wind.*

Hills of Eternity Memorial Park
Here lies Wyatt Earp.

1301 El Camino Real on the east side of the road. To reach the grave, go up the main road until you pass five intersecting sidewalks. At the sixth sidewalk, turn right (south). Pass one intersecting sidewalk and turn left just before the second. From here the marker is in the third row (plot D, section 2, lot 12, grave 2). Open Sun.–Fri., 9:00 A.M.–4:00 P.M. (650) 756-3633.

Yes, it's a Jewish cemetery. And, no, famous gunfighter and Wild West hero Wyatt Earp wasn't Jewish. His wife was. Josie Marcus Earp ran away from her parents' San Francisco home to join a theatrical troupe in 1879. In Tombstone, Arizona, she met lawman Earp and married him. In 1881 he and his brothers, with their friend Doc Holliday, faced the Clanton Gang at the O.K. Corral—a bloodbath that has become the stuff of legend. In real life it landed the Earps and Holliday in court. Acquitted, they were targeted by the surviving Clantons, then in turn began quashing outlaws. Mr. and Mrs. Earp roamed the West, eventually settling down as real estate speculators in southern California. Wyatt died in Los Angeles in 1929, and Josie in 1944. Their cremated remains lie together in the same grave.

Holy Cross Cemetery
Here lies Joe DiMaggio.

1500 Mission Road, south of Colma's other cemeteries. Open daily 8:00 A.M.–5:30 P.M. (650) 756-2060.

Most famous among this Catholic cemetery's permanent residents is Joe DiMaggio (section I, row 11, area 6/7, grave OGV—practically smack in the middle of the spread). Also here is slain mayor George Moscone (in the St. Michael section). This is the oldest and largest cemetery in a city that is positively riddled with cemeteries.

East Bay

OAKLAND

USS *Potomac*
FDR's "Floating White House."

> On the FDR Pier across from the Potomac Visitor Center, 540 Water Street, on the Oakland
> Estuary, in a corner of Jack London Square. Open for dockside tours Wed. and Fri., 10:00
> A.M.–1:15 P.M.; Sun., noon–3:15 P.M. Two-hour cruises spring–fall, selected Sat. and Thurs.,
> 10:00 A.M. and 1:30 P.M. Dockside tours: adults, $3; children ages 6–17, $1; under age 6,
> free. Cruises: adults, $30; children ages 6–17, $15; under age 6, free. (510) 839-7533.

FDR hated to fly. When D.C. got too hot and humid for comfort, he conducted business on board this 165-foot ship, originally built as a Coast Guard cutter in 1934. One of the disabled president's greatest phobias was dying in a fire, so he preferred his all-steel *Potomac* to traditional wooden yachts. By 1995 the meticulously restored ship was permanently berthed here in Oakland, of all places. Now a National Historic Landmark, it recalls the countless hours FDR spent on board enjoying poker games and poring over his treasured stamp collection.

THX-1138 Escape Tunnels

> The Webster Street Tube and the Posey Tube connect Oakland and Alameda; the Webster
> Street Tube access road starts at the intersection of Webster and 7th Streets in downtown
> Oakland; access the Posey Tube via Webster Street in northern Alameda. The Caldecott Tun-
> nel connects Oakland and Orinda; enter the tunnel via Highway 24 just east of Highway 13.
> The Berkeley BART station is in the center of downtown Berkeley, at the intersection of Shat-
> tuck Avenue and Center Street.

The climactic chase scene of George Lucas's sci-fi magnum opusculum *THX-1138* takes place in the bowels of a futuristic underground city. Eponymous hero Robert Duvall steals a rocket-powered hot rod and escapes robotic policemen through a seemingly endless maze of tunnels. The pursuit, in fact, merely goes back and forth along the Webster Street and Posey tubes below Oakland's Jack London Square, and through the Caldecott Tunnel at the other end of town. The final ascent was filmed in an unknown section of the BART system, but an earlier scene of shaved-headed drones going to work was filmed at the Berkeley BART station while it was still under construction—back when BART itself still seemed like a futuristic rapid-transit marvel.

Dunsmuir House
As seen in A View to a Kill.

2960 Peralta Oaks Court, off Peralta Oaks Drive, just south of 106th Avenue. Open February–October, Tues.–Fri., 10:00 A.M.–4:00 P.M. Admission: adults, $5; children ages 6–13, $4; under age 6, free. (510) 615-5555.

This Neoclassical Revival mansion appears in the 1985 James Bond extravaganza *A View to a Kill,* in which Roger Moore fights off baddies bent on harming the beautiful lady of the house. Boasting no less than thirty-seven rooms, ten fireplaces, and a shimmering Tiffany-style glass dome, it basks in the midst of a vast estate. Also shot here was *So I Married an Axe Murderer,* with Mike Myers.

Mountain View Cemetery
Here lies the Black Dahlia.

5000 Piedmont Avenue, at the northern end of the street, just north of Pleasant Valley Avenue. Open Mon.–Fri., 8:00 A.M.–4:30 P.M.; Sat.–Sun., 10:00 A.M.–4:00 P.M.; tours given the second Saturday of every month at 10:00 A.M. (510) 658-2588.

Good-time girl Elizabeth Short was nicknamed the Black Dahlia for her raven hair. Her savage 1947 murder in Los Angeles was one of the most sensational in California's history. Hers is reportedly one of the hundreds of graves scattered around this lushly landscaped acreage designed by Frederick Law Olmsted, the same man who brought you New York's Central Park. Twisting lanes meander up and down terraced hillsides dotted with the graves of California's key movers and shakers. Steel guy Henry J. Kaiser, novelist Frank Norris, and railroad and bank guy Charles Crocker are here. So are architects Julia Morgan and Bernard Maybeck, as well as the Ghirardelli (chocolate) family.

Bruce Lee's Kung Fu School Location
Now Downtown Toyota, part of Downtown Auto Center, 4145 Broadway, between 41st and 42nd Streets, Oakland. Open Mon.–Fri., 7:30 A.M.–5:30 P.M.; Sat., 8:00 A.M.–3:00 P.M. (510) 547-4635.

Though born in San Francisco, Bruce Lee spent most of his childhood in Hong Kong. He returned to the United States in 1959, moved to Seattle, and founded the Jun Fan Gung Fu Institute there in 1963. This small martial arts school proved so popular that Lee came to Oakland in the summer of 1964 and founded a second school here, at 4145 Broadway. In December of that year, the twenty-four-year-old Lee was challenged to fight by a local kung fu master named Wong Jack Man. By some accounts, the master was upset because Lee was teaching martial arts to Caucasians. The fight between the two—which took place here at Lee's Oakland school—is the stuff of kung fu legend. Of the handful of eyewitnesses, only four have ever discussed what happened that day. Lee claimed that he pounded Man into submission in less than three minutes. Lee's wife Linda gave a similar account in the biography she wrote about her husband, saying Man was so overwhelmed by Lee's attack that he turned and fled. Man, on the other hand, admits he spent the entire fight on the defensive but claims he was holding back so as to avoid seriously hurting Lee and thereby getting into trouble with the police. The only neutral witness ever to grant an interview says that the fight lasted twenty minutes, that Lee was on the attack the entire time, and that the fight ended more because both combatants were exhausted rather than because one defeated the other. Whatever the truth, Lee was unhappy with his performance—he felt he should have won after the first few strikes. It was because of this fight that he devised his own fighting style, for which he would later become world-famous. Sadly, the site of this historic battle is no more. The building that housed Bruce's gym was torn down in 1966 to make way for an auto showroom; a Toyota dealership now occupies the site.

BERKELEY

Allen Ginsberg Cottage Site
1624 Milvia Street, at Lincoln Street, on the west side of the street.

In 1956, soon after finishing *Howl*, Allen Ginsberg was living at this address with fellow poet Gary Snyder. An unforgettable party scene in Jack Kerouac's novel *The Dharma Bums* takes place here, recounting a strange night of Tantric sex and scholarly allusions. In his poem "A Strange New Cottage in Berkeley," Ginsberg writes fondly of the cottage's "scarlet bushes" and "tottering brown fence," and of hiding his pot stash. Yet the sunny little hideaway he enjoyed is long gone. Today a blockish stucco apartment building stands sullenly in its place. In 1999 the Berkeley Arts Magnet School (at 1645 Milvia) installed an Allen Ginsberg Poetry Garden directly across the street from where the cottage used to be. Children's poems are affixed to a bulletin board in front of the garden.

Jack Kerouac Cottage Site

*Former address: 1943 Berkeley Way, between Milvia Street and
Bonita Avenue. Address of new building: 1945 Berkeley Way.*

In the spring of 1957 Jack Kerouac and his mother rode
a bus cross-country and moved into what he called "a
little rose-covered cottage" which they rented at this address. *On the Road* would be published in a few months,
and in this cottage he worked on *Book of Dreams*. But
Berkeley's climate did not suit Kerouac's mother, who was
by all accounts an anti-Semitic alcoholic and the only
woman he ever loved. In practically no time at all they
packed up again, bound for points south and east. The
cottage is now gone, replaced by apartments.

*Modern apartments on the
site where Kerouac once lived*

The Bancroft Library

Guardians of the Wimmer Nugget and Drake's Plate of Brass.

> The Bancroft Library is located in the rear of Doe Library, in the center of the University of
> California campus, about 100 yards northwest of the can't-miss Campanile (Sather Tower).
> The nugget is on display in the administrative offices, which are on the left as you enter.
> Office hours: Mon.–Fri., 8:00 A.M.–5:00 P.M. (510) 642-3781. The brass plate is across the
> hall in the foyer of the library reading room, on the right as you enter. Library hours: Mon.–
> Thurs., 9:00 A.M.–6:00 P.M.; Fri., 9:00 A.M.–5:00 P.M.; Sat., 1:00–5:00 P.M., shorter hours when
> school is not in session. (510) 642-6481.

Libraries aren't just for books. The Bancroft displays two of the most significant
artifacts from California history: one of dubious authenticity, the other genuine.
In a glass case in the administrative offices lies the nugget that started the California
gold rush. Though it was found by James Marshall, it is known as the Wimmer
Nugget because within minutes of his discovery Marshall handed it to his colleague
Peter Wimmer. Wimmer and his wife Elizabeth then boiled it in soap lye; when the
nugget emerged unscathed, they knew it was gold. Marshall described the nugget as
being about half the size of a pea, yet the one displayed here is somewhat larger, leading some to question its authenticity. We know, however, that the Wimmer Nugget
was pounded and flattened out during various tests so it may have originally appeared smaller. Maybe peas were bigger in those days, or maybe Marshall just wasn't
very good at approximating size, as meticulous records confirm that this nugget is indeed the real thing (see **Coloma,** page 189).

In another glass case across the hall lurks a more dubious artifact. Explorer Francis Drake discovered California in 1579 and claimed the land for England, as he described in his diary, by nailing a "Plate of Brass" to a post (see also **Sir Francis Drake**

Landing Site, Point Reyes, page 260). The "plate" was lost for centuries until apparently found by accident in 1936 near San Quentin prison. The small rectangular slab of brass, with rustic inscriptions like TO BEE KNOWNE VNTO ALL MEN AS NOVA ALBION, was thought at first to be genuine, a significant historical find. But tests in the late 1970s proved the brass was manufactured in the twentieth century, dashing all hopes of its authenticity. The hoaxer who created the plate has never claimed credit.

Cyclotron Invention Site

In room 329 of LeConte Hall, on the third floor. A plaque marks the site. LeConte Hall is adjacent to the Campanile (Sather Tower), east of the Bancroft Library, on the University of California campus.

A cyclotron is a device that accelerates subatomic particles to the point that they can smash apart atomic nuclei. Esoteric, yes, but the cyclotron was the crucial machine that made the nuclear age possible; with it, physicists could take apart and examine the building blocks of matter. Without the cyclotron the world would have no nuclear power, nuclear bombs, transuranic elements, radiation therapy, or any real knowledge of how the universe works. Ernest Lawrence invented the cyclotron in this room at the back end of the physics department: his first model was literally held together with sealing wax. Between 1930 and 1934 he built successively larger models until they got so big he had to move out. Glenn Seaborg used a cyclotron to discover plutonium nearby (some say in LeConte Hall; others say in a temporary building alongside it, now gone). Rumor also has it that the very first meetings of what would become the Manhattan Project—the crash program to build the first atomic bomb—were held in LeConte as well.

Ted Kaczynski Office Site

Room 211 of building T-4, and room 219 of building T-9, on the University of California campus. See below for current status.

A ssistant professor of mathematics Theodore J. Kaczynski—later to gain worldwide fame as the Unabomber—had his offices in a row of rickety shacks known as the "T Buildings." This series of nine bungalows was built after World War II as a stopgap measure to handle the influx of postwar students. In 1967 Kaczysnki had his first office in T-4; in 1968 he was moved to T-9. But the buildings were never meant to last—the "T" stood for "Temporary"—and they were torn down in the 1990s to make way for an underground library expansion. The site of T-4 is now marked by a rectangular depression in a lawn on the west side of Evans Hall. The site of T-9 is now the northwestern edge of the wide lawn called Memorial Glade, about a hundred yards north of Doe Library. The T Buildings were, in retrospect, constructed rather similarly to Kaczynski's hut in Montana.

People's Park

Surrounded on 3 sides by Haste Street, Dwight Way, and Bowditch Street, just east of Tele-graph Avenue. James Rector was shot on the roof of a building whose entrance is on Tele-graph just south of Dwight, currently occupied by Body Time (2509 Telegraph) and Lhasa Karnak (2513 Telegraph).

In 1968 UC Berkeley—which owned the property—arranged for some houses to be bulldozed on this block. Local hippies were inspired to turn the resultant empty lot into a park that would serve as both a communal garden and community center. An April 1969 article in the radical *Berkeley Barb* urged supporters to bring tools and work together to create "Power to the People Park." Stunned, the university erected a fence surrounding the property. On May 15 a crowd of three thousand furious protesters stormed from campus down Telegraph Avenue to the empty lot, where they faced off with equally angry police. The cops had come prepared with guns, tear gas, buckshot, and birdshot, and the ensuing melee has come to be known as "Bloody Thursday." Over one hundred were injured that day, and a policeman's gun mortally wounded bystander James Rector, who was watching the action from a nearby rooftop. The fence stayed up for several years more, but the park faction eventually won out. Today the lawn and gardens are a magnet for down-and-outers, fringe dwellers, and the homeless.

Ted Kaczynski House

2628A Regent Street, between Parker and Derby Streets; 2628A is a cottage behind a larger house at 2626 Regent, on the west side of the street.

Future Unabomber Theodore Kaczynski moved into this modest stucco cottage in 1968 when working as an assistant professor of mathematics at nearby UC Berkeley. At that time he was just mild-mannered Ted, an introverted young mathematician whose only peculiarity was a tendency to be awkward in social situations. But while he was living here a year later in 1969 something snapped inside him: he abruptly resigned, fled to Montana, and started a new career as an ecoterrorist. The small, square cottage must be cursed: two decades after Kaczynski moved out, radical activist Rosebud DeNovo moved into the same lodgings. She was killed while attempting to assassinate the university's chancellor.

Patty Hearst Abduction Apartment

2603 Benvenue Avenue, #4, at Parker Street, on the east side of the street.

In February 1974 a nineteen-year-old heiress named Patricia Hearst was living here when a band of self-styled revolutionaries burst in one night, surprising the girl and her boyfriend, Steven Weed. The intruders beat Weed, and bullets flew as they dragged Hearst away. What followed was one of the century's most sensational true-crime stories. The Symbionese Liberation Army, as Hearst's kidnappers called themselves, imprisoned and abused her. Within a few months she had joined them, robbing a bank with her comrades before finally being captured in September 1975. Claiming the SLA had brainwashed her, she was nevertheless convicted of bank robbery. Jimmy Carter commuted her sentence after she had served nearly two years in prison. This dark-shingled quadruplex was new when Hearst lived here; today it looks like countless other college-town dwellings.

Philo T. Farnsworth Home

2910 Derby Street, above Warring Street, across from UC Berkeley's Clark Kerr Campus student housing.

Entirely on his own, twenty-one-year-old Philo T. Farnsworth invented television. A Utah farm boy, Farnsworth moved west, settled in Berkeley, and worked on his project in a San Francisco lab. In 1927 he introduced his creation to the world. And in 1927 he was living at this address, where it is believed he did some crucial work, or at least a lot of creative thinking. Thus 2910 Derby is sometimes known as "the house where television was invented." But which house? Whether the graceful, becolumned home now standing here was Farnsworth's is up for debate. Built in 1908, it is clearly old enough. But there is evidence that this house, which some attribute to the brilliant architect Julia Morgan, was actually moved here sometime in the last few decades from somewhere else, replacing the actual building where Farnsworth lived.

CONCORD

Port Chicago Disaster Site

The entrance to the Port Chicago U.S. Naval Magazine is on Port Chicago Highway in the community of Clyde, north of Highway 4, on Suisun Bay in northern Concord. To get access to the memorial and the actual site of the disaster, call the National Park Service at (925) 838-0249 at least 24 hours ahead of time; they will arrange a free Navy escort who will meet you at the gate and lead you to the site; otherwise the gate is locked and guarded, and there are no regularly scheduled tours.

Port Chicago was the Navy's primary ammunition loading dock during World War II. Cargo ships bound for the Pacific Theater stopped here to take aboard the bombs, shells, and depth charges used by the Allied forces in combat. On the night of July 17, 1944, two ships—the SS *E. A. Bryan* and the SS *Quinault Victory*—were loading ammunition at the dock when something went terribly wrong. The first sign of trouble was a peculiar metallic *ping* coming from the vicinity of the load-ing dock. Moments later a tremendous explosion blasted the pier to splinters. Sev-eral smaller blasts ensued. Then, for an instant—nothing. It seemed the worst was over. But that terrible roar was a mere warning for what was to come. Six seconds later the entire cargo of the *E. A. Bryan* detonated en masse as a single charge. The percussive force of that final explosion was so powerful that it reached all the way to Arizona. People throughout California and even in Nevada felt the shock wave. At least 320 dock workers and crew members were vaporized instantly. The *E. A. Bryan*—a 7,200-ton solid steel ship—was reduced to shrapnel. The *Quinault Victory* flew through the air like a toy. Windows imploded and buildings buckled all around the Bay Area. A plane flying nine thousand feet over Port Chicago was nearly knocked from the sky by pieces of white-hot steel rocketing upward. Historians later calcu-lated that the explosion was about one-fourth as powerful as the atomic bomb blast at Hiroshima a year later. But there was no time to mourn: U.S. forces needed a steady supply of ammunition for a desperate final assault against the Axis powers. So the surviving dock workers—all of whom were African American—were ordered back to work a short time later at a new facility. Naturally they refused, pointing out that they had never been properly trained to load ammunition and that there were essentially no safety precautions. Two hundred fifty-eight black Navy sailors were court-martialed for disobeying orders, fifty of whom were convicted of mutiny and sentenced to years of hard labor. Their case remains a major source of controversy to-day; as of this writing only one of the surviving black workers has received a pardon. A battle to overturn the racially tinged courts-martial continues. Port Chicago is still Navy property (at least for the moment) but is in the process of being turned over to the Army and the National Park Service, which manages the memorial. Whoever owns it, Port Chicago will always be remembered as the site of the worst World War II disaster on the U.S. mainland.

LIVERMORE

Altamont Speedway
Where the sixties came crashing to an end.

> 17001 Midway Road, technically in Tracy, but usually thought of as being in Livermore; the track is on the east side of Midway Road, a few hundred yards south of Highway 580, in a rural area between Tracy and Livermore. The concert took place not on the track itself but at the bottom of the hill on the eastern side of the property, in a natural amphitheater next to the track. (925) 606-0274.

A free concert here on December 6, 1969, with the Rolling Stones, Jefferson Air-plane, the Grateful Dead, and others, was intended to be the West Coast's answer to Woodstock. But something went awry, and now the very word "Altamont" symbolizes all that went wrong with the '60s. As revealed in *Gimme Shelter,* a documentary filmed at the concert, the show was organized haphazardly; other venues fell through days before the deadline, and everything had to be moved to Altamont at the last minute. A huge crowd—some estimates say four hundred thousand—swarmed over the property like locusts.

To control the chaos the organizers, at the suggestion of the Grateful Dead, allowed the Hell's Angels to act as security guards. *Oops.* During Jefferson Airplane's set, drugged bikers started abusing hippies. Singer Marty Balin jumped into the crowd to calm things down and was beaten unconscious by an Angel. As the Stones prepared to play, fists flew and the Angels attacked people with pool cues. Shortly after the Stones began, eighteen-year-old Meredith Hunter drew a gun during some kind of dispute in the crowd and was stabbed and beaten to death by Hell's Angels directly in front of the stage. Cameras caught the whole thing.

It is often said that the stabbing took place during "Sympathy for the Devil," but *Gimme Shelter* shows it happening as the Stones finish their next song, "Under My Thumb." The show fell apart after that—the Dead never came on. Three others died accidentally at Altamont as well, but in truth most of the audience had a great time, unaware of the violence. Still, the concert went down in history as the debacle of the decade. The track is still open for business (racing season is March–November; tickets range from $10 to $15). Former owner Dick Carter, the very person who allowed the concert to take place at Altamont, still shows up here to race cars.

World's Oldest Functioning Lightbulb
Proof that they don't make 'em like they used to.

> Fire Station 6, 4550 East Avenue, Livermore. From central Livermore, head out East Avenue toward Lawrence Livermore National Laboratory until you reach the fire station on the north side of the street at Loyola Way. The bulb is hanging from the ceiling of a locked area where equipment is stored, so visitors must ask to see it. (925) 454-2346.

Ever notice how cars falls apart the day their warranties expire? Or that shoes don't last as long as they did when you were a kid? It's no accident. The theory of planned obsolescence posits that well-made products are bad for the economy. If your toaster oven worked forever, why would you need to buy a new one? And, see, factories wouldn't need to keep producing, and the whole economy would go down the unclogged drain. If you believe contemporary manufacturers' claims that they make the best products possible, come to Livermore. Fire Station Number 6 has a lightbulb that has been burning continuously since 1901. When was the last time one of *your* lightbulbs lasted a century? Modern bulbs are purposely designed to burn out after a couple of years (or a couple of months). Or did the Shelby Electric Company possess some kind of advanced technology in 1901 that eludes modern electrical engineers? The truth is, this rather dim bulb was made with very primitive techniques, but it has lasted this long because it *was* made as *well* as possible. All lightbulbs would last essentially forever if they weren't purposely designed to wear out. And the same holds true for most other products as well. Shame on us.

Marin County

ANGEL ISLAND

Angel Island State Park
Immigration detention center and prisoner-of-war camp.

> Angel Island is just south of Marin County off the coast of Tiburon. Blue & Gold Ferries run to the island from Pier 41 in San Francisco, and from the Tiburon Ferry Terminal. Call (415) 773-1188 for current Blue & Gold schedule and rates; call (415) 435-2131 for the schedule from Tiburon. Park office: (415) 435-5390 or (415) 435-3522.

Angel Island was optimistically dubbed "the Ellis Island of the West" when a new immigration station opened here in 1910. But it became the Ellis Island from hell. European immigrants arriving in New York were basically processed and ushered into the mainstream; Chinese arrivals at Angel Island were harassed, humiliated, imprisoned, and usually sent back. In the nineteenth century, Congress passed the racist "Chinese Exclusion Act," barring all Chinese immigrants except those with relatives already living here. But the 1906 earthquake and fire destroyed most government records in San Francisco, so there was no way to tell who was who anymore. Hundreds of thousands of Chinese tried to take advantage of this loophole by claiming kinship with Chinese Americans who had sent forged papers to friends or potential employees in China. This resulted in a tragic game of cat and mouse: all Chinese immigrants between 1910 and 1940 were held on Angel Island, where immigration officials assumed they were lying and tried to trap them with trick questions and brutal interrogation sessions. While their cases were being settled, the Chinese were imprisoned on the island for weeks, months, even years, after which they were more often than not shipped back to China. Even those with legitimate claims were imprisoned and shipped back if they didn't know the system or couldn't answer the questions. During their imprisonment some detainees carved poignant poems into the walls of their cells; some of these survive to this day. After the immigration station closed in 1940, it found a cheery new use as a POW camp for captured German and Italian soldiers in World War II. Did somebody say "bad karma"? Later the Army installed a missile base here during the cold war, with nuclear-tipped short-range NIKE missiles ready to launch at the press of a button. (Since these warheads couldn't reach all the way to Russia, was the government planning to fight a nuclear war *on U.S. soil* if the Commies invaded?) Thankfully, the missiles were decommissioned in 1962, and the island was finally converted into a park. The Immigration Station is now open to visitors and even features a small museum that displays some of the detainees' poems. The station, also known as North Garrison, is at the northwest corner of the island. The ferry will drop you off at Ayala Cove, from which you can walk along a well-marked trail to the buildings for free (the walk takes about fifteen minutes), or pay $10 to take a tram and audio tour of the facility.

LARKSPUR

Larkspur Landing
Location for the climactic scene in Dirty Harry.

> *At the intersection of Sir Francis Drake Boulevard East and Larkspur Landing Circle, between San Quentin and Highway 101, in eastern Marin County. Golden Gate Ferries go from San Francisco directly to the Larkspur Landing ferry terminal, across the street from the site.*

D*irty Harry*'s edge-of-the-seat finale has relentless cop Harry Callahan pursuing a serial killer to an abandoned quarry in Marin County. Early in the scene Harry (portrayed by Clint Eastwood) stands on a railroad trestle and looks down on his prey as the killer passes underneath, unaware of his fate. Later, a block away in an old quarry with a murky pool, Harry catches the villain and metes out justice. The railroad trestle is still there, but you won't find the slightest trace of the quarry: developers got their hands on the property and turned it into a shopping mall-and-condo complex called, not surprisingly, Larkspur Landing. The only clue to how this place looked back in 1971 is the name of the street behind the shopping center: Old Quarry Road. But *Dirty Harry* fans still like to drive under the trestle and imagine Harry squinting malevolently down at them.

SAN RAFAEL

Marin County Civic Center
As seen in Gattaca *and* THX-1138.

> *3501 Civic Center Drive, at N. San Pedro Road, on the east side of Highway 101. Open Mon.–Fri. 8:00 A.M.–5:00 P.M. Tours: Wed. at 10:30 A.M. (meet in the second-floor gift shop). (415) 499-6358.*

Black Panther George Jackson was an inmate at this facility's jail when, on August 7, 1970, his younger brother arrived fully armed and attempted to rescue him by force. The bloody melee erupted in Courtroom D, then continued in the parking lot. When it was over, four were dead, including a judge; five were injured. Angela Davis was later one of those implicated. The futuristic building, sporting a distinctive dome and a 172-foot golden tower and set dramatically against a hillside, was designed by Frank Lloyd Wright, who did not live to see the finished product. Its courtrooms are circular, its jail subterranean; a pond hides the building's heating system. Sci-fi fans can see this place, inside and out, in the films *THX-1138* (where Robert Duvall and Donald Pleasence stroll around and ascend an escalator) and *Gattaca*.

OLEMA

1906 Earthquake Epicenter

> *Near the Bear Valley Visitor Center. From Highway 1 in western Marin County, take Bear Valley Road at Olema to the Bear Valley Visitor Center. The Earthquake Trail starts from the center's parking lot on the north side of the driveway; look for the entrance between the picnic area and the restrooms. Always open. (415) 663-1092.*

The devastating 1906 quake has since been known worldwide as the San Francisco Earthquake, but its epicenter was farther north. Because seismographic monitoring equipment had not yet been invented, the exact location and magnitude have never been exactly determined. Modern scientists approximate the magnitude at 8.1 on the Richter scale, making it the most powerful quake to strike California in the twentieth century. Most experts agree that the epicenter must have been in or near Olema, a tiny village in Marin County that sits directly on top of the San Andreas Fault. One thing is sure: the shaking, damage, and earth movement were most severe right here. An "Earthquake Trail" just west of town at the Bear Valley Visitor Center traverses the approximate area of the epicenter. Markers along the half-mile trail show the location of the fault line, and signs explain the theory of tectonics. As the Pacific Plate and North American Plate jerked past each other on April 18, 1906, the land on one side of the fault leaped twenty feet northward. After almost one hundred years, there's very little evidence of the quake, but you can still see a fence that was displaced sideways eighteen feet.

POINT REYES

Sir Francis Drake Landing Site

In Drake's Estero, on the southern side of Point Reyes National Seashore, in Marin County. From either Highway 101 or Highway 1, take Sir Francis Drake Boulevard west into Point Reyes; you can see the back end of Schooner Bay by turning off at the Oyster Farm, or see the mouth of the Estero by continuing on to Drake's Beach and walking along the beach eastward. Two different hiking trails, the Estero Trail and the Bull Point Trail, lead from Sir Francis Drake Boulevard to the shore of the inlet. If you don't have a map, stop off at the Bear Valley Visitor Center (see above) for information about Point Reyes.

Sir Francis Drake was the first Englishman to sail around the world, and he earned accolades for his naval explorations and his bravery in battle. He was also a privateer—a government-sponsored pirate—who raided and plundered Spanish ships and ports whenever he got the chance. In 1579, halfway through his round-the-world voyage, he rested for a while on the North American coast before heading home across the Pacific (after a quick side trip to search fruitlessly for the Northwest Passage). Using the era's primitive instruments, he recorded his approximate location as well as he could, and he nailed an inscribed brass plate to a post marking the site and claiming the continent for the queen of England. If this story is true, Drake would have been the first European to set foot in northern California, a historically significant event considering that more than a century later the Spanish claimed the whole Pacific side of North America for themselves.

Here's the catch: no one can figure out where Drake landed. Possible locations are scattered up and down the coast, from Santa Barbara to Oregon, but this one is the most likely; not only does it match the location Drake gave in his measurements, but its physical surroundings also match his description. Archaeologists have even found shards of Ming china in the area, and it was known that Drake had stolen some Ming china from Spaniards earlier in his trip. (Naysayers claim the china came from a later shipwreck.) But what of the brass plate that Drake described leaving behind? Pranksters claimed to have found it on the other side of the Marin peninsula, near San Quentin, in 1936, but their "discovery" was later shown to be a forgery (see **The Bancroft Library, Berkeley,** page 251). But some remnant of the plate apparently *was* found: Drake said he affixed a coin to the plate before nailing it up, and in 1974, by sheer chance, a sixteenth-century English coin was unearthed a few miles away (see **Olompali State Historic Park,** below). The theory runs that local Indians pried out the coin after Drake departed, then brought it back to their village. Aside from the coin, the shards, the fake plate, and a few crumbling pieces of timber that could have come from anywhere, there are no remnants now of Drake's visit—except place names all over Marin County (including the name of this inlet where he supposedly stayed), which are more the result of twentieth-century wishful thinking than anything else. At Drake's Beach you can see the chalky cliffs that reminded Drake so much of the White Cliffs of Dover and that led him to name this new land *Nova Albion,* or New England.

NOVATO

Olompali State Historic Park
Former home of the Grateful Dead, and of an important little coin.

> *Two and a half miles north of Novato, on the west side of Highway 101. The entrance is accessible only to southbound traffic, so if you are heading northward to the park, you must go past it, turn around, and come back south. Open daily 10:00 A.M.–6:00 P.M. (415) 892-3383.*

The Grateful Dead encamped on this rural estate in 1966, turning an abandoned Victorian ranch into a major nexus of the burgeoning hippie scene. Their parties, attended by the likes of Janis Joplin and Grace Slick, were notorious: sex, drugs, and certainly lots of rock 'n' roll, with Dead-led jam sessions lasting for days; a picture of Olompali even appears on the cover of one of their albums. After the Dead moved on, the site was taken over by a cultlike utopian commune ominously known as the Chosen Family. What they really should have chosen was a better electrician, since faulty hippie-style wiring caused a fire that burned the main mansion to the ground. After the state bought the land and turned it into a park, archaeologists discovered that the site had been a major Native American village, one of the Bay Area's largest. During excavations in 1974, to everyone's utter astonishment, a silver English sixpence dated 1567 was unearthed under a layer of packed dirt many centuries old. Since there was no known contact between local Miwok Indians and Europeans at that early date, historians have concluded that the coin must have come from the brass plate left by Sir Francis Drake on Point Reyes in 1579 (see above). Presumably, after the Miwoks watched the strange intruders sail away, they went down to the beach, removed the plate Drake had left, pried out the coin he had attached, and brought it back to the main village farther inland, where it was eventually lost. The coin now rests in Berkeley's **Bancroft Library** (see page 251), though it is not on display.

The Wine Country and Nearby

VALLEJO

ZODIAC KILLER TOUR

A madman calling himself "Zodiac" murdered at least five people in the late 1960s. Four were killed here in the North Bay, leading police to believe Zodiac was a resident of Vallejo or somewhere else nearby. He taunted the media and police with coded communiqués in which he claimed to have killed thirty-seven victims in a quest to collect "slaves" who would serve him in the afterlife. He also terrified the Bay Area by threatening to massacre a busload of schoolchildren. But after promising to thenceforth disguise his crimes as suicides or accidents, Zodiac faded away, never to be caught or heard from again. Like a modern-day Jack the Ripper, the Zodiac is a favorite subject for amateur sleuths and conspiracy buffs. Author Robert Graysmith (among others) claims to know Zodiac's true identity, yet no arrest has ever been made. Clint Eastwood finished off a fictionalized version of Zodiac in *Dirty Harry*. Hoping some long-lost witness would come out of the woodwork, *America's Most Wanted* recently reenacted the crimes, with no results. Wanna crack the case? Here's a rundown of the Zodiac's deadly spree.

- **December 20, 1968.** Zodiac shoots teenagers David Faraday and Betty Lou Jensen to death after he finds them parked in an isolated lovers' lane. The site was the entrance to a short, unmarked driveway that leads south from Lake Herman Road in Benicia, about 200 yards east of what is now called the Lake Herman Recreation Area. Some writers say the crime happened on Water Way, the access road to a city-owned water treatment plant, but that's wrong: it happened a mile farther west up the road, a little more than half a mile west of Reservoir Road. (This killing is often described as taking place in Vallejo, but the site is technically in Benicia.)
- **July 5, 1969.** Two more young lovers, Darlene Ferrin and Michael Mageau, are shot just after midnight in the parking lot of Blue Rock Springs Park, near the clubhouse of Blue Rock Springs Golf Course, at 655 Columbus Parkway on the outskirts of Vallejo. Mageau will survive and provide some vague clues to investigators that will fail to produce a suspect.
- **September 27, 1969.** Picnickers Bryan Hartnell and Cecilia Shepherd are accosted by a hooded assailant who ties them up and stabs them repeat-

edly with a long knife. The crime happened on the western shore of Lake Berryessa, in a rural area of Napa County east of St. Helena. To reach the site: From Highway 128 take Knoxville Road north past Spanish Flat Resort to a spot known as Zodiac Island, a little less than a mile north of the Bureau of Reclamation offices on the lakeshore. Park in the Twin Oaks parking lot and walk to the Oak Shores Day Use Area; look for a small peninsula with a picnic table on it. (The "island" is a peninsula when the lake level is low, which is often. The picnic table is a recent addition; at the time of the crime the peninsula had two large oak trees, now gone.) As he left, Zodiac scribbled the dates of his crimes on the victims' car. Hartnell survived but could provide few clues to his attacker's identity.

- **October 11, 1969.** Zodiac's last known attack takes place in San Francisco (see **Zodiac Killer Murder and Escape Site,** page 225).

NAPA

Bubbling Well Pet Memorial Park
As seen in Gates of Heaven.

> 2462 Atlas Peak Road. From Trancas Street in Napa, go northeast on Monticello Road, then turn north on Atlas Peak Road, and continue 2 miles past the Silverado Country Club. Open Mon.–Fri., 8:00 A.M.–4:30 P.M.; Sat.–Sun., 9:00 A.M.–3:00 P.M. (707) 255-3456 or (800) 794-PETS.

Perhaps the most entertaining documentary ever made, *Gates of Heaven* explores an extravagant pet cemetery and its owners and patrons. Director Errol Morris lets them tell their own stories, by turns unself-conscious, touching, and uproarious. (Watch for the word "neutered.") *Gates of Heaven* (not to be confused with Michael Cimino's awful *Heaven's Gate*) does for the pet-burial industry what Evelyn Waugh's novel *The Loved One* did for its human counterpart. Though in the film it seems too much of a self-parody to be genuine, Bubbling Well is definitely real, and has grown to become the nation's largest pet cemetery. The film was shot throughout the grounds, including the Garden of Companionship, the Mermaid Pool and the St. Francis Garden.

PETALUMA

American Graffiti Filming Location
Along Petaluma Boulevard, downtown.

Sleepy Petaluma's main drag has preserved its 1950s small-town ambience so perfectly that it's been the filming location of choice for dozens of movies re-creating
the Eisenhower era. The first—and most famous—was George Lucas's *American
Graffiti,* a disjointed tale of graduation-night frolics. (The movie sparked a '50s
nostalgia craze in the 1970s, though it was set in 1962.) The time-travel fantasy
Peggy Sue Got Married also showed off Petaluma Boulevard to its best advantage. *Basic Instinct* and *Phenomenon,* among many others, were filmed here as well.

SANTA ROSA

Shadow of a Doubt Locations
904 McDonald Avenue, and the Historic Train Depot, at 9 4th Street, Santa Rosa.

In Alfred Hitchcock's *Shadow of a Doubt,* which the director once described as his
favorite, a girl named Charlie idolizes her uncle Charlie. But when he pays the
family a visit in their Santa Rosa home, she begins to sense something sinister is going on. Hitchcock shot parts of his 1943 film on location, using a gracious white
Victorian at 904 McDonald as young Charlie's home, and using Santa Rosa's Historic Train Depot for a key scene. The Victorian is still here, on a street lined with
grand homes. The depot is still here as well, though a courthouse and library that appeared in the film have long since been torn down.

Snoopy's Gallery and Gift Shop
*1665 W. Steele Lane, near Range Avenue, at the Redwood Empire Ice Arena, Santa Rosa.
Opening hours are unduly complicated; generally open afternoons and evenings. (707) 546-
3385.*

Cartoonist Charles Schulz owned and operated this upscale ice rink. Attached to
the rink are Snoopy's Coffee Shop, better known as "the Warm Puppy," and an
all-Peanuts-themed souvenir store called Snoopy's Gallery and Gift Shop. Charlie
Brown, Linus, Lucy, Shroeder, Sally, Woodstock, and Snoopy assail your senses from
every direction. It's an explosion of Peanutsiana: dolls, clocks, videos, stationery,
clothing, figurines, stuffed toys, posters, rugs, and mugs, all printed with those lov-

able Schulz characters. Charles Schulz himself dropped by fairly frequently to play hockey and used to ensconce himself in a nearby studio, where he drew his daily strip, until he finally went to meet the Great Pumpkin early in 2000, the day before his final cartoon was published.

MONTE RIO

Bohemian Grove
Millionaires' campground.

> *One mile east of Bohemian Highway, just east of the bridge leading to Monte Rio, on the south side of the Russian River.*

For two weeks every summer, usually in late July or August, over one thousand of the most powerful men in America (and thus in the world) gather here in the woods for a superexclusive campout, complete with cabins and five-star chefs. Whether or not these presidents, cabinet members, and millionaires practice archery, plait lanyards, and make s'mores while networking and pondering international affairs is very hush-hush. Rumors circulate of naked frolics and pagan rituals. Within the grove's high-security gates, outsiders are strictly banned, as are TVs and radios. The campers are members of San Francisco's Bohemian Club, an intimidating all-male and nearly all-white confab with a very long waiting list. (Ironically the club was launched by the likes of Ambrose Bierce and Jack London—intellectuals, not magnates.) Past campers have included Herbert Hoover, Dwight Eisenhower, Richard Nixon, George Bush, Henry Kissinger and David Rockefeller. Protesters often gather outside the gates, lambasting its right-wing, rich-guy ethos.

BODEGA BAY

Filming Locations for *The Birds*
The Tides Wharf and Restaurant: 835 Highway 1, in the center of Bodega Bay, on the water-front. Open Mon.–Fri., 7:30 A.M.–9:30 P.M.; Sat.–Sun. 7:00 A.M.–9:30 P.M. (707) 875-3652. Potter Schoolhouse: on Bodega Lane in the town of Bodega, 5 miles inland from Bodega Bay; it's clearly visible near the top of the hill.

Alfred Hitchcock's horror classic *The Birds* was filmed on location in and around Bodega Bay, on the Sonoma Coast. Ground zero is the Tides Wharf and Restaurant, where Tippi Hedren's character retreats after the first bird attack, and where the townspeople hide from their avian tormentors later in the film. The restaurant was rebuilt from the ground up a few years ago, but photos on display recall the filming, and *Birds* mementos decorate the walls. The film's "Bodega Bay School" (called the Potter Schoolhouse in real life), where a sultry schoolteacher played by Suzanne Pleshette comes under attack, is actually five miles away from Bodega Bay, in the town of Bodega. (The building is now a private home.) The house where Hedren's character takes refuge with leading man Rod Taylor is now gone—it was on Bay Flat Road across the harbor west of Bodega Bay, where the Marine Lab housing now stands.

Benbow

Benbow Inn
Hideaway of the rich and powerful.

445 Lake Benbow Drive, just west of Highway 101, 3 miles south of Garberville, Humboldt County. (707) 923-2124.

This rustic Tudor-style country inn opened in 1926 and immediately attracted a celebrity following, despite—or perhaps because of—its isolation. Movie stars, politicians, and high-society jet-setters mingled and frolicked. President Herbert Hoover slept here, as did archrival Eleanor Roosevelt, whose husband picked up a broken nation from where Hoover had dumped it. Basil Rathbone kept a *Hound of the Baskervilles*–sized Doberman in his room against house rules, and Jack Benny pedaled around on a child's tricycle. Zillionaire buffoon William Randolph Hearst found refuge here from his many palaces. Charles Laughton, Clark Gable, and Spencer Tracy also prowled the hallways. The background scenery in Disney's *Bambi* was supposedly inspired in part by the scenery around the inn, which was sketched by a Disney animator when the film was in production. Things at Benbow have settled down a bit now, but the prices are reasonable and the place is aging gracefully.

Ferndale

Outbreak Filming Location
On and around Main Street in Ferndale, Humboldt County. Ferndale Chamber of Commerce: (707) 786-4477.

Dustin Hoffman was wildly miscast as an action hero in 1994's paranoiac thriller *Outbreak,* in which a killer virus threatens to wipe out first a quaint small town, and eventually—if left unchecked—the whole world. Aside from the odd spectacle of Hoffman stomping around in an army uniform, the film is taut and terrifying. The prototypically quaint small town used in the film was Ferndale, just south of Eureka. The rows of flawlessly preserved Victorian buildings marching down Ferndale's Main Street are a slice of picture-perfect Americana that couldn't be reproduced on a back lot.

Weaverville

Site of the Weaverville Tong War

A plaque marking the site is on the south side of Trinity Lakes Boulevard (Highway 3), adjacent to Weaverville Elementary School, between Center and Washington Streets, in Weaverville, Trinity County.

The gold rush brought thousands of Chinese to California, looking—like everyone else—for quick riches. Over two thousand Chinese prospectors flocked to the Weaverville area in the early 1850s and quickly reestablished many of the social structures they had left behind in China. One of these was the system of tongs, associations designed to mutually benefit members of a particular area or clan. In the best of times each tong functioned as Rotary Club, union, and fraternity rolled into one. When times were tough, rival tongs sometimes fought for honor, like Mafia families or gangs. In 1854 a conflict over mining rights to a sluice (which separated gold from river gravel), possibly exacerbated by a gambling dispute, erupted into what is now known as the Weaverville Tong War. The Young Wo (known to white miners as "the Cantons") and the Ah You (called "the Hong Kongs") challenged each other to battle. White miners for miles around placed bets on their favorites. Blacksmiths worked overtime making vicious-looking pronged battle weapons, and excitement rose to a fever pitch. Hundreds of fledgling warriors streamed onto the field next to what is now the Weaverville Elementary School, scarlet and gold banners streaming behind their upraised tridents. A huge crowd watched. But when the time came to fight, both tongs just stood there glaring, apparently having second thoughts. The white miners wanted to see a clear winner, not a double forfeit. Just as the tongs were about to cancel the fight, the whites gathered behind each group and chased them toward each other with rocks, intent on inciting bloodshed. It worked. Prongs and blades found their marks, and at least twenty-seven men bled to death. Scores were seriously injured. One white miner started firing a gun indiscriminately and was himself shot dead. When it was over, "the Cantons" claimed victory, helped in part by the miners who had bet on them. This strange "war" still ranks as one of the most idiotic and bloody days in California history. A plaque on the site commemorates the event.

Newell

Tule Lake Internment Camp

The site is marked by a memorial on the east side of Highway 139, just north of the Newell Elementary School in the town of Newell. The fenced-off electrical substation in front of the brick memorial sits on part of the former camp. The cross on the top of the hill on the other side of the road also has at its base a memorial marker. Newell City Hall: (530) 667-5522.

Tule Lake was the Buchenwald of Japanese internment camps, where trouble-makers and dissidents were segregated in a special high-security facility with extra guards and no chance of escape. It started its shameful career as one of ten "re-location centers" for Japanese Americans forcibly detained for the duration of World War II, on the theory that they might secretly side with their ancestral homeland. More prisoners here than at any other camp refused to sign an insulting "loyalty oath" in 1943, after which Tule Lake became the only "segregation center" to which "No-Nos"—those who answered "no" to both loyalty questions, often as a symbolic protest—from all the other camps were sent. Tule Lake was beset by demonstrations, strikes, gang harassment, and generalized hostility. Many internees were jailed in a stockade without trial. The camp was surrounded by tanks and military police. In-justices at the camp enraged the Japanese Americans trapped here, and over five thousand eventually renounced their U.S. citizenship rather than return to civilian society after the war. Most of the camp is now gone, marked only by two memorials. A jailhouse and a few barracks are still standing and can be seen in the distance, but they are fenced off and cannot be inspected up close. (See also **Manzanar Intern-ment Camp, Lone Pine,** page 193, and **Tanforan Park Shopping Center, San Bruno,** page 246.)

Tulelake

Captain Jack's Stronghold
Where the United States almost lost a war against a handful of Indians.

In Lava Beds National Monument, just south of Tule Lake and the Oregon border. From the town of Tulelake, go south on Highway 139 and turn south on Great Northern Road. Follow the road as it turns right (west) around Tule Lake (the lake, not the town) and enters Lava Beds National Monument. Captain Jack's Stronghold is clearly marked on the south side of the road, about 3 miles into the park. A sign and walking-tour brochures lead you to various highlights of the stronghold. Canby's Cross is 3 miles west of the stronghold along the same road. Lava Beds National Monument: (530) 667-2282.

During the 1860s white settlers around Tule Lake forced the local Modoc Indians off their ancestral land. The Modocs were resettled against their will on a nearby reservation that they had to share with their traditional enemies, the Klamath Indians. The situation on the reservation was intolerable and dangerous, so over the next few years many Modocs left and returned home. Finally, on November 28, 1872, the U.S. Army sent troops to herd the Modocs back onto the hated reservation. The Modocs fled. The Army followed. *Big* mistake. The Modocs, under the leadership of Kientpoos (whom the whites called "Captain Jack"), had entrenched themselves in the fissures and crags of an ancient lava bed. On January 16, 1873, troops marched into the stronghold and were nearly massacred by Indian snipers firing from hidden perches. Now the Army fled, abandoning weapons and wounded. The conflict was quickly dubbed "the Modoc War" and became an international cause célèbre. Much to everyone's surprise, the Modocs were superb guerrilla fighters and could not be dislodged. When the Indians killed an actual U.S. Army general (at the site now called Canby's Cross) during a failed peace talk, the government sent in over one thousand troops to surround them. Starving, the Indians easily slipped through the siege but were later arrested in small groups after the tribe had broken up into feuding bands. Captain Jack and three others were hanged for murder, and most of the rest were shipped off to Oklahoma, where they quickly succumbed to disease and poverty. Now the site of the battles has been turned into a walking trail. Despite its ignominious conclusion, the Modoc War was one of the most successful ever waged against U.S. troops, and Captain Jack has emerged from the black pages of history as a popular antihero.

SELECTED BIBLIOGRAPHY

Alleman, Richard. *The Movie Lover's Guide to Hollywood.* New York: Harper and Row, 1985.

American Heritage, eds. *A Guide to America's Greatest Historic Places.* New York: American Heritage Press, 1985.

Anger, Kenneth. *Hollywood Babylon.* London: Straight Arrow Books, 1975.

———. *Hollywood Babylon II.* New York: Plume, 1984.

Anonymous. *The Suppressed Mooney-Billings Report.* New York: Gotham House, 1932.

Arbeiter, Jean, and Linda Cirino. *Permanent Addresses: A Guide to the Resting Places of Famous Americans.* New York: M. Evans and Company, 1983.

Barrett, Liz. *Frommer's Irreverent Guide to San Francisco.* New York: Simon and Schuster, 1998.

Barth, Jack. *Roadside Hollywood.* Chicago: Contemporary Books, 1991.

———, Doug Kirby, and Mike Wilkins. *Roadside America.* New York: Simon and Schuster, 1986.

Behlmer, Rudy. *Behind the Scenes.* Hollywood: Samuel French, 1990.

Bergheim, Laura A. *Weird, Wonderful America: The Nation's Most Offbeat and Off-the-Beaten-Path Tourist Attractions.* New York: Macmillan, 1988.

Blackburn, Daniel J. *Human Harvest.* New York: Knightsbridge, 1990.

Blanche, Tony, and Brad Schreiber. *Death in Paradise: An Illustrated History of the Los Angeles County Department of Coroner.* Los Angeles: General Publishing Group, 1998.

Bock, Duncan, ed. *Spin Underground U.S.A.: The Best of Rock Culture Coast to Coast.* New York: Vintage Books, 1997.

Brandon, Jim. *Weird America: A Guide to Places of Mystery in the United States.* New York: Dutton, 1978.

Bravin, Jess. *Squeaky: The Life and Times of Lynette Alice Fromme.* New York: Buzz/St. Martin's, 1997.

Burk, Margaret, and Gary Hudson. *Final Curtain: Eternal Resting Places of Hundreds of Stars, Celebrities, Moguls, Misers, and Misfits.* Santa Ana, Calif.: Seven Locks Press, 1996.

Culbertson, Judi, and Tom Randall. *Permanent Californians: An Illustrated Guide to the Cemeteries of California.* Chelsea, Vt.: Chelsea Green, 1989.

Delahanty, Randolph. *San Francisco: The Ultimate Guide.* San Francisco: Chronicle Books, 1989.

Denver, Bob. *Gilligan, Maynard, and Me.* New York: Citadel, 1993.

Dickerson, Jr., Robert B. *Final Placement: A Guide to the Deaths, Funerals, and Burials of Notable Americans.* Algonac, Mich.: Reference Publications, 1986.

Farrin, Mick. *Conspiracies, Lies, and Hidden Agendas: Our Deepest Secret Fears, from the Antichrist to the Trenchcoat Mafia.* Los Angeles: Renaissance Books, 1999.

Fein, Art. *The L.A. Musical History Tour: A Guide to the Rock and Roll Landmarks of Los Angeles.* Los Angeles: 2.13.61 Publications, 1998.

Fortunate Eagle, Adam. *Alcatraz! Alcatraz!: The Indian Occupation 1969–1971.* Berkeley, Calif. Heyday, 1992.

Gaberscek, Carlo. *Cinema Western in California.* Udine, Italy: Trib. di Udine, 1991.

Gebhard, David, and Harriette von Breton. *L.A. in the Thirties.* Layton, Utah: Peregrine Smith, 1975.

Gehman, Pleasant, ed. *The Underground Guide to Los Angeles.* San Francisco: Manic D Press, 1999.

Genthe, Arnold, and John Kuo Mei Tchen. *Genthe's Photographs of San Francisco's Old Chinatown.* New York: Dover, 1984.

Gentry, Curt. *Frame-up.* New York: Norton, 1967.

Gilmore, John, *Severed: The True Story of the Black Dahlia Murder.* Los Angeles: Amok Books, 1994.

Gordon, William A. *Shot on This Site.* Secaucus, N.J.: Citadel Books, 1995.

———. *The Ultimate Hollywood Tour Book.* Toluca Lake, Calif.: North Ridge Books, 1992.

Graysmith, Robert. *The Sleeping Lady.* New York: Dutton, 1990.

Grenier, Judson A. *Historic Places in Los Angeles County.* Dubuque, Iowa: Kendall/Hunt, 1978.

Harris, Richard. *Unique California: Guide to the State's Quirks, Charisma, and Character.* Santa Fe, N.M.: John Muir Publications, 1994.

Herron, Don. *The Literary World of San Francisco and Its Environs.* San Francisco: City Lights Books, 1985.

Hoffman, David. *Very L.A.: The Native's Guide to the Best of Los Angeles.* San Francisco: Chronicle Books, 1989.

Hollywood Homes of the Stars! Glendale, Calif.: JBM Publications, 1999.

Jarvis, Everett G. *Final Curtain: Deaths of Noted Movie and TV Personalities.* Secaucus, N.J.: Carol Publishing Group, 1998.

Jencks, Charles. *Daydream Houses of Los Angeles.* New York: Rizzoli, 1978.

Jensen, Jamie. *Road Trip U.S.A.* Chico, Calif.: Moon Travel Handbooks, 1999.

Johnson, Marael. *California: Why Stop?: A Guide to California Roadside Historical Markers.* Houston, Tex.: Gulf, 1995.

Johnson, Troy R. *The Occupation of Alcatraz Island.* Urbana: University of Illinois Press, 1996.

Koenig, David. *Mouse Tales.* Irvine, Calif.: Bonaventure Press, 1995.

Lawson, Kristan, and Anneli Rufus. *America Off the Wall: The West Coast.* New York: John Wiley and Sons, 1989.

Legarde, Lisa. *Frommer's Walking Tours San Francisco.* New York: Macmillian, 1995.

Lewis, Richard. *Poor Richard's Guide to Non-Tourist San Francisco.* San Francisco: Unicorn, 1958.

Logan, William Bryant, Susan Ochshorn, and Chuck Place. *The Smithsonian Guides to Historic America: The Pacific States.* New York: Tabori and Chang, 1989.

Lovett, Anthony R., and Matt Maranian. *L.A. Bizarro: The Insider's Guide to the Obscure, the Absurd, and the Perverse in Los Angeles.* New York: St. Martin's Press, 1997.

Mallan, Chicki. *Catalina Island Handbook.* Chico, Calif.: Moon Publications, 1992.

Maltin, Leonard, and Richard Bann. *The Little Rascals.* New York: Crown, 1992.

Miller, Luree. *Literary Hills of San Francisco.* Washington, D.C.: Starhill Press, 1992.

Morino, Marianne. *The Hollywood Walk of Fame.* Berkeley, Calif.: Ten Speed Press, 1987.

Mungo, Ray. *San Francisco Confidential: Tales of Scandal and Excess from the Town That's Seen Everything.* New York: Birch Lane Press, 1995.

O'Brien, Robert. *This Is San Francisco.* New York: Whittlesey House, 1948.

Papanek, John L., ed. *Death and Celebrity.* Alexandria, Va.: Time-Life True Crime, 1993.

Parr, Barry. *San Francisco and the Bay Area.* New York: Compass American Guides/Fodor's, 1994.

Pashdag, John. *Hollywoodland U.S.A.: The Moviegoer's Guide to Southern California.* San Francisco: Chronicle Books, 1984.

Perry, Charles. *The Haight-Ashbury: A History.* New York: Random House, 1984.

Perry, Tim, and Ed Glinert. *Fodor's Rock and Roll Traveler U.S.A.: The Ultimate Guide to Juke Joints, Street Corners, Whiskey Bars, and Hotel Rooms Where Music History Was Made.* New York: Fodor's, 1996.

Pierson, Robert John. *The Beach Towns: A Walker's Guide to L.A.'s Beach Communities.* San Francisco: Chronicle Books, 1985.

Pike, Jeff. *The Death of Rock 'n' Roll.* London: Faber and Faber, 1993.

Pitcher, Don, and Malcolm Margolin. *Berkeley Inside Out.* Berkeley, Calif.: Heyday Books, 1989.

Pittmann, Ruth. *Roadside History of California.* Missoula, Mont.: Mountain Press, 1995.

Poshek, Lucy, and Roger Naylor. *California Trivia.* Nashville: Rutledge Hill Press, 1998.

Rasmussen, Cecilia. *Curbside L.A.* Los Angeles: L.A. Times, 1996.

Reavill, Gil. *Hollywood and the Best of Los Angeles.* New York: Compass American Guides/Fodor's, 1994.

Reynolds, Richard D. *Cry for War: The Story of Suzan and Michael Carson.* San Francisco: Squibob Press, 1987.

Richards, Rand. *Historic San Francisco: A Concise History and Guide.* San Francisco: Heritage House, 1997.

Ristow, William, ed. *San Francisco Free and Easy.* San Francisco: Downwind Publications, 1980.

Roberts, George, and Jan Roberts. *Discover Historic California.* Baldwin Park, Calif.: Gem Guides, 1994.

Sangwan, B., ed. *The Complete Monterey Peninsula and Santa Cruz Guidebook.* Tahoe City, Calif.: Indian Chief Publishing House, 1993.

Schlesser, Ken. *This Is Hollywood: An Unusual Guide.* Redlands, Calif.: Universal Books, 1988.

Selvin, Joel. *San Francisco: The Musical History Tour.* San Francisco: Chronicle Books, 1996.

Sieflein, David. *Meet Me at the St. Francis: The First Seventy-five Years of a Great San Francisco Hotel.* San Francisco: St. Francis Hotel Corporation, 1979.

Siegel, Jeff. *The Casablanca Companion: The Movie and More: The Behind the Scenes Story of an American Classic.* Dallas: Taylor Publishing, 1992.

Smith, Leon. *Famous Hollywood Locations: Descriptions and Photographs of 382 Sites Involving 289 Films and 105 Television Series.* Jefferson, N.C.: McFarland and Company, 1993.

Spade and Archer. *Fifty Maps of San Francisco.* New York: H. M. Gousha, 1991.

Staten, Vince. *Unauthorized America: A Travel Guide to the Places the Chamber of Commerce Won't Tell You About.* New York: Harper and Row, 1990.

Sternfeld, Joel. *On This Site: Landscape in Memoriam.* San Francisco: Chronicle Books, 1996.

Swift, Harriet. *The Virago Woman's Travel Guide San Francisco.* Berkeley, Calif.: Book Passage Press, 1994.

Taliaferro, John. *Tarzan Forever.* New York: Scribner, 1999.

Time Out magazine, eds. *Time Out San Francisco Guide.* 3d edition. New York: Penguin, 2000.

Vertikoff, Alexander, and Robert Winter. *Hidden L.A.* Layton, Utah: Gibbs Smith, 1998.

Vestner, Heinz, ed. *California Nelles Guides.* Munich: Nelles, 1991.

Vorpagel, Russell, as told to Joseph Harrington. *Profiles in Murder: An FBI Legend Dissects Killers and Their Crimes.* New York: Plenum Press, 1998.

Wach, Bonnie. *San Francisco As You Like It.* San Francisco: Chronicle Books, 1998.

Wagner, Walter. *Beverly Hills: Inside the Golden Ghetto.* New York: Grosset and Dunlap, 1976.

Weimers, Leigh. *Leigh Weimers' Guide to Silicon Valley: An Insider's Tips for Techies and Tourists.* Santa Cruz, Calif.: Western Tanager Press, 1993.

Dr. Weirde. *Dr. Weirde's Tours: A Guide to Mysterious San Francisco.* San Francisco: Barrett-James Books, 1995.

Wilcock, John, ed. *Insight Guides Northern California.* New York: APA Publications, 1995.

Wilkins, Mike, Ken Smith, and Doug Kirby. *The New Roadside America: The Modern Traveler's Guide to the Wild and Wonderful World of America's Tourist Attractions.* New York: Fireside/Simon and Schuster, 1992.

Wolf, Marvin J., and Katherine Mader. *Fallen Angels: Chronicles of L.A. Crime and Mystery.* New York: Ballantine, 1986.